San Francisco's Ultimate Dining Guide

A survey of over 300 Bay Area restaurants by the REAL experts: chefs, concierges, cafe critics and community leaders

By Don W. Martin and Betty Woo Martin

Illustrated by Robert Gumpertz

Pine Cone Press • 587 Europa Court, Walnut Creek, CA 94598

Guidebooks by Don & Betty Martin:

THE BEST OF SAN FRANCISCO • Chronicle Books © 1986
THE BEST OF THE GOLD COUNTRY • Pine Cone Press © 1987
SAN FRANCISCO'S ULTIMATE DINING GUIDE • Pine Cone Press © 1988

Library of Congress Catalog-in-Publication Data
Martin, Don and Betty—
San Francisco's Ultimate Dining Guide
Includes Index
ISBN: 0-942053-03-6
Library of Congress card catalog number: 87-62336

Book design and production • Charles L. Beucher, Jr.

Typesetting • Crosby Associates, P.O. Box 248, Sutter Creek, California 95685
(209) 267-0115

CONTENTS

1: THE SELECTED RESTAURANTS 9
San Francisco dining places surveyed by our guest critics

2: THE OUTSIDE GUIDE 151
Selected restaurants in other Bay Area communities

3: WHERE THE ELITE MEET TO EAT 179
Favorite restaurants of personalities and community leaders

4: THE PROFESSIONALS' PICKS 188
Favorite cafes of celebrity chefs and restaurateurs

5: THE BEST OF THE FINEST 194
The Bay Area's highest rated restaurants

6. EVERYBODY'S FAVORITES 196
Top ten lists from various panel members

7: DINING VARIETY 198
The selected restaurants listed by type

8: WHAT PRICE GUMBO? 206
Budget restaurants; eating well while dining cheaply

9: MIDNIGHT DINERS 210
For prowling night owls: places that serve after 11 p.m.

10: SPECIAL PLACES FOR SPECIAL FACES 213
Romantic, special occasion & view restaurants; outdoor dining

11: A GUIDE TO THE GUIDES 220
Reviews of other dining directories

JOIN THE CLUB

Be the first person on your block to become a member of our restaurant reviewers' panel. If you're part of the restaurant, hotel or visitor trade, or just someone who enjoys eating out, we'd like you to be a guest critic for the next edition of *SAN FRANCISCO'S ULTIMATE DINING GUIDE.*

Send us your name and address and we'll supply you with a set of survey forms when we're ready to start the next issue. Your reward for returning a completed questionnaire will be an autographed copy of that edition. Isn't that exciting?

QUANTITY SALES AT A DISCOUNT

Incidentally, the dining guide makes a great packet stuffer, premium or gift for conventions, club gatherings, social functions, large weddings, wakes and similar affairs. For details on special discount prices for autographed copies, contact the publisher at the address below.

NOBODY'S PERFECT, BUT WE TRY

There are several thousand facts in this book, and a few of them are probably wrong. So if you catch an error, or learn that a restaurant has changed its name, chef, hours or become a laundromat, we'd certainly like to know.

Address all letters to:

Pine Cone Press
587 Europa Court
Walnut Creek, CA 94598
(415) 945-6774

A BIT ABOUT THE AUTHORS

This is the third guidebook by the husband and wife writing team of Don and Betty Martin. Don, who provides most of the adjectives, has been writing for a living since he was seventeen, starting as a printer's devil for a small newspaper in Idaho. He served as a Marine correspondent in the Orient, worked for assorted California newspapers and functioned for years as associate editor of Motorland, the travel magazine of the San Francisco-based California State Automobile Association. He now devotes his time to writing, travel, photography and the operation of Pine Cone Press.

Betty, who does most of the research, comes equipped with the curious credentials of a doctorate in pharmacy and a California real estate broker's license. A first-generation Chinese-American, she's also an expert on Oriental cuisine, a freelance writer and photographer, and she is a student of the culinary arts and food service program at California's Columbia College.

AND THE ARTIST

The drawings of Robert Gumpertz of Mill Valley have been scampering about the world for decades, bringing smiles to readers of *Playboy, Punch, Paris Match* and other publications. His cartoons are a weekly feature in the *San Francisco Chronicle's* "This World" section; his book credits as author and illustrator include *Professor Twill's Travels* (Houghton Mifflin), *The International Dog* (Golden Press) and a book about oddball American place names, *From Fiddletown to Tuba City* (Workman Publishing).

Occasionally, he puts down his pen and picks up a spoon to pursue his avocation as a gourmet chef, creating such culinary curiosities as Loquot Kumquat Compote Des Dieux.

INTRODUCTION

"Ultimate?"

Certainly.

We'll admit that it's a rather strong word to place on the cover of a mere book. But then, this is a rather significant dining guide. Instead of relying on the opinions of a cafe critic or two, it digests the culinary wisdom of hundreds of people closely allied with the Bay Area dining scene.

SAN FRANCISCO'S ULTIMATE DINING GUIDE is a distillation of restaurant surveys from three knowledgeable sources:

- Restaurant owners, chefs and employees.
- Hotel executives, concierges, barkeeps, cabbies and others allied with the visitor industry, who are frequently asked to recommend dining spots.
- Community leaders, personalities and other citizens who love to eat out and who follow the Bay Area dining scene.

When we wrote *The Best of San Francisco* (Chronicle Books, 1986), we devoted several chapters to the city's restaurants. Almost as an afterthought, we asked concierges and cab drivers to nominate *their* favorites. After a couple of years (sometimes, brilliant ideas take a while), it occurred to us that they—not we—are the better authorities.

So we sought their opinions again. This time, we broadened our base to include hundreds of others. As a final ingredient (seasoning, perhaps?) we included many of our personal dining experiences. For three decades we have eaten hundreds of meals, ranging from awesome to awful, in Bay Area bistros. Also, mostly for the fun of it, we've included a chapter that analyzes other restaurant guides and their selections.

In the interest of unbiased reporting, we didn't stuff the ballot box by voting in any of the "ten best" categories. Also for reasons of fairness, we did not permit restaurant and hotel people to nominate their own establishments.

THE WAY THINGS WORK

We're practitioners of the KISS formula for guidebook writing: "Keep It Simple, Silly." Someone thumbing through our listings shouldn't be required to return to this introduction to decipher assorted codes, abbreviations and little squiggly figures. So we require that you memorize very little. In case you *do* need to return to "Go," we've cleverly given this section a black border so you can easily thumb back to it.

Each restaurant is listed alphabetically and in bold face, followed by the address and (in parentheses) the cross street or other geographic reference, then the phone number. All are (415) area code unless otherwise indicated, but you probably know that. And in the interest of saving ink, we don't say "street" when it's part of the address, but we do say "boulevard," "avenue," "lane" and such.

On the next line, you'll discover the style of food and a "spoon rating" for overall quality, based on a measure of food preparation, ambiançe and service:

— Outstanding: Consistently great in all categories
— Excellent: A fine place to dine, with no major flaws
— Good: Well-run, pleasant, with generally tasty food
— Fair: Acceptable but substantially short of awesome

One or more symbols follow the ratings, and their meaning should be obvious:

— A smoke-free restaurant or dining room
— Non-smoking section available in dining room
— Separate bar or lounge
— Early-bird budget dinners
— Night owl service: food offered after 11 p.m.
— Outdoor tables available

Next, we estimate the price of a typical dinner with the main course and a soup or salad, not including drinks, dessert or tips:

$ — Under $10
$$ — From $10 to $19
$$$ — From $20 to $29
$$$$ — $30 or more

We don't list specific hours (except in a few instances where they were temptingly simple); they're often rather complicated and may be changed at a manager's whim. Instead, we indicate what meals are served and what days the place is functioning. Our "dress codes" are suggestions, based on what the typical diner wears in a particular place: casual, casual to sport jacket or dressy. "Dressy" indicates that the restaurant has specific dress requirements, or that you'll feel more comfortable in coat and tie or cocktail wear. Some have different dress codes for lunch and dinner, so ask if the place has specific standards when you make reservations.

This is followed by a description of bar service, and a list of credit cards accepted, using these obvious abbreviations: MC—MasterCard; VISA—VISA; AMEX—American Express; DC—Diner's Club; CB — Carte Blanche; DIS—the Discover Card. "Major credit cards" indicates the ubiquitous MasterCard-VISA-American Express plus one or more of the others. "All major credit cards" literally means that, including that new Sears one called Discover.

If reservations are recommended, we say so. Either way, it's a good idea to call ahead, since the place may be closed that day, or it may have become a parking lot.

CLEARING THE AIR

In July, 1987, the San Francisco Board of Supervisors passed an ordinance requiring all restaurants to set aside areas for non-smokers. We applaud this move, since nothing ruins a good meal more thoroughly than a cloud of tobacco fumes drifting from a nearby table. Also, many diners are allergic to cigarette smoke; one whiff and they can't tell marsala sauce from mayonnaise. The law doesn't require *partitioned* non-smoking areas, and that's reasonable. Many places are too small, or the owners simply can't afford to erect barriers.

But even with the new ordinance, there's trouble in clean air paradise: Most restaurants we visited ignored the specifics of the law. The statute states that "an eating establishment shall allocate *and designate by appropriate signage* an adequate amount of space...to meet the demands of both smokers and non-smokers, and shall inform all patrons that non-smoking areas are provided."

We dined out dozens of times as we gathered background for this book and only about one in ten restaurants volunteered the information that they had a non-smoking section. Rarely did we see areas designated "by appropriate signage."

So the rule is simple: Don't wait to be asked. Request "non-smoking" and insist that you be seated as far away from smokers as possible. If someone challenges you, remind them to read Part II, Chapter V, Section 19A of the San Francisco Municipal Health Code.

The non-smoking symbols in our San Francisco listings aren't redundant; they indicate restaurants that clearly mark their tobacco-free sections and/or advise patrons on arrival that such areas exist. And the double symbol marks those few places that have declared their entire dining area off limits to smokers, or provide a separate dining room for non-puffers.

Closing introductory thoughts: Keep in mind that the restaurant reviews which follow are based on opinions of people whose tastes and temperament may differ from yours. We get nervous when one of our critics gives an establishment a scathing review, for even in well-run places, good chefs occasionally singe their sauces. It's unfair to condemn a cafe because a waiter had a bad night—or is recovering from one. So when a critic really pans a place, we try to check it out ourselves. Also, we're quite familiar with the San Francisco dining scene, so we're confident no one has slipped any turkeys into our book—unless they're rated as such.

But enough of this. There are more than four thousand dining spots in San Francisco and the Devil knows how many more in the rest of the Bay Area. Let's go find a good place to eat.

Chapter One
THE SELECTED RESTAURANTS
San Francisco places surveyed by our guest critics

A. SABELLA'S • 2766 Taylor (Fisherman's Wharf) • 771-6775

Seafood • $$

Lunch and dinner daily; reservations accepted; casual; full bar; major credit cards • We've long since given up on honky-tonk Fisherman's Wharf, which has become rife with wax museums, T-shirt shops and sidewalk trinket peddlers. But blame the city for poor planning control, not the family-owned Italian seafood restaurants that have been serving tourists and residents there for decades. These nautically-trimmed fish houses and the pleasantly aromatic sidewalk crab pots are about all that survive of the Wharf's original ambiance. Many of the restaurants serve rather ordinary tourist fare; perhaps they've been lulled by a market that isn't too demanding.

A. Sabella's, which received more votes in our survey than any other Wharf restaurant, is as good as the rest and better than some. Ask for fresh fish, lightly done, and you'll probably get it that way. The menu is a simple balance of fish, shellfish and pasta; nothing fancy but the portions are generous. The place was established in 1920 and a fourth-generation Sabella, Antone, runs it these days. "Clean, good food at reasonable prices," says one of our critics, adding, however that it's "not a place for a romantic interlude." But Antone tries; he's put candles on the tables.

ACT IV • 333 Fulton (Inn at the Opera, near Franklin) • 863-8400

California/French • $$$$

Breakfast, lunch and dinner daily, post theater service to 1 a.m.; dressy; full bar; MC, VISA, AMEX • Act IV and its adjoining Inn at the Opera are examples of the elegantly coifed boutique restaurants and hotels currently emerging in San Francisco. The tiny dining room with its paneled columns and floral wallpaper can be more intimate in appearance than in fact, however. The room is so small that it's hard to tune out the conversation at the next table.

The fare is French with strong California underpinnings; Chef Christian Janselme calls it his "new nouvelle cuisine." Most of our crew called it tasty. We found it just a bit uneven; a fish dish was overdone but veal in port sauce was excellent. A block or so from Davies Symphony Hall and the Opera House, Act IV serves a $33 prix fixe dinner starting at 6 p.m. "My very favorite place for a romantic, but expensive, evening," says one reviewer. Sorry, Sabella's.

ADOLPH'S • 641 Vallejo (Columbus) • 392-6333

Italian • $$

Lunch weekdays, dinner Tuesday-Sunday to 11:30; reservations recommended; casual to sport jacket; full bar; major credit cards • Adolph's is one of those comfy little North Beach Italian cafes decorated mostly with wine bottles, but it has a chandelier for a touch of class. One of our crew described the food as "excellent," then gave it a six on a scale of ten; we wonder what sort of score he awards to *mediocre* fare. Others of our critical crew agreed that Adolph's offers good, occasionally outstanding Italian food—the typical and tasty mix of chicken, veal and pasta. For dessert, the *zabaglione* is almost awesome.

The kitchen has had plenty of practice; things Italian have been emerging from there since 1956. It has been sold by the original Adolph, but it appears to be doing well under new ownership.

ADRIATIC • 1755 Polk (Washington) • 771-4035

Seafood/French • $$

Lunch Tuesday-Saturday, dinner Tuesday-Sunday; casual; full bar; MC, VISA, AMEX • "Cozy corner cafe" is the proper cliche to describe the Adriatic—a little gem in green and white with bentwood and wicker chairs and lace cafe curtains. It's a popular lunch stop with the Polk Gulch group; a favorite of ours is cheese-topped crab shrimp on a bit of baguette, toasted under the broiler. The French accent is apparent in the dinner menu, which isn't limited to seafood; offerings include sea bass in *amandine* sauce, Prawns Miramar sauteed with brandy and Pernod, steak in red wine and shallot sauce, and the requisite

Veal Cordon Bleu.

"Intimate neighborhood restaurant with excellent food and attentive service," commented one of our volunteers, and our own experiences confirm this.

ALEJANDRO'S SOCIEDAD GASTRONOMICA • 1840 Clement (19th Avenue) • 668-1184

Latin Mix • $$

Dinner nightly; reservations recommended; casual to sport jacket; full bar; major credit cards • Alejandro Espinosa's fare is supposedly Peruvian-Spanish-Mexican, but it's assembled with a bit of Espinosan creativity. Start with deep-fried "Alejandros", pastries stuffed with mild chilies, egg and cheese, or have some *tapas* (Spanish hors d'oeuvres), then wander at will through the large menu. The *Paella Valenciana* rice dish with mussels and cracked crab, oregano chicken, and trout with dried ham are memorable. The entrees are complex and spicy but rarely mouth-burning. The place is a visual delight, too—high-backed carved Peruvian chairs, lots of bright Spanish tile, busy-bordered Latin mirrors and pre- Columbian artifacts.

Sociedad Gastronomica, incidentally, is an association of Latin epicures that has convened at the restaurant and blessed certain of the foods, which carry the "S.G." initials on the menu. Blessings from our crew included "Food consistently good", "Very good *paella*", "Nice atmosphere" and "The only alternative to a trip to Spain. A single sour note—one of our secret agents reported getting cold food; presumably, it should have been hot.

ALEXIS • 1001 California (Mason) • 885-6400

French/Continental • $$$$

Dinner Monday-Saturday; reservations recommended; dressy; major credit cards • This ornately attired restaurant, a Nob Hill fixture since 1953, is almost over-dressed with its busy Byzantine decor accented with the odd Russian artifact. The Continental-Eastern theme carries into the menu, where Lamb Karski and Squab Byzantine lend Asian accents to the European fare. The lamb, says one judge, is particularly noteworthy. But others were less enthusiastic; they found this posh place to be a bit stuffy and the food uneven.

Although opulent old Alexis is predictably pricey, it does offer an early bird full-course prix fixe dinner for $22.50, including dessert and coffee or tea.

Its cellar lounge, once a Truman Capote hangout, is a delightful little hideaway. It becomes a disco on Friday and Saturdays from 10 p.m. to 2 a.m. but we prefer it at other times, when we can relax to the sounds of Gypsy music. Sipping to the measure of a gentle violin in this cozy den, one almost expects an over-dressed Russian noble to step boldly through the door. Capote would've liked that.

ALFRED'S • 886 Broadway (Mason) • 781-7058

Steakhouse/Italian • $$$

Dinner nightly; reservations recommended; sport jacket; major credit cards • Alfred's is another of those San Francisco institutions that's showing its age, yet it has maintained a high level of consistency since its founding in 1928. The decor, crystal chandeliers, glossy red leather booths and white tablecloths, is a blend of Victorian, American Thirties and British men's club. Steaks here are nothing short of exceptional; only prime is served and it's dry-aged and seared over mesquite. "Fine quality and large portions," exulted one of our crew, who promptly gave the food a nine. The beef-oriented menu has a strong Italian accent, although our agents gave the pasta mixed reviews.

A full dinner will sink your boat; in addition to the entree, it includes a huge antipasto tray, salad, soup and a choice of ravioli, spaghetti or cannelloni. While waiting for the next course, one can stare into a glassed-in cooler and admire dinner-to-be.

ALIOTO'S RESTAURANT • #8 Fisherman's Wharf • 673-0183

Italian/seafood • $$

Lunch and dinner daily; reservations accepted; casual; full bar; major credit cards • One of the original Fisherman's Wharf restaurants, Alioto's has been issuing fish to tourists since 1928. Present owners Nunzio and Joe Alioto (no, not the former mayor) have upgraded the fish menu, offering what they call "new traditional seafood"—lighter sauces, more lightly grilled. And they offer a full range of Italian dishes.

The decor is just what you'd expect of a venerable Wharf restaurant—old European with nautical tones.

ALLEGRO • 1701 Jones (Broadway) • 928-4002

Italian • $$

Dinner Monday-Saturday; reservations suggested; casual to sport jacket; wine and beer; major credit cards • This small Russian Hill cafe, with a sort of upscale Italian bistro look, focuses more on lightly grilled fish and meat entrees than heavy pastas, and they tend to be more reliable than the *tortellini* and *spaghettini.*

"Reasonably priced Italian food in a charming, intimate setting," offers one of our agents. "Well worth the fact that there's no parking in the area, and the restaurant has no valet." Are you listening, new owner Angelo Quantara? A valet parking set-up couldn't hurt.

AMELIO'S RESTAURANT • 1630 Powell (Union) • 397-4339

French/Continental • $$$$

Dinner nightly; reservations essential; dressy; full bar; major credit cards • Influenced perhaps by the innovative cuisine of Alice Waters of Chez Panisse and Stars' Jeremiah Tower, several long-established restaurants are shifting to lighter, more innovative fare. Opened in 1926, Amelio's is an excellent example of a venerable restaurant attaining new luster in San Francisco's changeable feast. Chef Jacky Robert, late of Ernie's, arrived in 1985 as co-owner and chef de cuisine, and began performing small miracles in Amelio's kitchen. The "French/Continental" label falls short of describing innovative, artfully presented dishes that include influences of the Orient and nouvelle California, such as pastry-encased sea bass and lamb in honey-soy marinade.

"Especially liked Robert's 'sampler' type dinner," said one critic, who gave the place straight tens. The samplers are four or five-course prix fixe "tasting menus" offering a delicious cross-section of his creativity. Incidentally, Amelio's polished "Old San Francisco" look—crystal chandeliers, guilt-edged mirrors and brocade banquettes—is wearing well.

ANGKOR WAT • 4217 Geary Boulevard (6th Avenue) • 221-7887

Cambodian • $$

Dinner nightly except Monday; reservations suggested; casual; full bar; MC, VISA • In San Francisco's culinary sea of Asian restaurants, only four or five are Cambodian, and this one is a pearl. Angkor Wat is handsomely fashioned, avoiding the Formica look of many Oriental cafes. Its tasteful Asian decor is accented by carvings simulating the ancient temples of Cambodia's Angkor Wat.

Cambodian cooking is similar to Thai and Vietnamese but it's more complex, at least in the Angkor Wat style. Aromatic herbs, oils, lemon grass, mint and the ubiquitous Southeast Asian peanut are among ingredients used to create savory but difficult to define tastes. An excellent broiled chicken, for instance, is marinated for hours in a busy blend of sesame oil, soy sauce, garlic, ginger and honey. The dishes are artfully presented, unlike those in many Asian restaurants, where the offerings look like flattened haystacks. One reviewer did complain that the servings were small for the price.

BAKERS SQUARE • 2353 Lombard (Scott) • 931-1174

American diner • $

Breakfast, lunch and dinner daily, service to 1 a.m. Friday and Saturday; casual; wine and beer; MC, VISA • "Surprisingly good food for a chain restaurant," said one of our spies. "Very good quality for semi-fast food," offered another. We agree. The big menu is all things to all appetites, but with some interesting twists—bacon-avocado omelets; burgers on French bread with parmesan cheese, sauteed onions and Dijon mustard sauce; and stir fried chicken with crisp broccoli, snow peas and other veggies. We tried a "stir fry shrimp pita" and were pleased with the results. The shrimps were plump and the busy blend of vegetables was fresh and lightly cooked.

Our only disappointment—even with their properly flaky crusts, the much-heralded pies were something short of awesome. We tried a boysenberry and later a pecan; the fillings were tasty but not rich and full, as the table tent card led us to believe. For nearly $2 a slice, we expected more. But the place offers 27 varieties; maybe we should go back for thirds. The decor is simple, bright and, with upholstered instead of plastic-skinned booths, it's a notch or two above Denny's.

BALBOA CAFE • 3199 Fillmore (Greenwich) • 921-3944

California • $$

Lunch and dinner daily; casual; full bar; MC, VISA • Jeremiah Tower refurbished the menu in this refurbished San Francisco bistro before moving on to Stars. Owner Jack Slick, aided by fresh young California Culinary Academy graduates, has kept the faith. The "small but changing, delightful menu" offers appealing nouvelle savories like fresh and complex salads, carrot-tarragon soup, black pepper *fettucini* with bay scallops, and sausages with lentils. The Balboa's 'burgers, installed in a dugout mini-sourdough loaf, are the stuff of legends.

This is a popular, noisy hangout that doesn't take reservations, so just shoulder up to the bar and settle your fingers around a glass of good California wine. The old fashioned bar, the restored antique tables and warm woods give it the proper look for a turn of the century bistro. "Good food but a little loud for pleasant dining," one of our agents shouted over the noise.

BANKOK EXPRESS • 907 Irving (10th Avenue) • 759-9238

Thai • $

Lunch weekdays, dinner nightly; casual dress; full bar; MC, VISA • When you turn into 907 Irving, you think you've made a mistake. This is an Old San Francisco style pub with wicker and leaded glass and potted palms, not a Thai restaurant. But walk to the rear and you'll emerge into a sunny glass-roofed dining area, with light wood and mirror strip walls and some Asian artifacts. Bankok Express is remarkably inexpensive, considering that the place is rather handsome and the food is tasty, ample *and* artfully presented. Most dinners are under $7 and lunch goes for less than $5.

My recent *kao pad grapow* lunch of chicken over rice garnished with strips of red and green peppers was attractive, tasty and hot. Order lots of beer here. Sundry other dishes with those strange chopped up Thailand names are equally tasty, many with that spicy hint of peanuts and lemon grass typical of Southeast Asian cooking. One of our group calls it "the best Thai in the Bay Area."

Incidentally, the restaurant has that familiar (and not really unpleasant) tropical musty aroma found in most enclosed buildings in Southeast Asia. Perhaps the management had it bottled and sent over for authenticity.

BARDELLI'S RESTAURANT • 243 O'Farrell (Mason) • 982-0243

Italian/Continental • $$

Lunch weekdays, dinner Monday through Saturday; reservations advised; casual to sport jacket; full bar; major credit cards • Even as the marble columns hold up its high coffered ceiling, the quality has held up well through the years in this old-fashion dining institution. Dating from 1909, it has gone through sundry transitions from oyster house to grill to, in 1949, an Italian restaurant established by Charles Bardelli. He's since departed but his old world ambiance of linen napkins and tuxedoed waiters survives.

Beef tips, sweetbreads with mushrooms and sundry savory veal dishes are among the kitchen offerings. An early bird dinner is served from for $11.75. Our group's comments reflect the solid, reliable (if not exciting) nature of this place: "Nice atmosphere" and "accommodating staff."

BASTA PASTA • 1268 Grant Avenue (Vallejo) • 434-2248

Italian/seafood • $$

Lunch and dinner daily, service to 2 a.m.; reservations accepted; casual; full bar; MC, VISA, AMEX • There is a kind of restaurant, not unique to San Francisco but certainly popular here, that can create ambiance out of noise. Not irritating noise, but a kind of irrepressible, happy hour mix of urgent voices talking over background music. But a lively crowd isn't enough; the place should be in an atmospheric building not yet ruined by an interior decorator, and the food should be reliable and at least occasionally excellent. Otherwise, such an establishment would just be a bad joke on the ear drums. We've already touched on one specimen, the Balboa Cafe, and the best example—or worst, if you're the quiet type—is yet to come, the Cadillac Bar and Grill.

Basta Pasta (Italian for "Enough spaghetti, already"), a two-story, open kitchen bistro on a North Beach street corner, meets all of the above criteria. Basta's pastas are uneven, according to our scouts and our own experience, but they can be excellent. The strongest part of the menu is the seafood, fresh, simply prepared and lightly cooked, as seafood should be. The reason for this sounds like a PR man's fantasy, but it's true. Owners Bruno Orsi and Lorenzo Petroni also own a piece of a fishing boat called the *North Beach Star.* So when you hear the term "fresh off the boat" in this lively place, they aren't talking about the new busboy from Hong Kong.

BEETHOVEN RESTAURANT • 1701 Powell (Union) • 391-4488

German • $$

Dinner Tuesday through Saturday; casual to sport jacket; wine and beer; MC, VISA, AMEX • You step from busy Powell Street into an elegant oasis of old Germany when you enter this pleasant restaurant with its wainscoting, fine print wallpaper and softly ticking cuckoo clock. Yet for all its Black Forest refinement, this romantic, family-owned restaurant is surprisingly inexpensive.

The menu is obviously German, but with some creative twists by host Alfred Baumann, like *Paprikaschnitzel* (veal in a paprika and mushroom sauce). He also offers a lightly-done catch of the day. When we tried his *rindsrouladen* (the classic stuffed rolled beef), it was tasty but a bit dry. Most other dishes have been excellent. Baumann serves the best apple strudel in the city; it's like a deep-dish apple pie in vanilla sauce.

"Just superb," extolled one spy. "Consistently outstanding food, preparation, presentation and service."

THE BIG FOUR • 1075 California (Huntington Hotel, near Taylor) • 771-1140

American/Continental • $$$

Breakfast, lunch and dinner daily; reservations advised; sport jacket to dressy; full bar; major credit cards • Since this isn't a history book, we'll not get involved with Central Pacific railroad barons Stanford, Hopkins, Crocker and Huntington for whom this restaurant is named, except to say that after they made their fortunes, these "nabobs" lived in baronial splendor on Nob Hill. The Big Four Restaurant in the Huntington Hotel reflects this opulence, with its rich oak paneling, high-backed leather banquettes, rams horn wall sconces, polished copper bar and railroading memorabilia. It may be, in fact, the most comely example of 1880 restaurant decor in the country.

Amid all this pomp and posh, the food is refreshingly light and innovative; the changing menu wanders culinarily from grilled buffalo with wild mushrooms to Peking duck to Texas antelope with corn griddle cakes and glazed kumquats. Such experimentation can have its weak moments, but generally, most of Chef Gloria Ciccarone's culinary surprises are good.

THE BILLBOARD CAFE • 299 Ninth (Folsom) • 558-9500

Funky nouvelle • $

Lunch and dinner Monday through Saturday, service to midnight Friday and Saturday; casual; wine and beer; no credit cards • "The best defense is a cultural offense" reads the canvas sign at Ninth and Folsom streets. Or it may suggest that we stay the hell out of Nicaragua. The art-on-canvas marks the location of a curious corner cafe concoction called the Billboard. For all of its attempts at punk goofiness and its Mohawk-haired waiters, the place serves remarkably good California cuisine. Quiche with watercress and red union slices, mesquite-grilled fresh fish and calamari in *marinara* are among its memorable and inexpensive offerings.

The cafe was created through the fortunate union of Middle Easterner Ali Ghanbarian, who had some ideas about food, and artist Mark Rennie, whose concept of interior decoration is a sort of surrealistic explosion. Most of the employees are artists between sales; the punk look is for show and quite harmless. There's little point in describing the interior. Except for a giant hand sculpted by Rennie and clocks giving the proper time in Kabul, Managua, Berlin and Petaluma, the place is redecorated at the slightest artistic whim. "Not an especially attractive restaurant," one reviewer said, but he liked the Greek salad.

BILL'S PLACE • 2315 CLEMENT (24th Avenue) • 221-5262

American/mostly hamburgers • $

Lunch and dinner daily; casual; wine and beer; no credit cards • "Great hamburgers, excellent milk shakes, good old American staples," writes one member of our cartel. But we hold an advantage over our volunteer critics; we're writing the book, so we can disagree with them occasionally. Bill's hamburgers are good but not great and certainly not, as some insist, the best in San Francisco. On several occasions, they've arrived more medium than medium rare as requested, and the accompanying red wine (an essential companion to a fine burger) was thin and uninteresting.

His milkshakes? Now, they *are* great, and so is the friendly, family ambiance. We also like the little outdoor dining patio out back that has a sort of Japanese garden look. It's a pleasant place to relax when the Richmond District fog occasionally retreats.

THE BLUE FOX • 659 Merchant (off Montgomery) • 981-1177

Continental • $$$$

Lunch and dinner daily; dressy; full bar; all major credit cards • In early 1988, the venerable Blue Fox locked its doors for a couple of months, then re-opened with a new decor and new management. We understand that the menu is still basically Continental, but the unveiling came too close to press time for an analysis. The restaurant received several votes, both good and bad, but these referred to the old Fox, so we must withhold judgment. Comments ranged from "elegant dining" to "out of touch and over the hill."

We'll assume the new Blue Fox is back in touch, although we hope the architects and interior decorators preserved the opulence of Ionic columns, Florentine gold and Venetian crystal that drew luxury-loving diners for more than four decades.

BOMBAY PALACE • 600 Beach (The Cannery, Leavenworth & Columbus • 776-3666

Northern India • $$

Lunch and dinner daily; casual to sport jacket; full bar; major credit cards • Compared with most East Indian restaurants, such as Gaylord and the Peacock, Bombay Palace is almost stark. It's located in a corner of the Cannery, and the lofty ceiling and bare brick walls give it a rather cheerless look. A few India prints, the odd potted palm and worn gray carpet don't help.

But we're not here to nibble on the scenery. Our regiment gave the cuisine and service excellent ratings and our own visit bore this out. The cooking is *tandoori* style. Tasty things emerge from a hot, circular clay oven, usually served with a warm, chewy bread that's cooked quickly by being slapped against the oven's side. We were particularly enamored with a dish called chicken *tikka*—chunks of fowl marinated overnight in chili, yogurt, red pepper and other spices. It emerged from the *tandoor* with a delicious smoky, sweet-spicy flavor.

Bombay's portions are generous and prices are modest. Large meals with all the spicy accents are well under $20, and a 5 to 6:30 early bird dinner is only $10.95. Incidentally, the restaurant also features several tasty vegetarian dishes.

BON TEMPS LOUISIANA RESTAURANT • 1963 Sutter (Fillmore) • 563-6300

Cajun/Creole • $$

Dinner Tuesday-Sunday; reservations recommended; casual to sport jacket; wine and beer; AMEX only • Come here for the blackest, spiciest gumbo and the best sweet potato tart in town, but don't come looking for blackened redfish. Bon Temps, spare in decor but warm in reception and spicy of menu, serves *real* Cajun food, not the trendy stuff of currently in-vogue (but fading) Cajun/Creole places. Co-owner and Chef Brad Borel's cuisine includes properly prepared classics such as thick, casserole-like jambalaya; shrimp or crayfish *Etouffe* and a spicy, poached Louisiana catfish dish called *Couboullion*, served over rice. And his cornbread muffins are the best this side of my late Aunt Lydia's Idaho farm kitchen. The decor in this narrow refurbished Victorian is simple—a potted plant or two and a few prints and sketches spotlighted along the walls, with white linen and candles on the small tables.

A big, friendly bear of a man, Borel ambled out of his kitchen during one of our visits and generously recited his cornbread recipe for my wife and co-author, while I furiously scribbled down ingredients and measures. And no, he didn't know we were restaurant reviewers. We left with his cornbread secret and only two minor complaints. Carpeting is needed to help muffle the happy conversation and the place accepted, at this writing, only American Express.

BRANDY HO'S • 217 Columbus Avenue (Pacific Avenue) • 788-7527

Hunan • $

Lunch and dinner daily, service to midnight Friday and Saturday; casual; wine and beer; MC, VISA, AMEX • This lively spit-level restaurant is decorated mostly with "NO MSG" signs, plus the usual Chinese filigree on the walls and the odd lantern or two hanging from the ceiling. The Hunan food, as assertive and outgoing as the luncheon crowd that pushes in here daily, is generally well-prepared and generously laced with those tongue-igniting bits of dried red peppers. But a few milder Cantonese dishes are on the menu, and you can request that the peppers be held back on the Hunan entrees.

"Great, spicy Chinese food," says one judge. "Wait staff very helpful and knowledgeable," offers another. But the best quote comes from Brandy S.C. Ho; it was written on the form that we send all restaurants after our volunteers have nominated them:

"Opening second cafe at 450 Broadway in late spring (1988). Beautiful decor, expanded menu, spending lots of money but will keep prices within reason."

BULL'S TEXAS CAFE • 25 Van Ness Avenue (Market) • 864-4288

Texas barbecue/Tex-Mex • $

Lunch Monday-Saturday, dinner nightly, service to 11 p.m. Friday and Saturday; casual; full bar; MC, VISA • Urban (but not necessarily urbane) cowboys will feel at home in this former auto parts shop converted into an upbeat Texas-style bar and restaurant. It's a Hard Rock Cafe turned Country and Western, with cactus, pitchforks, plank floors, rough-finished wood furnishings and a Houston Yellow Cab sign. And if the juke box gets too loud and it isn't raining, you can retreat to a patio out back.

"Best nachos in town," exudes one agent; "great variety of Tex/Mex cooking," adds another. The variety includes a rather rich Texas-style chili (lots of meat, no beans) that can be spiced to order, *fajita* steak and many things barbecued. We found the barbecue sauce to be almost too rich, to the point of being cloying, but many of our judges disagree. So y'all go on down there, stick your feet under one of the wooden tables and decide for yourselves. Y'hear?

CADILLAC BAR AND GRILL • 1 Holland Court (off Howard, between Fourth and Fifth) • 543- 8226

Mexican/seafood • $$

Lunch weekdays, dinner Monday-Saturday, service to midnight Friday and Saturday; casual; full bar; major credit cards • Patterned after a similar place in Nuevo Laredo, just south of the Texas border, the Cadillac is decorated mostly in noise, with an occasional potted and painted cactus. Fortunately, the mesquite-grilled seafood and other authentic Mexican dishes here are excellent, so you'll be too busy eating to attempt conversation. An overnight success as a Yuppie hangout when it opened a few years ago, this barn-like restaurant in an old warehouse is jammed with San Franciscans craving an escape from refried beans and the occasional bewildered tourist. This is noisy ambiance at peak output.

Fresh broiled fish in a curiously spicy white salsa is the premiere offering here; *carnitas* with seasoned, shredded pork and mesquite broiled chicken also were recommended by our crew. And the light, grease-free *quesadillas* are excellent. However, erratic service and extended waits, even after you've put your name on the list, keep the Cadillac from earning a third spoon.

"Noisy, crowded and lively; it wouldn't work any other way." Well said, Spy #HT-14.

CAESAR'S • 2299 Powell (Bay) • 989-6000

Italian • $$

Lunch and dinner Tuesday-Sunday; casual; full bar; MC, VISA, AMEX • This pleasant little Italian family restaurant with a clean Art Deco look serves generous multi-course dinners at reasonable prices, mostly well under $20. A la carte versions are available for even less. All the Italian regulars are here—chicken *cacciatore*, veal *scaloppine* and *parmigiana* and *scampi*, plus the usual pastas and a selection of fresh fish. The place offers early bird dinners (Tuesday-Friday from 4:30 to 6 for $7.95) and several senior citizen specials.

"I eat there often because other members of my family like it," one reviewer says, then adds, apparently as an afterthought, "and the food is good."

CAFE D'ARTS • 205 Oak (Gough) • 626-7100

California/Mediterranean • $$$

Dinner Wednesday-Saturday; reservations suggested; sport jacket; wine and beer; MC, VISA • Can something that's good for you really taste this good? The Cafe d'Arts adds no salt to its dishes, which feature an abundance of freshly prepared vegetables. Yet the clever use of spices such as cloves and ginger and fresh herbs produces some of the Bay Area's finest examples of nouvelle cuisine. Further, smoking isn't permitted in this small dining room, so nothing will interfere with the refreshing tastes of ingeniously seasoned, simply prepared food. A clove salmon, sauteed rabbit liver and eggplant parmesan are among the offerings in this intimate boutique cafe.

One diner suggests it's *too* intimate: "Tables too close together," he complained and he found the portions "a tad small."

The decor is modern European with, appropriate to the name, changing art exhibits.

CAFE MAJESTIC • 1500 Sutter (Gough) • 776-6400

California nouvelle • $$

Breakfast, lunch and dinner Tuesday-Sunday; reservations suggested; casual to sport jacket; full bar; MC, VISA, AMEX • What a curious setting for new-wave cooking. Former theater critic Stanley Eichelbaum's cozy cafe recently earned *San Francisco Focus* magazine's "Most Romantic Restaurant" award for its Victorian decor. But it's more California Victoriana than typical Victoria and Albert—a busy study in floral wallpaper, crystal and warm woods that you might find in a restored bed and breakfast inn.

The decor goes with Chef Eichelbaum's cuisine—a mix of nouvelle and early California dishes (turn-of-the-century, not Spanish mission). Our group revealed uniform affection for his place, giving it an average score of 7.8 out of 10. "Marvelous oyster sandwich on excellent house-baked brioche", "Great! Room is lovely", "California cuisine in the 'olden days,' updated."

CAFE RIGGIO • 4112 Geary Boulevard (Fifth Avenue) • 221-2114

Italian • $$

Dinner nightly; reservations only for 5-5:30 dining times; casual to sport jacket; full bar; MC, VISA • We went for the calamari, and stayed for the upbeat ambiance. Our introduction to Cafe Riggio came by way of an overheard conversation at Hayes Street Grill. Two patrons were discussing this place "way out in the avenues" that served great calamari. In addition to the city's best calamari *fritti*, John Riggio's cafe also serves excellent, rich *minestrone*, a really fine *cannelloni* and lightly sauced versions of classico entrees—steamed clams with tomato and sweet basil, Milanese veal, and prawns with garlic.

The decor might be called "old world nouvelle"—wood paneling, white walls with framed menus, bentwood chairs and white-clothed tables with dropped lights. Located in the Richmond District, Cafe Riggio is yet to be discovered by many Bay Areans, and tourists almost never trip across it. "Our favorite 'sleeper' restaurant," says one member of our regiment. But once you've found it, the calamari and the noisy enthusiasm will draw you back. With a no-reservation policy, it's best to go during week nights or plan on spending time enjoying one of the fine Italian or California wines at the happily boisterous bar.

CAFE SAN MARCOS • 2367 Market (Castro) • 861-3846

Seafood/Cajun • $$

Lunch and dinner daily, service to midnight; casual to sport jacket; full bar; major credit cards. • This intimate three-level cafe is bright and pretty, with large windows, doweled polished-food furniture, lots of potted plants, gleaming blue strips of Spanish tile and other old world Latin touches; the management describes the look as "Spanish deco." Focal points are an antique Spanish fountain and a striking wall mural depicting the portals to San Marcos Gardens in Mexico's fabled spa city of Agua Caliente.

The food earned an average rating from our panel and one spy called the service "slipshod." We found the service to be all right, but we also rated the food as average. It's an interesting menu—fresh seafood, with strong Cajun accents. A champagne buffet is served Sundays and a deejay spins music in the main bar Friday and Saturday nights and Sunday afternoon; complimentary hors d'oeuvres are served.

CAFFE SPORT • 574 Green (Front) • 981-1251

Southern Italian • $

Italian; lunch and dinner Tuesday-Saturday with 6:30, 8:30 and 10:30 dinner sittings; reservations essential (see below); casual; wine and beer; no credit cards • Why do people keep pushing and shoving into this cluttered, noisy restaurant with a reputation for indifferent service and rude waiters? And why do restaurant critics keep enticing more people into this cycle of punishment by writing about it?

Perhaps it's the excellent but garlicky Sicilian-style food that arrives in huge servings, or the eclectic cluttered chaos that passes for decor. Or perhaps we're all just a bit masochistic.

Getting to that wonderful food is a bit of a challenge. Advance reservations are taken only for parties of four or more, and day-of-service (this is service?) reservations are grudgingly accepted for couples. But there's no guarantee that the couples will get in, so find a pair of friends before you attempt the Caffe Sport Experience. Or go for weekday lunch, when things are slightly less chaotic.

One of our crew members says it all: "Great pasta; the most arrogant, indifferent staff; bizarre, wonderful junk shop atmosphere; fun to sit at the bar and watch the scene."

CALIFORNIA CAFE BAR & GRILL • 900 Bush (Taylor) • 775-2233

American nouvelle •  $$

Lunch weekdays; dinner nightly, service to 11:30 Friday and Saturday; reservations advised on weekends; casual; full bar; MC, VISA, AMEX • California Cafe is a Bay Area chain that combines a sleek Art Deco look with generally tasty but not terribly innovative versions of the New Cuisine. We first tried its blackened redfish several years ago at the Walnut Creek branch (1540 N. California Boulevard) and decided it was quite tasty and novel. We've since had our fill of carcinogens, and have moved on to more interesting nouvelle dishes.

But the California Cafes (there are about seven now) remain reliable, efficient and pleasing to the eye. You'll get well-prepared food and efficient service, if you're not bothered by the restaurant management school mentality in these places. ("Hi! My name is Jeffrey and I'll be your waiter tonight. In addition to our regular menu items, let me recite our lengthy and impossible to memorize list of specials.")

CALIFORNIA CULINARY ACADEMY • 625 Polk Street (Turk) • 771-3500

Continental •  $$

Lunch and dinner weekdays, various sittings so call for times; reservations required for dinner; sport jacket; full bar; major credit cards • The California Culinary Society recently moved its school from Fremont Street to the soaring spaces of the old Germania Hall (changed to California Hall during World War II), where its students have more room to learn things gastronomic, and diners have more space in which to enjoy the results.

Patrons sit in a huge grand hall, and expanses of glass open the teaching kitchens to their curious eyes. The Academy is one of America's leading schools for chefs; all food preparation and service in its restaurant are handled by students. Booking a table is a bit of a wager, like getting your hair done at a beauty college, but the food is generally quite good and sometimes exceptional. Instructor-chefs probably intercept an artgum eraser fish or broccoli boiled to a pulp before it gets to your table. As you may surmise, this "classic" cooking school concentrates on Continental dishes.

Our experience there was quite satisfactory and our group gives it generally high ratings. Thus, the CCA earns three spoons despite the risk of getting a student chef who just flunked French Sauces 1-A.

CALZONE'S PIZZA CUCINA • 430 Columbus (Vallejo) • 397-3600

Pizza and pasta • $$

Lunch and dinner daily, service until 1 a.m.; casual; full bar; MC, VISA, AMEX • Owner Mario Abruzzo created an "instant old Italian" bistro when he opened Calzone's in 1986. It's housed in a 1940s high-ceiling grocery store and the upper walls are lined with narrow shelves stuffed with Italian groceries; the usual garlic, pepper and salami strands hang from the rafters. The long storefront with its big windows give patrons an excellent view of the passing parade of Italian San Francisco. The windows are opened during warm weather and a clever electrical retracting awning keeps the sun out of diners' eyes.

Calzone's is named for its specialty, a sort of oversized Italian *flauta*. Some describe it as a folded over pizza, with typical pizza toppings tucked inside. Mario does pizzas as well, baked in an old-fashioned wood-fired oven. His *ratatouille* pizza with a tasty squash, Swiss chard, bell pepper, tomato and *mozzarella* is handy for vegetarians. Mario also offers the usual assortment of home-made pastas. Our only complaint—wines are overpriced. A glass of ordinary chianti goes for $3.25, which offsets the reasonable food cost.

"Good, excellently presented Italian food with a San Francisco flavor," extols one agent, who ends with a great punch line: "Lots of *fresh* garlic; good thing the windows open."

CAMPTON PLACE • 340 Stockton (Campton Place Hotel, near Sutter) • 781-5555

American nouvelle • $$$$

Breakfast, lunch and dinner daily; reservations essential; dressy, jacket and tie; full bar; all major credit cards • "American nouvelle" is our attempt to put a label on Chef Bradley Ogden's creations, which are a delicious mix of Middle America/California Nouvelle/French Nouveau. The menu is changed frequently as Ogden draws from America's corners to find the freshest ingredients. A typical dinner might consist of onion tart appetizer, corn and oyster soup, chicory salad with garlic and pepper dressing, breast of pheasant or grilled wild turkey with bacon and Black Bottom Raspberry Mousse for dessert.

The decor is a beautifully executed version of the modern hotel look, with salmon colored fabric walls, a bit of gold leaf and brass, mirrors and potted palms, and Chinese porcelains for color accents. The table service is equally opulent—Wedgwood china, crystal glassware and silver flatware.

"Elegant, great service", "Great atmosphere", "Excellent service, superb ambiance."

CARLOS GOLDSTEIN'S • 282 O'Farrell (Mason) • 397-3356

Gringo Mexican • 

Lunch weekdays, dinner Monday-Saturday; casual; full bar; MC, VISA • "Carlos Goldstein's was named for a little known, inept lieutenant of Pancho Villa's army. He is remembered primarily for his enormous capacity for tequila and the senoritas."

And the mood goes upbeat from there. This place is a parody on Mexican/American restaurants, taking nothing seriously except its food, which is basic Mexican but quite good. A silly favorite of ours is the Goldstein Special Kosher Burrito with a spicy pastrami filling. This huge burrito arrives with a knife and fork, a green onion and a chili pepper inserted into a lemon slice, so you know these people are trying to tell you something. The O'Farrell Goldstein's, incidentally, is a clone of a larger version at 52 Belden Place in the Financial District.

"Informal atmosphere; service slow to inattentive," accuses one agent, but we've gotten average-to-prompt service during a dozen or so visits to the Belden and O'Farrell Goldsteins through the years. (We go all the way back, in fact, to the original Goldsteins located near Market Street.)

The decor is Gringo funk, consisting primarily of black and white blow-ups of scenes from Pancho Villa's army. The rawhide and rough wood chairs are surprisingly comfortable, with deep, curved backs that encircle you like a thirsty senorita in a bordertown cantina.

THE CARNELIAN ROOM • 555 California (at Montgomery, atop Bank of America Building) • 433-7500

Continental • $$$$

Dinner nightly, Sunday brunch from 10:30; reservations essential; dressy; full bar; all major credit cards • Bay Area restaurant critics don't have the old Carnelian Room to kick around anymore. When it opened in 1970, the skyroom restaurant's original operators seemed more concerned with selling the spectacular view than decent food, and the kitchen rating varied from ordinary to awful. But new management has elevated the Continental cuisine to fairly reliable heights. Some restaurant reviewers say the menu is still a bit too cutesy with curious fruit-based sauces, but we've found them to be delicious, and most of our guest reviewers agreed. And the 35,000-bottle wine cellar is one of the best in the country.

The vista is spectacular; the 52nd story perch is so high it looks down on other city skyrooms; it affords an awesome panorama of this fragile peninsula upon which a city has been thrust. One of our tricks is to arrive early and have a drink in the cocktail lounge to get a different vantage point before dinner; obviously, an after-dinner brandy will do as well. The inside view is impressive too—a splendid mix of French antiques, tapestries, crystal chandeliers and marble buffets.

Plan to part with around $60 per person for a full dinner with wine, or come early and get the same view with a $23 prix fixe "Sunset Dinner" from 6 to 7.

Our troops were almost but not quite unanimous. "Superb San Francisco-type experience", "Delighted to find a view restaurant with such excellent food", "Can't beat the view; outstanding service." And finally: "What a view! My lobster paled in comparison."

CENDRILLON • 1132 Valencia (22nd Street) • 826-7997

American nouvelle • $$

Lunch weekdays, dinner Monday-Saturday; casual to sport jacket; wine and beer; MC, VISA, AMEX • "Very good food, beautifully presented in a nice, quiet restaurant," commented a member of our regiment. Prompted by our agent's enthusiasm, we visited this relatively new cafe (1984) and discovered a place that pleases both the eye and the palate. The changing menu is California cuisine with an obvious French influence. Our duck breast in orange Grand Marnier sauce and phyllo-wrapped coho trout stuffed with shrimp were delicious and beautifully presented; the accompanying veggies were fresh and crisp. A tortellini with crab and shrimp sauce appetizer was tender, fresh and very tasty!

Classical background music sets the proper audio mood for the clean, cool interior with Art Deco prints on salmon walls and matching gray tablecloths, chair upholstery and carpeting. For a sampler of the kitchen style, Cendrillon offers a four-course prix fixe dinner for $20, or one can order from the eclectic menu.

CHA CHA CHA • 1805 Haight (Shrader) • 386-5758

Caribbean • $

Lunch Monday-Saturday, dinner nightly; casual; wine and beer; no credit cards • It could pass for one of the intimate little alley cafes in Jamaica or the Dominican Republic, with its palm-and-tile decor. Spanish *tapas* are served at the neat little bar, and assorted items with Latin/Caribbean accents appear in the dining room— trout in Spanish sherry, garlic chicken wings and a kind of *ceviche* style cold mussels.

CHATEAU SUZANNE • 1449 Lombard (Van Ness Avenue) • 771-9326

Continental with Chinese accent • $$$

Dinner Tuesday-Saturday; reservations advised; sport jacket to dressy; full bar; MC, VISA, AMEX • Our team led us to a wonderful restaurant that has thus far been ignored by most other Bay Area guides. Chateau Suzanne is the creation of 70-plus-year-old Stanley Toy. After a varied career that ranged from houseboy to secret service agent to restaurant manager (most recently at the Empress of China), he built this place by hand, fashioning it by expanding an old Lombard row-house. The dining room is an understated French jewel—chandeliers, Provincial furniture, thick green carpets, silver candlesticks and fresh flowers in bud vases on pink linen tables. It avoids the curlicue clutter of other formal food parlors.

The cuisine is a creative blend of classic French with Oriental seasonings, using no butter, salt, preservatives or egg yolks. And it's almost too pretty to disturb. A carrot and cauliflower soup arrives in a perfect orange and green yin-yang pattern; the salmon pate is a delicate pink rose with spinach pate leaves and stems. Toy's Chinese influence is evident. His Duck

L'orange is crispy like the Peking variety; ginger and curries are used as spices and crisp snow peas form pretty patterns in the food presentations. One flaw—a rolled and sliced chicken dish, while pretty as a picture, was over-cooked.

"Beautiful and romantic setting; service, food and presentation are excellent."

CHINA MOON CAFE • 639 Post (Jones) • 775-4789

California/Chinese • $$

Dim sum lunch Monday-Saturday, dinner Monday-Saturday; reservations advised for dinner; wine and beer; MC, VISA, AMEX • After years of fascination with the Orient and its foods, Chef-owner Barbara Tropp has cleverly concluded an eclectic marriage between California and Chinese cuisine in her Art Deco restaurant. Her innovative fare earned uniform praise from all of our agents, including the celebrity chefs, who cried "Brilliant!" and "Great flavors!" My co-author points out that the dishes are neither Chinese nor Californian, but a fascinating mix of fresh Chinese and American ingredients with Chinese and other Asian herbs, spices and condiments. Try deep-fried soft shell crabs with lemon sauce, Beijing antipasto, lettuce-wrapped chicken with almond, or spring roles with chili and you realize that Ms. Tropp has invented a new cuisine.

She recently began serving dim sum lunches, again using clever but never clashing combinations to create these Chinese "little hearts."

Only one complaint, also uniform—her cafe matches her diminutive proportions and the booths are rather cramped. Hopefully, her continued success will allow her to expand, even as her patrons' waistlines do the same.

CHRISTOPHE • 320 Mason (Geary) • 433-7560

French • $$$

Lunch weekdays, dinner nightly; reservations advised; sport jacket; full bar; MC, VISA, AMEX, DC • Theater crowds like this pretty French Art Deco cafe with touches of elegance in the crisp linen tablecloths, cut flowers, crystal and silver.

Owner-chef Patrick Grepon studied culinary arts in France and cooked in several Michelin-rated restaurants; his skills are evident in his exemplary French fare. Examples of his culinary classics include chicken breast stuffed with veal mousse in mustard seed sauce, scallops *provencales* and a sole *quenelle* with champagne sauce. A special prix fixe dinner is offered from 5:30 to 10:30 for $16.95, with a choice of three entrees, plus soup, salad and dessert.

"Excellent food", "Very pleasant and relaxing", "Fabulous desserts," came the cries from our regiment.

CIAO • 230 Jackson (Battery) • 982-9500

Northern Italian • $$$

Lunch Monday-Saturday, dinner nightly, service to midnight; reservations advised; casual to sport jacket; full bar; MC, VISA, AMEX, CB • This white, bright and deliberately cheerful restaurant attracts a trendy crowd to match its upscale look. The food is essential Italian but with a California influence—charbroiled shrimps, lightly seared fresh fish and a busy *antipasto misto* of calamari, sardines, cheese and meats with fresh garden vegetables. The pasta, voted best in the city by *San Francisco Focus* magazine, is freshly made.

The decor, "bright, clean, fresh and white," reflects a careful corporate conception of a cheerful, upscale Milanese restaurant. The white-walled, wicker-chaired, brass-railed dining room is striking; strings of sausages and garlics, requisite olive oil tins and hanging hunks of ham provide earthy accents.

CIRCOLO • 161 Sutter (off Kearny, in Crocker Galleria) • 362-0404

Italian • $$$

Lunch and dinner daily, service to 11:30 p.m.; reservations advised; casual to sport jacket; full bar; major credit cards • We lamented the passing of the reincarnated Old Poodle Dog, which lasted less than two years in stylish new quarters off the Crocker Galleria. But the new Circolo appears to be a worthy successor, in both appearance and cuisine. The restaurant is a pretty "modern-deco" vision with its marble entry, rose-colored wall fabric in the dining room, concave ceiling and intimate high-backed booths.

"Excellent pastas and fish," said one spy; "Excellent filet of sole and pasta" echoed another. Pastas are fresh, as are the grilled fishes, and the place specializes in an upscale pizza. Diners nosh to the pleasant tinkle of a piano nightly.

CITY OF SAN FRANCISCO — see Hornblower Cruises

CLEMENT STREET BAR & GRILL • 708 Clement (Eighth Avenue) • 386-2200

California nouvelle • $$

Lunch and dinner Tuesday-Sunday; casual; full bar; major credit cards • "Very creative" says one of our group, describing the daily-changing menu in this warm, comfortable Richmond District restaurant. The place occasionally develops a Southern accent, with some blackened items on the menu, but the best dishes are new Californian—lightly grilled fresh fish, calamari in marinara, grilled chicken wings *gorgonzola* and angel hair pasta. The B&G also does an excellent hamburger.

Owner Rico Nappa calls the look Old San Franciscan—wooden booths, a brick fireplace, skylights in the high ceilings and crisp white linens on the tables. The modest priced menu becomes even more modest during the 5 to 6 p.m. early bird hour, when dinners are 15 percent less.

CLIFF HOUSE (SEAFOOD AND BEVERAGE CO.) • 1090 Point Lobos (Great Highway) • 386-3330

American/Continental • $$

Lunch and dinner daily, Sunday brunch; casual; full bar; MC, VISA, AMEX • One of our critic's reviews sounds like an apartment ad: "Beautiful ocean view w/sea lions." And that just about sums up the historic Cliff House, which has perched precariously above Seal Rocks in various architectural manifestations since 1850. It has been a tourist attraction all those years, with a menu to prove it—shrimp cocktails, Eggs Benedict, New York steak and jumbo prawns. Ask what fish is fresh, then tell the chef when to pull it from the griddle and you'll have a passable dinner to go with that spectacular view of crashing surf and yelping *lobos del mar.*

The best part of the Cliff House is its rustic, funkily contrived Phineas T. Barnacle saloon, with a fireplace and picture windows on the Pacific. It is, without argument, the best place in the city to sip a drink and watch the sunset.

COMPADRES MEXICAN BAR & GRILL • Ghirardelli Square (North Point and Polk) • 885-2266

Mexican/American • $$

Lunch and dinner daily, breakfast weekends and holidays; reservations advised on weekends; casual; full bar; MC, VISA, AMEX • Compadres is a restaurant chain with consistently good but not necessarily exciting Mexican-American food, but this place earns an extra spoon for its ambiance and its impressive cliff-hanging location in Ghirardelli Square. Outdoor patios, a glassed-in terrace and the open dining room all take advantage of the bayside panorama.

Light woods, lots of tropical plants, Mexican handicrafts and a pair of macaws named "Syd" and, naturally, "Cesar" elevate Compadres from corporate complacency to a festive hangout. A *pan hana*, sort of a Mexican happy hour, occurs each Friday, to the ringing thump of Jeff Narell's steel drums.

"Good food, pleasant surroundings—especially the terrace."

COMPASS ROSE • 335 Powell (at Geary, in the Westin St. Francis) • 774-0167

Continental/Oriental • $$

Lunch daily; sport jacket; full bar; major credit cards • Most folks think of the Compass Rose as that opulent cocktail lounge on the ground floor of the St. Francis. Indeed, we took one look at its fluted columns, ornate carved woods, scalloped drapes and European antiques and selected it as the city's most elegant bar in *The Best of San Francisco*. But it also serves fine, light lunches and fashionable high tea (from 3 to 4:30). The fare is Continental-American with Asian accents, including dim sum, spicy chicken sachets, petit fillets and a caviar cart. It's not inexpensive, around $10 an entree, but the service is exquisite.

"Excellent lunch; one of the elegant rooms in San Francisco."

CORDON BLEU VIETNAMESE RESTAURANT • 1574 California (Polk) • 673-5637

Vietnamese • $

Lunch and dinner Tuesday through Sunday; casual; no alcohol; no credit cards • "Tiny, fast; mountains of good, CHEAP food. Cable Car drivers stop on the run to order, then pick up food on the return trip." "Small, yet very popular; counter dining; good view of the cook; friendly service."

Thus did two of our crew do a thorough job of summing up this diminutive one-counter, two-table restaurant. It's one of the best of the many remarkably inexpensive and remarkably austere Vietnamese cafes around the city. Many are in the Tenderloin, where the hard-working Viet immigrants are transforming the old slum into a livable, safe neighborhood. But until the transformation is complete, many people migrate toward this better-located hole-in-the-wall cafe in boutique-lined Polk Gulch.

A larger twin, started by the same family but now under different ownership, ladles out similar inexpensive fare at 771 O'Farrell near Larkin. It offers a couple of advantages—MasterCard and VISA are accepted and, for those of us who like to sip Tsingtao with our five-spice chicken, beer and wine are served.

CORONA BAR & GRILL • 88 Cyril Magnin (Ellis, across from the Ramada Renaissance) • 392-5500

Southwestern/Mexican • $$

Lunch and dinner daily; reservations suggested; casual to sport jacket; full bar; all major credit cards • This "contemporary Mexico" designer restaurant opened in late 1987 and received few votes, but when an agent praised its "excellent food with impressive decor and service," we decided to check it out. The look *is* impressive. A creation of Fog City designer Pat Kuleto, it's a big, high-ceiling place done in a soft rainbow of pinks, turquoise and autumn browns. Turquoise drop lamps brighten white-clothed tables and booths; potted palms and cactus bring desert greenery indoors. Bright colored tribal masks decorate the long bar, adjacent to an open kitchen.

The food was interesting but portions were meager for the price. We ordered a "small plate" of shrimp *relleno* and were advised that it would be too small for an adequate lunch; we nodded and added smoked duck *quesadillas* with sour cream from the appetizer list. Both were tasty. Little *jalapeno*-flecked cornbreads baked in the shape of corn were excellent; we quickly devoured a basket of two and were brought another pair. Service was almost too attentive; a busboy turned our water glass into an endless font, the waitress popped by every few minutes and the hostess checked on our welfare as she walked past with a fresh pair of patrons.

A big, irritating minus—waitpersons recite a list of six to eight specials, without volunteering prices.

THE CULTURED SALAD • #3 Embarcadero Center (Sacramento and Davis) • 781-1922

Salad 'n' soup lunches • $

Lunch from 10 a.m. to 5 p.m. weekdays, 10 to 4:30 Saturday; casual; wine and beer; no credit cards • Fitness enthusiasts will love this place that sells health by the pound. For around $4 a pound, you can build your own salad, picking and choosing from one of the largest and most varied salad bars we've ever seen. Pass up the ordinary lettuce and go for the fresh spinach leaves, sprouts, pickled beets, raisins, cherry tomatoes, cold cooked corn and peas, bacon bits, sunflower seeds and whatever. Soups and a meaty but rather flaccid chili are also offered, and a small dessert bar serves good frozen yogurt.

You build your salad in one of those styrofoam take-home containers, so it's easy to close the lid, balance a drink on top and head for one of Embarcadero Center's sunny patios. Or dine in the surprisingly well-designed blonde, pink and green cafe, with carpeting and bentwood chairs; sprigs of dried flowers add nice touches to the small tables.

"Very fresh, efficient, economical."

DA SANDRO • 347 Presidio Avenue (Sacramento) • 929-0402

Italian • $$

Dinner nightly; reservations suggested on weekends; casual; full bar; MC, VISA, AMEX • Da Sandro is a neighborhood family trattoria that serves a mix of Italian and American fare. "Very buttery pasta, excellent tomato sauce and fresh shellfish." Our phantom diners agree that pastas are the strongest thing here; the veal dishes can be tasty or tasteless, chicken is often quite good. Desserts, done elsewhere but carefully chosen, are uniformly good.

The look of the high-ceiling twin dining rooms and cocktail lounge is Italian-American, with the typical Italianate deli display case and garlands of garlic and red peppers.

DES ALPES • 732 Broadway (Stockton) • 391-4249

Family style Basque • \⊘Y$

Dinner Tuesday through Sunday; reservations advised; casual; full bar; MC, VISA • One of the oldest of the city's several Basque family-style restaurants, Des Alpes has been serving staggering portions of soup, salad and hearty entrees since 1908. The food has a strong Italian accent although the owners are Spanish Basque. Fare ranges from cooked-to-death vegetables to wonderfully spiced meats and fresh salads large enough to feed the cast of *Watership Down*. Each evening's pre-set menu features two entrees, plus a parade of soups, salads and crusty Italian bread, so one never waddles away hungry. In no other Bay Area restaurant can you eat so much, and so much variety, for so little. At last report, owner Ciriaco Iturri's prix fixe dinner was $9.

The decor is what you'd expect—plain, wood paneled and rather weathered walls, pictures of Basque dancers and the characteristic checkered oilcloth tables. One enters via a long, cluttered bar out front.

DOIDGE'S KITCHEN • 2217 Union (Fillmore) • 921-2149

American • \\$$

Breakfast and lunch daily, dinner Thursday-Sunday; reservations advised on weekends; casual; no alcohol but wine or beer can be brought in; MC, VISA • Doidge's serves some of the city's best breakfasts—tasty things like honey-cured ham, curried apples, corned beef hash with fresh mushrooms, and creative omelets. And you can get these wake-up meals most of the day. "Fantastic breakfast; always fresh fruit." In the evening, the scene shifts to items such as basil-seasoned meat loaf and other "good old American" dishes, and some really delicious desserts.

Take your pick of decor. This cheerful, airy place with patchwork tablecloths wears a country French look for a few months, then, like an affordable Four Seasons, becomes a slice of English countryside.

DONATELLO • 501 Post (at Mason, in the Donatello hotel) • 441-7182

Northern Italian • $$$$

Lunch and dinner daily; reservations essential; dressy; full bar; major credit cards • When we wrote *The Best of San Francisco* in 1986, we nominated Donatello as the city's finest restaurant. Now, the best has been improved—not by hiring a new chef or switching to California cuisine, but by banning smoking in its two stunningly refined dining rooms. Puffing is permitted only in the cocktail lounge.

Nothing now disturbs the subtle sauces of the finest Italian cooking west of Emilia-Romagna, the northern district that is inspiration for Chef Renato Rizzardi's creations. Proprietor Cal Rossi has provided Italian-born Rizzardi with an exquisite arena—two comely dining rooms done in Fortuni silks, Venetian glass, Carpaccio lamps and all those other impressive-sounding Italian names. We'll not dwell on the menu, for it changes frequently.

We will dwell briefly on the restaurant's *table d'hote*, a four-course dinner with a regional Italian wine to compliment each service. Incidentally, the restaurant brings fresh ideas into its kitchen and keeps abreast of culinary proceedings in the mother country by importing top Italian chefs for week-long stays at this sophisticated hotel. Meanwhile, our critics (who gave Donatello a 9.916 out of a possible ten and selected it as the city's top restaurant) say it best:

"Ambiance, food and service all rate a ten", "Very expensive but fantastic for special occasions", "The most classic cuisine; the most professional operation."

DOROS • 714 Montgomery (Washington) • 397-6822

Continental • $$$$

Lunch and dinner daily; reservations essential; dressy; full bar; all major credit cards • Unlike red wines, most restaurant don't improve with age, but Doros is an exception. Don A. Dianda has been greeting regulars and newcomers and his chefs have been pleasing them at this San Francisco landmark for more than three decades. Chef Paul Bermani draws from northern Italy and elsewhere on the Continent for his consistently tasty cuisine— from *Escargots Farci* and *Zucchini Florentine* to dungeness crab Delmonico and *saltimbocca a la Romana.* And two thousand cases of California and European wines lie asleep in the cellar, awaiting pairing with the proper foods.

The restaurant remains a study in refined simplicity—rich red leather banquettes complimenting fabric-covered red walls and red carpeting, white lace tablecloths and gold-rimmed china with silver service. "Excellent," said Reviewer RE-36.

DUFFY'S TAVERN • 451 Pine (Montgomery) • 989-1239

American/Italian lunch • $

Lunch weekdays; reservations accepted; casual to sport jacket; full bar; MC, VISA, AMEX • This pleasantly noisy upstairs white-collar pub in the Financial District serves light lunches heavily tilted toward Italian—chicken *tortellini*, *fettucini* and prawns, *linguini* with calamari and clams and something called a shrimp and tomato burst. (Bite with care?) We recently tried chicken Jerusalem; the chicken was moist and tender; unfortunately, so were the over-cooked veggies. But the sauce was so rich and tasty that I even ate the mushrooms (not one of my favorite foods).

The place is very Old San Francisco, with a pressed tin ceiling from which fans dangle, raw brick walls, a weathered wooden bar, and skylights to allow a little daylight into the dark-wood interior, but not enough to spoil the atmosphere.

E'ANGELO RESTAURANT • 2234 Chestnut (Pierce) • 567-6164

Northern Italian • $$

Dinner Tuesday-Sunday; casual; wine and beer; no credit cards • Chef-owner Enzio A. Rastelli rises with the roosters each business day to personally prepare pasta for the more than twenty different dishes on his menu. He and his Milanese pasta machine obviously do wonders, since our experts have uniform praise for his *fettucini carbonera*, *tortellini papalina*, *lasagna* and similar fare. Another liked his "great eggplant parmesan." "Great Italian food; service is fast and friendly" was the cartel's summation.

When Rastelli purchased this Marina District landmark in 1978 (originally called Eduardo's), he quickly allayed fears that quality would suffer under new management. He has carried the Eduardo banner well, and improved on service, which was rather erratic in the old days. Decor is appropriately simple for this neighborhood pasta house—small paintings based on

Italian legends, candle-lit tables and an open kitchen with an old brick oven.

EDDIE JACK'S • 1151 Folsom (Seventh) • 626-2388

California nouvelle • $$

Lunch weekdays, dinner Tuesday-Saturday; reservations suggested; casual; wine and beer; MC, VISA • We almost hesitate to call this new south of Market place trendy, for the food is better than that catch-word suggests. "Rather new, but with a real impact," reported one reporter. "It's here to stay", "Great food, great people, fresh" and "Pleasant, upbeat atmosphere" were among the other endorsements, while *Food and Wine* magazine called it "a real cross-section of San Francisco's special world."

Opened in early 1987, this family-operated cafe features lightly grilled and lightly sauced seafoods, a kind of California *cioppino* and some items with mild Spanish accents. It *is* a lively place; "Too loud," said one of our group.

EL SOMBRERO • 5800 Geary Boulevard (22nd Avenue) • 221- 2382

Mexican • $

Lunch Tuesday-Saturday, dinner Tuesday-Sunday; casual; full bar; MC, VISA • El Sombrero has been serving ordinarily reliable Mexican fare since 1946; in that time it has settled into a predictable pattern preferred by its regulars, although it offers little for the adventurous diner. The decor is typical of such seasoned old margarita parlors; it's sort of Spanish colonial with a massive wrought iron chandelier, high-backed booths and woven strap-leather chairs, beamed ceiling and lots of blue Spanish tile.

The kitchen uses shredded instead of ground meats in its various tortilla-wrapped offerings; the chicken with rice, chicken *mole* and pure meat chili *con carne* are worth the long drive out Geary Boulevard.

EL TAZUMAL RESTAURANT & TAQUERIA • 3522 20th (Mission) • 550-0935

Mexican/Salvadorean • 

Lunch and dinner daily; casual; wine and beer; MC, VISA, AMEX • El Tazumal rises above the dozens of mom and pop refried beanries that line the tiled sidewalks of the Mission District. Both the creative fare and the pleasant potted plant decor set this friendly family-run place apart from the others, yet it's equally inexpensive. "Consistently the best Mexican, Salvadorean restaurant I know," says one of our associates.

The Salvadorean side of the menu is particularly intriguing, with entrees like *lomo de puerco asado*, pork with fried potatoes and bananas; *lengua en salsa*, beef tongue in a fresh tomato-onion sauce and *lomo saltado*, beef strips with fried potatoes and sweet peppers.

EL TOREADOR FONDA MEJICANA • 50 West Portal (Vicente) • 566-8104

Mexican • 

Lunch and dinner Tuesday-Sunday; casual; wine and beer; all major credit cards • A wonderfully funky clutter of Mexican excess fills this cheery little restaurant just outside the west portal of Twin Peaks Tunnel, such as pinatas, sombreros, paper flowers, bullfight posters and written testimonials from happy customers.

"Fine Mexican food at good prices." That comment from one of our associates is a fair appraisal of the place that has been serving south of the border fare for 35 years. The kitchen produces the usual array of tortilla wrapped items and adds some distinctive Jalisco touches, using cilantro and chocolaty *mole* in some of its dishes. *Gorditas*, thick tortillas with chicken or *chorizo* chunks, topped with sour cream, guacamole and chopped onion are tasty, as are the *chimichangas*, shredded beef or chicken rolled into flour tortillas with a generous dollop of sour cream and *guacamole* on top. Beer goes great with Mexican food and El Toreador offers 35 varieties, from Mexico to Jamaica.

THE ELITE CAFE • 2049 Fillmore Street (California) • 346-8668

Cajun/Creole/Seafood • $$

Dinner Monday-Saturday, Sunday brunch; sport jacket; full bar; no credit cards • The Elite accepts no reservations, but an oyster bar quells hunger pangs as the faithful wait for seating in this popular Art Deco bistro. The dark woods, enclosed booths, ceiling fans and etched glass windows give it the proper look for an upscale New Orleans bistro and the menu is equally convincing.

With strong emphasis on Louisiana seafoods (or suitable local substitutes), the kitchen generates an assortment of spicy Cajun and Creole creations. Redfish with pecan sauce, shrimp *remoulade,* fresh Louisiana crawfish and fresh delta catfish are among the offerings on a frequently-changed menu. The Elite was one of the first Bay Area restaurants to try New Orleans Chef Paul Prudhomme's blackened redfish. Using heavy cast iron to achieve the proper searing temperature, Chef Duane Mears turns out an excellent rendition of this curious carcinogenic creation.

"Not afraid to charge, but overall, the food is good and it's very well-run."

EMERALD GARDEN • 1550 California (Larkin) • 673-1155

Vietnamese • $

Lunch Monday-Friday, dinner Monday-Sunday, reservations advised Fridays and Saturdays; casual to sport jacket (no scruffies); wine and beer, and wine can be brought in for a $5 corkage fee; MC, VISA • Emerald Garden joins the growing list of small, inexpensive Vietnamese cafes that have graduated from Formica and chrome to a more attractive decor. The "garden" is a clever bit of interior work with green carpeting, bamboo plants and photo-murals of tropical flowers. Taped music ranging from classical to modern synthesizer provides a mellow background for the garden-like setting.

Like other Southeast Asian restaurants, Emerald Garden offers cuisine with a tropical flair—papaya, mint, shrimp and peanut salad; taro soup; and curried vegetables in coconut sauce. And we've got to try the Evil Jungle Prince with Prawns; it's stir-fried shrimp in a wicked red chili-coconut sauce.

"Delightful; excellent."

EMPRESS OF CHINA • 838 Grant Avenue (Clay) • 434-1345

Chinese • $$

Lunch and dinner daily; reservations advised; casual to sport jacket, full bar; major credit cards • Is it awesome or awful? Our reporters can't agree on this venerable Chinese landmark which stares over Portsmouth Square from its sixth floor perch. "Elegance at a good price," says one. "Tourist trap with cornstarch," counters another. Bearing in mind the old cliche which says truth lies somewhere in the middle, diners can order carefully and get tasty, fresh Cantonese flavors, or put themselves in the hands of a stoic Chinese waiter and receive ordinary fare.

Originally a Cantonese showplace, the restaurant now offers assorted Szechuan, Peking and even "Nanking" food, although some of it is Cantonese with peppers added. Dining here is a visual event. Picture windows offer a generous slice of city and bay, and the interior is a busy vision of things Asian—carved Oriental panels, magnificently garish chandeliers, Chinese lanterns and assorted Asian artifacts.

ENGLISH GRILL • 335 Powell (at Post in the Westin St. Francis) • 774-0233

Continental/seafood • $$$

Lunch Monday-Saturday, dinner nightly; reservations suggested; casual to sport jacket; full bar; major credit cards • "Outstanding seafood; swordfish with avocado was magnificent." Originally a Continental restaurant with a men's club ambiance, the Westin St. Francis "downstairs" restaurant now focuses on the fresh catch, offering ten or more seafood entrees. They can be accompanied by an array of crisp white California wines, poured by the glass. A few beef dishes also are on the menu.

The Grill still retains much of its clubby look, with wood paneling and English decor, but it's hardly stuffy. Many business types save the swanky upstairs Victor's for more formal evening occasions and use the handsome, comfortable Grill for their power lunches.

ENRICO'S RESTAURANT • 504 Broadway (Columbus) • 392-6220

American/Continental • $$

Daily from 11 a.m. to 3 a.m.; casual; full bar; reservations accepted; MC, VISA, AMEX • For years, Enrico Banducci's sidewalk cafe has been witness to the blinking nipples of the Condor Club marquee and the garish neon of Broadway's other strip and topless joints. It is both oblivious to, and part of, the jarring and jaded scene surrounding it. This is a gathering spot for writers, artists and other night owls; for Kansas tourists who ogle the freak parade along Broadway and horny conventioneers who retreat here to regain their composure after observing the Adam and Eve Love Act three doors down.

Opened in 1958, Enrico's was part of the Broadway scene long before Carol Doda's mammaries went public and it likely will remain long after the last bump and grunt show has been called on account of disinterest. When this area was the city's legitimate nightlife center, Banducci propelled Mort Sahl and other stars to fame in his hungry i, then he settled down to operate this Parisian-style sidewalk cafe. The American and Continental food, particularly the pasta, is surprisingly tasty, prepared by chefs who have worked with Enrico for years, and served with good-humored efficiency by his veteran waiters.

The only jarring note is the bus and truck traffic that growls and fumes up Broadway, but that isn't Enrico's fault. In Europe, a boulevard so rich in past glory and present decadence would be an historical site and a pedestrian mall by now.

ENZO'S • #3 Embarcadero Center (Sacramento and Davis) • 981-5530

Italian • $$

Lunch Monday-Friday, dinner Monday-Saturday; casual to sport jacket; full bar; MC, VISA, AMEX • Enzo's is a popular lunch spot for the lower Market white-collar crowd, featuring a predominately Italian menu with sundry pastas, upscale pizza and the usual veal, chicken and steak entrees. During a recent visit, we stuffed ourselves with a rich linguini with crab—a busy blend of fresh tomatoes, mushrooms, chives and onions, accompanied by a generous glass of wine. Unfortunately, wine prices are a bit generous, too. Enzo's is one of the many restaurants that slaps a severe markup on premium wines by the glass; the $3.50 to $5 tab drives up the cost of an otherwise moderately priced lunch. Stay with the house reds and whites; they're quite good.

The decor is San Francisco *moderne*, with impressionistic prints on off-white walls and a black-painted exposed ceiling of heating ducts and pipes. Big windows and planter dividers that break this large restaurant into smaller sections provide an airy yet intimate atmosphere.

"Food was good," was the simple comment of one of our phantom diners. He (and we) particularly liked the zucchini-garlic bread.

EQUINOX • #5 Embarcadero Center (in the Hyatt Regency) • 788-1234

American/Continental • $$$

Lunch and dinner daily; casual to sport jacket; full bar; major credit cards • "Mediocre; expensive for lunch."

It's amazing. The management of the Hyatt Regency, one of the city's most chic and exciting hotels with its stunning atrium lobby, monumental artworks and Friday tea dances, permits its Equinox revolving skyroom restaurant to function as an over-priced tourist trap. Perhaps a glitzy glass rotating cylinder is doomed to this role, like Seattle's Space Needle. Such novelties attract so many sightseers that it's difficult to maintain any sense of dignified dining decorum; employees must keep alert to discourage an occasional camera-clutcher from leaning over patrons to point his Pentax out a window.

It would help if the food were excellent and imaginative; unfortunately it's ordinary and overpriced, along with the drinks. The Equinox exhibits an expense account mentality; the delicate question of cost is often avoided. After our critics gave it bad marks, we stopped by for lunch and noted that a table card promoting daiquiris, Singapore Slings and such did not list prices. Our waiter arrived with a menu and a cold bottle of 1986 Chateau St. Michelle chardonnay (Washington State) in hand. He offered to pour a glass but neglected to mention that it was $4.75 per pour, the price of a good lunch in some places. Our lunch, breast of Petaluma chicken in a tart cream sauce, wasn't bad; it was merely ordinary. Regrettably, the price wasn't. The tab, including two glasses of wine (not considered excessive for someone of Scottish-Irish descent) was more than $25, plus gratuity.

An awesome view might blunt the shock of a $25 lunch, but the vista isn't that impressive. Since the Equinox sits at the foot of Market Street and is a mere sixteen stories high, one stares at the city's waistline, not its skyline. The slowly-twisting restaurant offers an unraveling panorama of the midsections of Financial District high-rises. Even its bay vistas are disrupted by an ugly, square concrete collar that rims this skyroom novelty. Maybe management should follow the lead of Oz at the Westin St. Francis and turn this architectural malediction into a disco.

ERNESTO'S RESTAURANT • 2311 Clement (24th Avenue) • 342-3932

Italian • $$

Dinner nightly, service to midnight Friday and Saturday; casual; wine and beer (and wine can be brought in for a corkage fee); MC, VISA • "Great pasta; attention to detail; never disappointed." And with that, one enthusiastic epicure gave this Richmond District bistro tens for food and service and a predictable five for the ordinary mom-and-pop Italian cafe look. The place ladles out generous portions of excellent home-made pastas, along with the usual veal and chicken dishes and some really fine pizzas.

You may have to wait for a table, but friendly employees ply you with a gratis glass of wine and garlic bread to encourage you to stick around.

ERNIE'S RESTAURANT • 847 Montgomery (Pacific) • 397-5971

French • $$$$

Dinner nightly; reservations advised; dressy; full bar; major credit cards • There is a temptation among diners and dining critics to assume that complacency sets in when a restaurant has been in business for decades. In the case of Ernie's, serving classic French fare since 1934, most of our experts heartily disagree. "The best of French", "Service impeccable; attentive but not intrusive", "The staff goes out of its way to provide a memorable dining experience." However, one fussed about a limited menu and small portions.

A few years ago, new chef Bruno Tison trimmed the ponderous menu and created interesting new sauces, producing a lighter French nouveau cuisine, such as grilled lobster with sea urchin coral butter, veal in a red bell pepper sauce and (with a touch of humor, perhaps) *Poularde de Petaluma* with truffles and duck liver sauce. (I lived in Petaluma for a decade one year, but I never did encounter a French chicken.)

One of the few old-time San Francisco restaurants still with the founding family, Ernie's was started by the grandfather of present-day proprietors Victor and Roland Gotti. It survives handsomely as an opulent Victorian dining parlor with plush red walls, high-backed chairs and tasteful globed light fixtures on a heavy-beamed coffered ceiling.

FAZ • 123 Bush (Battery) • 362-4484

California nouvelle • $$

Lunch weekdays, dinner Tuesday-Friday; casual to sport jacket; full bar; major credit cards • One is tempted to call this place trendy, with its California menu and sleek decor tucked into the narrow confines of a curious 20-foot-wide, ten-story mini-skyscraper. But Fazio Poursohi goes beyond trends to feature lightly smoked fishes, meats and birds as the heart of his menu. They range from smoked salmon appetizers and duck salad to an entree of smoked Petaluma duck (there's that town again). A mixed smoked fish platter appetizer at $6.95 is sufficient for a light meal. Faz's prices, in fact, are remarkably modest for his financial district location. In addition to the house-smoked specialties, Faz features fresh fish, steak and grilled jumbo shrimp.

The restaurant occupies two floors of this skinny building, with a bar and open kitchen on the lively ground floor and a more intimate dining room upstairs. Blue and beige booths and tables with white linen complete the lighter touch in this interesting new restaurant.

FESTA FESTA FESTA • 532 Columbus (Green) • 391-3800

Italian buffet • $

Lunch and dinner daily, service to midnight; casual; full bar; MC, VISA, AMEX • Is San Francisco ready for Italian smorgy?

"You can characterize it as such, if you wish, but we offer a lot more substance," commented one of the owners of this new-concept cafe. It opened in January, 1988, replacing Martinelli's which, in turn, had replaced the Dixie Cafe, an apparently popular yet short-lived Cajun/Creole place.

This is indeed a new angle in dining, with more substance than Smorgy Bob's. For a slim five-dollar bill, collected at the door, patrons have access to the following: an extensive Italian-style buffet with such goodies as marinated green beans, sauteed mild red chilies, calamari and rice salad and the usual antipasto scatter of olives, meats, cheeses, marinated artichoke hearts and onions, plus a choice of four or more hot entrees and several desserts. We can attest to the fine quality and variety of the cold dishes and we enjoyed a tasty lasagna, obviously made with fresh tomato sauce. We'd gone looking for Martinelli's (which had received favorable reviews from several cartel members) and walked in on the first day of business for "Feast, Feast, Feast."

One sour note, which is easily repaired (and perhaps it has been): ordinary and rather flaccid chianti was over-priced at $3.73 for a modest-sized goblet; our usual two glasses was considerably more than the cost of the meal.

The decor is Art Deco and mostly green; in fact it's as garish as green can get. One sits on green-upholstered chairs between a forest green ceiling and a black and green tile floor. Green-trimmed milk glass lamps dangle from the green ceiling and glittery neon graphics (not green) enliven one wall. The fair-sized restaurant attains a cheerful ambiance despite all that glowering green-ness.

FETTUCINI BROTHERS • 2100 Larkin (Vallejo) • 441-2281

Pastas and salads • $

Lunch Monday-Saturday, dinner Thursday-Sunday; casual; wine and beer; MC, VISA • Initially a deli and pasta bar, Fettucini Brothers expanded to include a small cafe at the insistence of its regular customers. A variety of Bob Battaglia and Don Woodall's fresh, sheet-cut pastas are featured for light lunches and dinners, with an exceptional herb-walnut tomato sauce and several other tasty sauces, along with fresh and crispy salads.

It offers one of the best buys in the city, with a dinner of richly sauced *fettucini ala marinara,* salad, crunchy rolls with sweet butter and glass of hearty Italian red for about for $10. The place is bright and sunny, yet it has the warm woods of an old Italian bistro.

FIOR D'ITALIA • 601 Union (Columbus Avenue) • 986-1886

Italian • $$

Lunch and dinner daily; reservations accepted; casual to sport jacket; full bar; major credit cards • San Francisco's senior Italian restaurant, Fior d'Italia is a grand old world North Beach dining cavern filled with glossy, high-backed booths, cut glass and dark-suited waiters. The food is good (if old fashioned); one agent rated it as "excellent." A dozen other North Beach Italian places serve equally good fare for less money, but one goes here for a touch of yesterday, for the place has been peddling pasta and veal since 1886.

"Everything is a la carte here, so it can get expensive," pointed out one of our spies. But he gave this landmark very high marks, and indicated an affection for the "truly delightful atmosphere."

There doesn't seem to be a culinary niche for these venerable, over-dressed and moderately costly restaurants in today's Italian mix of opulent and expensive places like Donatello, trendy and lower-priced cafes like Firenze and the inexpensive trattorias. But we respect and cherish them for their history; only a tiny handful of San Francisco restaurants have eclipsed the century mark, and we owe them an occasional visit, particularly when the quality of food is as durable as the place itself.

FIRENZE RESTAURANT • 1421 Stockton (Vallejo) • 421-5813

Italian • $$

Lunch weekdays, dinner nightly; reservations advised; casual to sport jacket; wine and beer; MC, VISA • This comely new restaurant brings trendy architecture to the yesterday look of North Beach—marble exterior, salmon interior with sculptured walls and patterned fabric on modern softly-rounded furniture.

The fare in this intimate restaurant is in vogue, too; it's upscale Italian with fresh ingredients and nouvelle touches such as garlic-basted grilled eel. The Salvadorean chef uses Tabasco (lightly, of course) and other New World spices to bring fresh flavors to old Roman standards. "Nice place; everything made to order", "Not your usual Italian fare; very imaginative."

565 CLAY RESTAURANT • 565 Clay (Sansome) • 434-2345

American regional • $$

Lunch and dinner weekdays, closed weekends; lunch reservations essential; casual to sport jacket; full bar; major credit cards • Think of this place as a Financial District Greens that serves meat. In fact, former Zen priest and 565 owner-chef David Cohn once managed Greens and its highly-acclaimed Tassajara Bakery. Located across from the Transamerica Pyramid, his new restaurant caters to trendier tastes with creative American fare such as grilled Gulf of Mexico prawns in vermouth and ginger sauce, and chicken breast with peppers, sage and green peppercorn butter. True to his Zen/Greens heritage, he serves only fresh fare, much of it organically grown. His bakery products come from Tassajara, of course.

The walls of the dining room and adjoining bar are intentionally stark to better focus attention on changing exhibits by contemporary artists. The serenity of this place is somewhat disturbed by busy lunch crowds; dinners are much more genteel. And Wednesday through Friday dinners are further mellowed by Renaissance music and classical guitar.

FLEUR DE LYS • 777 Sutter (Jones) • 673-7779

French • $$$$

Dinner Tuesday-Sunday; reservations essential; dressy; full bar; major credit cards • With its excellent *haute nouvelle* cuisine by three-star chef Hubert Keller and its exquisite decor topped by a canopied fabric ceiling, Fleur de Lys is one of San Francisco's premiere restaurants. We'll relax and let our reporters tell its story:

"Excellent food, service and ambiance", "Classic, nouvelle, innovative", "Highly touted cuisine actually lives up to its reputation", "Five-star in my book", "Great chef" and "Without doubt the best, innovative, pure French cooking." That last comment came from the head chef of another major restaurant.

Significantly, Fleur de Lys rated first in our restaurant executive/celebrity chef poll *and* in our tally of restaurant employees, and it finished second in popularity among all of our guest critics. It received not one negative comment and scored a 9.66 out of a possible ten.

FOG CITY DINER • 1300 Battery (Greenwich) • 982-2000

American regional • $$

Lunch and dinner daily, service to midnight Friday and Saturday; reservations essential; casual; full bar; MC, VISA • We struggled through the crowds when Fog City first opened, dined on mediocre catfish and gave it mediocre marks. But our cartel has out-voted us: "Great atmosphere", "Quality everything", "Inexpensive; small plates or appetizers make a great dinner," and even "Loads of fun."

Loads of fun?

It can be, as one spy said, rather inexpensive, for it features "small plates" sized and priced between an appetizer and an entree. In fact, one could sample a broad range of goodies from Fog City's creative kitchen by ordering an assortment of appetizers and little plates. Things like crabcakes and buffalo chicken wings and prawns in mustard sauce and *quesadillo* with green salsa.

With its sleek streaks of aluminum, curved coffered ceilings and inventive regional fare, Fog City appears to be the invention of a Yuppie chef who escaped from the kitchens of an upscale hotel. Or at least a run-away Zen priest, restaurant critic or gourmet architect. But this is a corporate creation, assembled by Real Restaurants, Inc., and staffed by eager, smiling and almost freshly-scrubbed young people. The unsigned corporate person who completed our questionnaire calls it a "luxury re-creation of a diner."

FOUR SEAS • 731 Grant Avenue (Sacramento) • 397-5577

Chinese • 

Lunch and dinner daily; reservations suggested; casual; full bar; major credit cards • This gym-sized restaurant appears at first glance to be a cavern of chaos, but the service is remarkably prompt and organized. One of Chinatown's long-time food palaces, Four Seas specializes in Cantonese fare but, like most Chinese restaurants these days, the kitchen sprinkles peppers into some dishes and calls them Szechuan or Mandarin.

My Chinese bride and other Asian acquaintances say the food isn't bad, in spite of (or because of) its location in the heart of touristy Chinatown. And the kitchen at times can be moderately innovative, serving prawns rolled in graham flower and garnishing some plates with little displays of cooked baby veggies.

Chinese nouvelle?

FOURNOU'S OVENS • 905 California (Powell) • 989-1910

Continental • 

Lunch and dinner daily; reservations suggested; sport jacket to dressy; full bar; major credit cards • A decade and a half ago, James A. Nassikas started the now-popular fashion of creating small, exquisite European style hotels when be built Stanford Court from an old luxury apartment building. Affixed to it, but with its own entrance and identity, is Fournou's Ovens, one of the city's most attractive restaurants. In a sense, it's two restaurants in one; the upper section features Latin-European decor with wrought iron filigree, ornate pillars and the namesake ovens faced with Portuguese tile; the lower level is Victorian lace, bathed in light from galleria-style glass.

Like many of today's chefs, Christian Iser has lightened the sauces and brought new blends to the Continental fare—roast duck in ginger-chili sauce and phyllo-spinach sweetbreads in mustard seed sauce are examples. The service, in keeping with a fine Old World hotel in the New World, is efficient without a hint of pretension. Fournou's, incidentally, has one America's great wine cellars that includes private bins for collectors.

THE GALLEON BAR AND RESTAURANT • 718 14th (Church and Market) • 431-0253

American/Italian • $$

Dinner nightly and Sunday brunch; reservations suggested; casual to sport jacket; full bar; MC, VISA • There's not a brass lantern or porthole in sight; the Galleon is a chic high-style restaurant with mirrored and carpeted walls, burgundy-clothed tables and a virtual forest of Ficus Benjamima. The hall of mirrors effect succeeds in giving the restaurant a roomy feel until you squeeze behind one of the under-sized tables, too many of which are crammed into this small space. Intimacy has its limits.

The food is uneven; after a critic said it was "less than fair," we stopped by for dinner. My veal *piccata* was lightly done and delicious, with a perfectly tart caper-lemon sauce. Betty's veal *rouladin* was interestingly seasoned and tasty, but very dry. Salads were excellent, crisp and made tangy with a fine Dijon mustard dressing. Prices, incidentally, are very reasonable for the fair-sized portions. The attractive little bar up front features live entertainment; as we dined, the lyrics of a fine tenor carried back to our table.

Although we requested a no smoking table, the puffing section started one table away; fortunately, the place is well ventilated. The Galleon strikes us as a restaurant that tries hard and is at least halfway to success.

THE GARDEN COURT • Sheraton Palace Hotel, 639 Market (New Montgomery) • 392-8600

American/Continental • $$

Breakfast, lunch and dinner daily, Sunday brunch; reservations advised, essential for Sunday brunch; sport jacket; full bar; major credit cards • Time was, "The Palace" was *the* hotel in San Francisco and the splendid glass-roofed Garden Court was *the* place to join one's friends for a hearty dinner. The handsome, airy Garden Court hasn't changed. Unfortunately, neither has the menu. We suspect the kitchen experienced its last surge of creativity in the early 1930s, perhaps to celebrate Repeal.

Still, be you visitor or resident, you should "do" the Garden Court at least once to absorb a little sunshine and yesterday splendor. There isn't much excitement in the Basic Hotel hot lunch and dinner menus, so we recommend the extensive and lavishly arrayed Sunday buffet. Also, this vaulted conservatory is more pleasant under daylight than the uncertain promise of San Francisco stars.

Secret Agent HT-113 summed it up very nicely: "The feeling of eating in an elegant old hotel was a fun experience."

GARIBALDI CAFE • 1600 Seventeenth (Wisconsin) • 552-3325

California nouvelle • $$

Lunch Monday-Friday, dinner Tuesday-Saturday; reservations advised; casual; full bar; MC, VISA • Our motive for writing this book was rather selfish. We scattered agents throughout the city, hoping they would unearth some exciting new cafe discoveries for us, and not just all converge on Stars and Ernie's. One of their best revelations came in a most unlikely place, *very* south of Market in a scruffy industrial area, across from Jackson Playground.

"Delicious! Inventive! Good portions!" one of our associates cried.

Garibaldi's has become a quick favorite. It's a cu-u-ute little place all done up in high tech gray and pink, brightened by mirror strips, with bonsai on the tables and artists' "constructions" on the walls. (One object looks like a set of Technicolor bed springs and another resembles a cuckoo clock on an LSD trip.) Following the tenets of California cuisine, owner Robert Weiss and Chef Daniel Mertes base their menu on seasonal veggies and fresh seafoods, meats and birds. Fish is their main focus, and they shop daily for whatever's coming off the boats. Mertes likes to experiment, and his nouvelle style is influenced by spices from his native Columbia. Considering the creativity and craftsmanship involved, the food is remarkably inexpensive.

On our first visit we tried breast of chicken in plum sauce; it arrived with a side of crisp snow peas, seared red pepper strips and cold tomato wedges. An odd blend, but it worked well. This was preceded by an excellent potato curry soup and wedges of French *baguettes* seasoned with garlic and assorted fresh herbs. Nearly everything on the wine list is poured by the glass and again, prices are pleasing. The cocktail lounge, separate from Garibaldi's and obviously older, looks more at home in this honest working man's neighborhood; it's a friendly and slightly scruffy pub called Maria Gloria's.

GAYLORD INDIA RESTAURANT • Ghirardelli Square (North Point and Polk) • 771-8822 • #1 Embarcadero Center • 397-7775

Northern Indian •  $$$

Lunch and dinner daily, Sunday brunch; reservations advised; sport jacket to dressy; full bar; all major credit cards • Somehow, Gaylord achieves an exquisite Eastern sense of intimacy with its potted palms, wall hangings and plush sofas while at the same time affording a dazzling view of the bay through its floor-to-ceiling picture windows. Gaylord began in India in 1941 when that nation was under British rule, and it reflects the opulence of the "class" society of that era. But Gaylord is very much Indian, not British. Its Delhi-trained chefs create wonderful dishes with their almost mystical blends of Eastern spices; examples are lamb in piquant hot sauce, chicken in savory cream spinach, and egg plant in onions, tomatoes and spices.

Much of the menu focuses on baked creations from the tandoor oven, accompanied by the puffy and chewy bread cooked on its hot clay sides. Several curry dishes also are featured, but these are the milder curries of northern India.

Incidentally, early arrivals can enjoy full dinners for about $5 off from 5 to 6:30 each evening.

A new Gaylord emerged recently at #1 Embarcadero Center; it shares its older sister's opulence, offering soft, richly upholstered booths, Chippendale furniture, Indian art and palms in pots.

GELCO'S • 1450 Lombard (Franklin) • 928-1054

Yugoslavian/lamb •

Dinner Monday-Saturday; reservations advised; casual; full bar; major credit cards • "Lamb is basically what is offered here. The rack of lamb is excellent."

Lamb isn't the sum total of Yugoslavian cooking, but it's what the Buich brothers do best at Gelco's, particularly the chops and roast rack of baby lamb. Both dishes are probably the best of their type in the city. Our diners didn't get too excited over the rest of the menu; it's a rather ordinary mix of veal, steaks and fish (although the fish of the day can be very good).

From the outside, Gelco's blends too well into Lombard's motel row and is overlooked by many. It's a bit more intimate inside with dim lighting and warm woods, suggestive of a cozy American roadhouse. Live Yugoslav folk music is featured once a month.

GOEMON JAPANESE RESTAURANT • 1524 Irving (16th Street) • 664-2288

Japanese • $$

Dinner nightly except Tuesday; reservations accepted; casual; wine and beer; MC, VISA • Goemon is a particularly pleasant example of the Bay Area's many little family-owned Japanese restaurants, which invariably seem to be more attractive (but slightly more expensive) than similar mom and pop restaurants of other Asian ilk. Slatted blonde woods, tastefully displayed Nippon artifacts and rice paper *shoji* create a mellow environment in which to enjoy really fresh sushi and flaky, grease-free tempura.

"Excellent sushi; attentive service," reports one of our judges. Our own experience confirm this, and prices are a bit better than similar spots downtown and in and about *Nihonmachi.*

GOLDEN TURTLE • 2211 Van Ness Avenue (Broadway) • 441-4419
• 308 Fifth Avenue (Geary Boulevard) • 221-5285

Vietnamese • $$

Lunch and dinner daily except Monday on Van Ness; dinner only on Fifth Avenue; reservations advised; casual; wine and beer (and wine can be brought in); MC, VISA, AMEX • Both branches of this popular Vietnamese restaurant received enthusiastic votes. We raved about the Fifth Avenue Turtle in an earlier guide, and one of our investigators says the Van Ness branch is even better. Even though they occupy modern buildings, both achieve Vietnamese village visions with raised dining areas, bamboo or burnished wooden columns and lots of thatch, plants and native artifacts. A koi pond greets visitors to the newer and much larger Van Ness branch. Creative decor and candlelit tables elevate the Turtles well above most family Vietnamese cafes.

We've commented earlier that things like lemon grass and peanuts influence the flavors of Southeast Asian cooking. It's a refreshing break from the omni-present Japanese tempura and Chinese soy-sauced stir fry. For a sampler of this distinctive cooking, try the Five Spice Chicken or Seven Jewel Beef; both show off the rich variety of Vietnamese spices. Excellent, too, are the appetizers with their distinctive blends of cool and crisp vegetables and hot spiced meats; *chao tom,* shrimp sticks served with rice pancakes and plum sauce with raw vegetables is a good example.

"Great Vietnamese!" exclaimed a restaurant executive who selected the Turtle as one of his five favorite dining spots. "Comfortable room and friendly service," added another, "Fanciful and fresh ingredients highlight the somewhat repetitive menu."

THE GRAPELEAF • 4031 Balboa (41st Avenue) • 668-1515

Lebanese • $$

Dinner Wednesday-Sunday; reservations suggested; casual; full bar (and wine or champagne can be brought in); MC, VISA, AMEX • We'll admit a prejudice here, but it is a prejudice born of good food and good times. Friends put us onto this place several years ago, and we return whenever we feel like partying to the tune of spicy Middle Eastern food. The pretty and properly provocative belly dancer doesn't exactly diminish the evening's excitement.

Gabriel and Suzy Michael stir up wonderfully savory lamb and *kebab* savories in the kitchen, then they move about their small cafe to ensure that everyone is passing a pleasant evening. Gabe has turned this early 1900s Clement District house into a pretty Mediterranean courtyard, replete with arches, lanterns and tile floors. One of the least expensive of San Francisco's Middle Eastern Restaurants, the Grapeleaf offers a spicy assortment of regional specialties, starting with a *maza* tray of appetizers that includes tiny *dolmas*, seasoned lamb and fresh veggies with yogurt and chick-pea dips. Meat dishes follow, usually lamb, along with baked veggie preparations so hearty and richly spiced that a vegetarian could dine here and waddle away with a happy smile.

The next time you feel the urge to celebrate a birthday, income tax return or new marriage, take a small herd of friends to the Grapeleaf, ask Gabe to push some tables together (call ahead, of course), then just put yourselves in his hands. You'll be wined, dined and entertained like sultans.

"Great food and belly dancing; the authentic feeling of Lebanon. And that great-looking waiter with the mustache really makes the place," exuded a lady critic. Uh, that was Gabe, miss.

GREENS AT FORT MASON • Fort Mason Building A (Marina Boulevard) • 771-6222

Vegetarian • $$

Lunch and dinner Tuesday-Saturday, Sunday brunch; reservations essential; casual to sport jacket; wine and beer; MC, VISA, AMEX • "I could eat here every day; everything is fresh, tasty and thoughtfully presented", "Very interesting menu, even for those who are not vegetarian, such as myself."

Greens is no longer the popular novelty nor the conversation piece among fitness freaks who've found a holistic, meatless source of protein. After nine years, it has settled in as one of the city's finest, most enduring restaurants. And fortunately, one no longer has to wait two months for dinner. Greens hasn't changed; we have merely accepted it as a bright part of the San Francisco culinary scene.

When we dine here, we forget that our meals are meatless. We're aware that they are innovative and richly flavored, that the service is attentive and friendly, and that the predominately white wine list is excellent (a concession by the Tassajara Zen Mountain Center operators, since they drink no alcohol). We enjoy the soaring ceilings, the expansive bay views, the natural wood partitions and elevations that successfully conceal the room's military warehouse heritage. And we certainly enjoy stopping by the Tassajara Bakery take-out counter to take home something multi-grained and delicious.

The best news about Greens is that it obviously is here to stay.

GRIFONE — see Ristorante Grifone

GRUBSTAKE II • 1525 Pine (Polk) • 673-8268

American cafe • $

Breakfast, lunch and dinner daily, service to 5 a.m.; casual; no alcohol; no credit cards • Where do you go to clear your head or satisfy your tummy after you've closed down the bar *and* the after-hours disco? Obviously, the Grubstake. Since 1966, this funky cafe in a converted old train car with a Gay Nineties mural out front has offered hamburgers, omelets, salads, hot coffee and sympathy to incurable night owls. We can attest that it serves excellent chilly-night chili burgers with rich, meaty chili that buries a sesame seed bun containing a perfectly seared medium-rare patty.

The 'Stake is "open almost always," from 7 a.m. to 5 a.m.; it might be open perpetually, but owners David Sisler and Arthur Reed say they need a couple of hours to clean the place and adjust the volume on the jukebox. "Great gathering spot; food OK", "Really good omelets; constant for food; it was a fun place."

Was?

HAMBURGER MARY'S • 1582 Folsom (12th Street) • 626-1985

All-American food and funk • $

Daily from 10 a.m. to 2 a.m.; so casual it's limp; full bar; MC, VISA, AMEX • We like everything about Hamburger Mary's but the hamburgers and the noise. We like the eclectic explosion that passes for decor, the charmingly punk waitpersons and bartender, and some of the bartender's innovative drinks. Our secret agents like Mary's, too. "Great burgers and fries; casual, fun place."

But unlike places such as the Balboa Cafe and Cadillac Bar where the noise is a happy babble of voices and background music, Hamburger Mary's noise is a temple-pounding, monotonous bass-thumping jukebox rock blast that attacks your eardrums like Excedrin Headache #13. My 26-year-old daughter Kim likes this audio assault; my 13-year-old son Dan can't stand it. Obviously, I'm either too young or too old for Mary's brand of noise.

The breakfasts are excellent, and the place now offers some interesting dinner entrees. Some folks like the 'burgers. We found them to be gloppy, organic gobs of beef, tomatoes, chopped lettuce, sprouts and mayonnaise stuffed between two defenseless slices of whole wheat bread that disintegrate in your hand, not in your mouth. On each of four visits, the patties were over-done.

Like most everything else here.

HANG AH TEA ROOM • #1 Pagoda Place (Sacramento) • 982-5686

Chinese/dim sum • $

Dim sum, lunch and dinner Tuesday-Saturday; casual; wine and beer; no credit cards • This weathered cafe with its Levitz Furniture Formica dinette decor has been serving good Cantonese food and rather tasty dim sum for more that sixty years, and it makes no effort to hide its age. Tourists rarely discover this place because they are intimidated by Chinatown's alleys (which are harmless, at least in daylight). If they were to venture within, they would receive a warm welcome and authentic Cantonese fare, not the stuff dished out at some neon-lit tourist parlors along Grant Avenue.

Dim sum, the "little hearts" that range from meat-filled dumplings to broiled chicken feet to sweet rice cakes, is the specialty here. Come early for a good selection, and enjoy the curious aromas as an endless parade of carts are wheeled past your Formica table.

"Friendly; very good food; fresh ingredients."

HAPPY VALLEY RESTAURANT • 2346 Lombard (Scott) • 922-9179

Cantonese/Mandarin • $

Lunch Monday-Saturday, dinner nightly; casual; wine and beer; MC, VISA • Henry Wong set up shop on Lombard Street's Motel Row far from Chinatown five years ago and his Happy Valley Restaurant soon became a happy neighborhood lunch and dinner hangout. The decor is typically low-budget Chinatown, however, with bamboo print wallpaper, Formica woodgrain tables and incongruous wagon wheel hurricane lamps probably left over from a previous tenant.

As soon as you hit your chair, a big pot of tea and a bowl of tasty hot and sour soup hit your table. The menu is Chinese eclectic, mostly Cantonese but with several north China dishes; it ranges from the typical Canton stir fries to hot Mongolian beef and equally spicy *Kung Pao* chicken. Portions are ample, prices are good and so is the food for the most part, although a recent lunch of Kung Pao shrimp was rather bitter flavored, a case of too many and too woody bamboo shoots. The rest of the meal was fine. And Happy Valley offers an advantage over its Chinatown kin; one can usually find a place to park along Lombard.

HARBOR VILLAGE • #4 Embarcadero Center (Front) • 398-8883

Chinese/dim sum • $$

Lunch and dinner daily; reservations accepted; casual to sport jacket; full bar; major credit cards • Alphabetical coincidence has dictated listing three Chinese restaurants in a row, and each represents the three primary types: old Chinatown, newer suburban and upscale downtown. Like Tommy Toy's, which we will encounter much later, Harbor Village is a dramatic departure from the basic family diner. The Village was opened in 1985 by Lawrence Lui, whose family operates a pair of upscale restaurants in Hong Kong. It's a handsome place, designed by renowned architect John Portman, divided into several cozy canopied dining areas, and it affords fine harbor views from its niche in the Embarcadero Center complex.

The emphasis is Hong Kong Cantonese, featuring delicacies from the Colony like shark's fin and bird's nest soup and steamed fish plucked live from a tank. There's also a certain Chinese nouvelle attitude in such entrees as catfish in black bean sauce and chicken salad. And in keeping with trends, the Village's five chefs, all Hong Kong trained, can whip up an assortment of spicy northern Chinese dishes. The restaurant also offers a startling variety of exotic dim sum savories at lunch time.

HARD ROCK CAFE • 1699 Van Ness Avenue (Sacramento) • 885-1699

American graffiti •

Daily from 11:30 a.m. to 11:30 p.m.; casual (and a casualty to the eardrums); full bar; MC, VISA, AMEX • Take a perfectly sane interior decorator, force him to sit through every Annette Funicello, Elvis Presley and Tab Hunter surfing movie ever released, then turn him loose on an empty automobile showroom. The odds are, you'll get a Hard Rock Cafe. When this garish, blaring showplace of 50s and 60s excess opened a few years ago, teenyboppers of all ages lined up around the block, waiting to get in the door. The joint's novelty has since worn thin, but it still bustles. Somewhat smaller crowds hang around the big center floor bar with coke or white wine in hand, just dying to get to those baby-back ribs in watermelon sauce or mushy hamburgers.

There's plenty to see while you're waiting for your name to be bellowed above the cacophony of rock music and shouting patrons, such as half a candy apple red Caddy fused to a wall, a plastic Holstein, Waylon Jennings' guitar, a cape worn by Elvis in concert, football helmets suspended from strings and an outlaw motorcycle (sans gang, although some of the patrons could pass for members).

The service from the bobby sox waitresses is quite good, even if the food isn't. This is another instance when we don't agree with our associates, who extol its "good quality food for the price." We said it in our earlier guide and it bears repeating:

"They should charge admission and give away the food."

HARRIS' • 2100 Van Ness Avenue (Pacific Avenue) • 673-1888

American/mostly steak • $$$

Lunch weekdays, dinner nightly; reservations essential; dressy; full bar; major credit cards • We have eaten in Denver's premiere steakhouses and the legendary Morton's of Chicago, but nothing can touch Harris' for absolutely prime steak. Proprietor Ann Lee Harris can choose the finest beef from California's largest feedlot, once operated by her and her late husband. The lot is located deep in the San Joaquin Valley, well beyond sniffing distance of civilization (but unfortunately close to Interstate 5, where it is the nasal dread of every passing motorist).

The handsome high-ceiling restaurant rimmed with plush oversized booths has a men's club look about it, but the friendly and attentive wait staff dispels any notions of stuffiness, and the piano bar is lively and cheery. Although steak is the item here, the menu offers well-rounded feasts, starting with sweetbread pate, crab cocktail or fried zucchini appetizers and ending with tasty desserts produced in the Harris kitchen. Best bet is the old fashioned apple pie.

It's a busy place but if you have a bit of a wait, you can enjoy a perfect martini at the mahogany bar, admire the monumental Barnaby Conrad mural or stare into a glassed-in cooler and watch next week's steaks age.

"Service and food were excellent, but I never issue 10's," said one; another praised its "very good beef" and gave it two tens and a nine.

HARRY'S BAR AND AMERICAN GRILL • 500 Van Ness Avenue (McAllister) • 864-2779

Italian • $$

Lunch weekdays, dinner nightly, service to midnight Friday and Saturday; reservations advised; casual to sport jacket; full bar; MC, VISA, AMEX • We received positive and negative votes on Harry's, which was fashioned somewhat after the originals in Italy. We agree with one diner, who reported good food and service, but he felt that "the helpings were small for the price." I experienced the same sensation; a recent lunch was painfully pricey, and I went away vaguely hungry.

On the other hand, others praised the "super old world atmosphere" and "creative offerings." Those offerings consist of some good pastas and typical upscale Italian veals, chicken and beef dishes.

It's certainly an attractive place, sort of Italian nouvelle sleek with wood paneling, burgundy drapes and crisp white linens. Corporate owner Spectrum Foods has made a noble attempt at bringing Harry's Bar from Italy to San Francisco. But at Harry's in Venice, Gringos such as ourselves found a bit of urbane yet friendly Americana in a foreign land. On lower Van Ness Avenue, it's rather a cultural redundancy.

HARVEY'S MAIN STEM • #2 Turk (Market) • 776-3330

Haufbrau • $

Daily from 10 a.m. to 11 p.m.; casual; full bar; no credit cards • The Main Stem is a San Francisco institution that defies progress, change and particularly nouvelle cuisine; it has been ladling out good, honest fare to the faithful for decades. The only thing that has changed in this venerable brauhaus is the name, and that because new generations of the same family have assumed management, from Tommy's to Sam's Original to Harvey's.

The "Stem" offers great dining bargains; our favorite is a huge "hand carved" corned beef sandwich with generous slices of savory beef on a thick roll for $2.99. Assorted haufbrau dinner plates go for $5.29, with sides of baked beans, potatoes or home made soup for 99 cents, all served 365 days a year. Sadly, Harvey provides only one mustard to accompany his beefs and pastramis, and that tastes suspiciously like French's. However, he does furnish a real creamed horseradish that will set your sinus free. The veggies are over-cooked in typical steam table fashion, but his meats are invariably high quality and rich with succulent juices.

The cafeteria-style serving counter with its wonderful kitchen smells fills one wall and a large wooden bar with a beautifully carved back bar occupies another. The Stem is a nostalgic slice of Old San Francisco with its dark wood columns and partitions that break up the large seating area, its thick paneled ceilings and walls busy with black and white photos of yesterday.

HAYES GARDEN CAFE • 482-A Hayes (Octavia) • 861-6044

American/Continental • $$

Lunch Tuesday-Friday, dinner Tuesday-Saturday, Sunday brunch; reservations accepted; casual; wine and beer; MC, VISA • One gets the impression here of an entrepreneurial effort with limited funds. This small cafe is sparse of decor and the chef operates out of a tiny kitchen that's merely a partitioned extension of a narrow room in a refurbished Victorian. Light peach walls beg embellishment, and the simple Art Deco style light fixtures contribute to this feeling of austerity. The overall effect isn't unpleasant, just a bit spartan. Hayes Garden can be delightful as a sunny day or warm evening place, since a pretty little patio with a wedge of real grass offers pleasant alfresco dining and after-work sipping.

Service is attentive and the kitchen offers an interesting regional menu that sometimes hits; sometimes just misses. A chicken jambalaya was generous, spicy and excellent; cornbread with cheese bits and green peppers was more of a novelty than a taste breakthrough. A corn and clam chowder was off-balanced by too much corn; the effect was niblets with clam bits.

The signals we received from the kitchen were those of a young chef who's still experimenting. But that's good, not bad, and we'll return frequently to see how he's coming along.

HAYES STREET GRILL • 320 Hayes (Franklin) • 863-5545

Seafood • $$

Lunch weekdays, dinner Monday-Saturday; reservations essential; casual to sport jacket; full bar; MC, VISA • Has it really been serving some of the finest seafood in San Francisco for nearly a decade? We still tell friends about this place that offers perfectly fresh fish, lightly mesquite-broiled, with a choice of complimenting sauces, as if we'd just discovered it. Yet, it was opened in 1979 and we've eaten dozens of meals there. And in all those years, we have never been served old fish; perhaps Patricia Unterman and her two co-owners have cats at home to take care of the day's unsold catch.

Now double its original size, the Grill has added sautees and enlarged its salad and dessert selections, but we're in a comfortable rut. We settle ourselves at one of the small tables, glance up at the blackboard to see what the fishing boat brought in that morning, then discuss with the waitperson which sauce and which wine to try this time.

"Excellent fish; simple, straightforward, perfectly prepared."

Minuses (as critic Unterman would say): tables are a bit small and close together; even with the addition of carpeting a few years back, the place gets noisy. Save those intimate evenings for Fleur de Lys; come here for the lively ambiance and the best seafood in San Francisco.

THE HILLCREST BAR AND CAFE • 2201 Fillmore (Sacramento) • 563-8400

American regional • $$

Lunch and dinner daily, "pub menu" from 10:30 to 3 a.m.; reservations accepted; casual; full bar; MC, VISA, AMEX • We liked this place the moment we stepped through the door: It's a cheery little cafe with high ceilings, off-white walls with bright blotches of modern art, and blue-gray bentwood chairs at small tables. The tiny cocktail lounge is an intimate corner sitting room with comfortable stuffed furniture. Manager Matthew Stocker calls the cafe "California modern."

The small menu is Americana nouvelle, featuring only fresh, natural ingredients—pastas, calves liver, Louisiana hot sausage with chutney, stuff like that. And it changes frequently. Our palates were pleased by a light lunch of fettucini with shrimp, fresh tomato sauce and fresh basil.

THE HOLDING COMPANY • #2 Embarcadero Center (Front) • 986-0797

American • $$

Lunch and dinner weekdays; reservations suggested; casual to sport jacket; full bar; major credit cards • We like this Yuppie luncheon spot for its excellent hamburgers, although it also offers a nicely edible selection of pastas, chops, the daily catch and other light meals. Even after the Crash of '87, Corona-sipping Financial District regulars can dine well on the hearty burgers with a choice of cheeses on a sourdough or onion roll, excellent skins-on fries and a lettuce-tomato dab of salad for under $7. Dinners, obviously, are more but they're generous for the $10 to $15 tab.

The ambiance is pleasant, too—a rich blend of woods and brass inside, with sunny patio tables on the perimeter.

HORNBLOWER DINING CRUISES • Pier 33, The Embarcadero • 434-0300

American/Continental • $$$$

Nightly dinner cruises on the "City of San Francisco" plus weekend brunch and weekday lunch cruises; reservations essential; sport jacket to dressy; full bar; MC, VISA, AMEX • It's odd that most other legitimate restaurant guides ignore the "City of San Francisco," apparently brushing aside dining cruises as gimmicks. But is a cafe with sushi-laden little boats in water troughs or a place with Reynolds Wrap palm trees any less gimmicky? Also, the ship and its dining room are quite handsome and the food is generally rather good. (Fish was overdone and bland on our last cruise, however. You might prefer to stay with the meats and fowls on the limited prix fixe menu.)

We have no problem parting with $100 per couple to cruise around the beautiful bay on this glossy new "old" ship fashioned after a turn of the century luxury yacht. The captain chooses a different route each outing, depending on the weather, the clarity of the view and his mood. "I've got the best job in the world," he boasted during our after-dinner visit to the wheelhouse, as he guided his ship up the Oakland Estuary. On another cruise, we prowled the Raccoon Straits, slipped under the Golden Gate Bridge and brushed the edge of Alcatraz.

HOT AND HUNKY • 4039 18th (Noe) • 621-6365 • 1946 Market (Duboce) • 621-3622

Hamburgers • $

Lunch and dinner daily, service to midnight Friday-Saturday on Market; to midnight Sunday-Thursday and to 1 a.m. Friday-Saturday on 18th; casual; wine and beer; no credit cards • The original 18th street Hunky and its new Market Street outlet offer nearly 20 different "square meals on a round bun" that are among the city's better 'burgers. Using a super hot grill and excellent timing, the cooks manage to produce perfect medium-rare yet thin and juicy patties nearly every time. The 'burgers arrive with slices of sweet Bermuda onions and thick-cut skins-on fries. Sundry other diner-type foods are offered as well.

The name suggests, accurately, that these are funky, informal and up-beat places; the original is decorated primarily with Marilyn Monroe visages and the new outlet has a nostalgic Fifties theme.

HUNAN • 924 Sansome (Broadway) • 956-7727
• 853 Kearny (Jackson) • 788-2234
• 5723 Geary Boulevard (21st Avenue) • 221-3388

Hunan • $

Lunch and dinner Monday-Saturday; casual; full bar; cash only at Kearny, major credit cards at the others • You'll find fifteen of them in the Yellow Pages now, from Hunan City and Hunan Shaolin to Hunan Village. One of the first and still the most popular of these suppliers of spice-laced north China cuisine is simply called Hunan Restaurant. It's not necessarily the best, however. Our critics give it mixed reviews and we found that each succeeding dish seemed determined to outdo the other in mouth-scorching spiciness. Yet the cavernous remodeled warehouse on Sansome is crowded nightly, and people push eagerly into the smaller versions on Kearny and Geary; obviously, lots of folks favor this gustatorial punishment.

Hunan's ingredients are fresh and lightly cooked and the three outlets use no MSG, but you might want to request that the dried red peppers be held to a minimum, or the fiery impact will drown any subtleties of spice and flavor.

"Fun, casual."

Some of our folks like it hot.

I FRATELLI • 1521 Hyde (Jackson) • 776-8661
I FRATELLI NORTH • 1896 Hyde (Green) • 474-8603

Italian • $$

Dinner nightly; reservations suggested; casual; wine and beer; MC, VISA • We're not sure why Giannini and Peter Huson chose to open twin *trattorias* three blocks apart on Hyde Street; perhaps it gave each of them something to do. Both received several votes, and we've eaten at Fratelli, uh, South. We are pleased to report that they are two pleasant little bistros with the attendant table candles, cozily dim light and occasional raffia bottle. Both are intimate places suitable for quiet conversations and lazy chianti sipping.

We enjoyed a tasty veal *parmigiana* and properly *al dente* fettucini at Fratelli. Our agents report "Food and service consistently good", "Very good fresh pastas; great linguini with clams; moderate prices and relaxed atmosphere" and "The best garlic bread in town" at I. North. Both have good wine lists with plenty of Italian reds to accompany their fresh pastas.

IL PIRATA • **2007 16th (between Potrero and Utah)** • **626-1845**

Italian • \\ Y $

Lunch Tuesday-Friday, dinner Tuesday-Saturday; casual; wine and beer; MC, VISA • The South of Market industrial area is the latest breeding ground for trendy restaurants, but the "Pirate" isn't one of them. It's a scruffy, friendly *trattoria* that has been around for more than twenty years. Despite its nautical Italian name, Il Pirata's seagoing decor is limited to a few fake plastic portholes mounted on the walls, along with a couple of ship's wheels. The decades-old restaurant, adjoining a weathered neighborhood bar, is trimmed mostly in *raffia* bottles and ingenious wainscoting made from end panels of old wooden wine cartons.

And the size of the meals! If Mrs. Columbus had fed Chris this way, he'd never had made it up the gangplank of the *Santa Maria.* We recently worked our way through a lunch of crusty French bread, two bowls of clam and whitefish soup rich and hearty enough to ward off a Minnesota blizzard, *rigatoni* perfectly *al dente* and a mound of excellent lightly cooked *calamari.* (We ignored the large serving of mushy zucchini that died enroute to our table.) All of this was an entire $8, washed down by two $1.50 glasses of wine. Dinners, such as rabbit with *polente,* roast beef or pork, or petrale sole are even more ample, for just a bit more money.

IL POLLAIO • **555 Columbus Avenue (Union)** • **362-7727**

Italian/Argentinian • \\\\ ⊘ $

Lunch and dinner daily except Sunday; casual; wine and beer; no credit cards • The food in this small *rosticceria* (rotisserie cafe) is remarkable not only for the price and ample servings, but for the quality. Slow-cooked, lightly marinated chicken and ribs and Italian sausages, accompanied by excellent fresh salads, provide hearty dinners for well under $10. It's a tiny wedge of a place just off Washington Square, sparkling clean with simple furnishings. The Italian *rosticceria* style cooking is enhanced by lively Latin spices.

"Great ribs!", "Good work-night dinner" and "Great grilled chicken!" numbered among our cartel's enthusiastic comments.

IRON HORSE • 19 Maiden Lane (Kearny) • 362-8133

Northern Italian • $$$

Lunch Monday-Saturday, dinner nightly; reservations accepted; sport jacket to dressy; full bar; major credit cards • Maiden Lane (named either for London's street of jewelers or in jest for its Gold Rush era bawdy houses, depending on your historian) is now a quiet little alley of select shops, galleries and restaurants. The dimly-lit, comfortable and stylish but unassuming Iron Horse has been serving proper Continental fare here since 1955.

Owner John Kukulica's current focus is on "contemporary Northern Italian," including appetizers like Malpeque oysters in champagne, Italian onion soup, spinach *ravioli*, veal with *fontina* and basil, and broiled rabbit with roasted peppers. The menu changes daily, depending on the availability of fresh ingredients and the chef's mood.

"Elegant, traditional old San Francisco atmosphere."

IRON POT • 441 Washington (Sansome) • 392-2100

Italian • $

Lunch weekdays, dinner Monday-Saturday; casual; full bar; MC, VISA • First opened in 1934, the Iron Pot was moved to its present site in 1961 and the owners preserved its weathered old wooden European decor. Italian five-course dinners with soup, antipasto, pasta, an entree such as veal, chicken *Luciano* or the Pot's special baby steak, and dessert will send you away smiling for under $20. And if you're caught between paydays, early bird dinners are served from 4:30 to 5:30 for $5.75 to $7.75.

"Very filling; lots to eat", "Wonderful food, good prices, noisy, old San Francisco" our epicures said of this casual *ristorante.*

IRONWOOD CAFE • 901 Cole (Carl) • 664-0224

American • $$

Lunch weekdays, dinner Monday-Friday; casual; wine and beer; MC, VISA, AMEX, DISC • It's refreshing, in the midst of California cuisine and blackened this or that, to see a cafe that issues simple, fresh American-style dishes. This charming Early American knotty pine place in an old San Francisco Victorian serves full-course Americana dinners for about $17. A typical home-cooked meal might include sweet potato soup, bacon and oyster pasta, ham with locally-grown fresh basil, garden salad (is there any other kind?) and peach-nectarine pie.

RE-89 describes this old-style yet innovative restaurant between Haight-Ashbury and the University of California Med Center as "a wonderful place to eat." Another agent calls the fare "above average but a bit pricey" for a neighborhood cafe.

ISOBUNE SUSHI RESTAURANT • 1737 Post (in Japan Center, near Buchanan) • 563-1030

Sushi • $$

Lunch and dinner daily; casual; wine and beer; MC, VISA • Isobune doesn't offer the best nor the cheapest sushi in town, but it's certainly the most entertaining. In gimmick-oriented Japan, conveyer-belt sushi parlors are quite common, but this place goes a step beyond; your lunch is launched aboard tiny wooden flatboats that float by in a water trough. Sushi chefs inside an oval bar craft the Oriental delicacies and set them adrift in the surrounding moat; diners make their choices as they pass. We've found the sushi to be fresh and generally good, with prices only a bit higher than more conventional Oriental raw bars.

Costs are calculated by the style of the serving plates, which can stack up alarmingly fast, so it might be best to blunt your appetite with a bowl of hearty noodle soup. Waitresses work the perimeter of the big oval bar, bringing non-sushi fare and drinks. "A really fun restaurant to 'do' sushi."

IT'S TOPS COFFEE SHOP • 1801 Market (McCoppin) • 431-6395

American diner • $

Breakfast and lunch daily; casual; wine and beer; no credit cards • Bruce Chapman's old fashioned diner is stuck in a time warp, featuring Formica counter tops with juke box players, vinyl booths and block-lettered menus plastered about the walls. Happily, his prices are nearly the same vintage. Complete dinners with soup, salad and a meat entree with veggies and a dollop of mashed potatoes and dessert range from $4 to $8. It rivals Il Pollaio as the city's most inexpensive non-Asian restaurant, and portions are generous.

This little place on upper Market has been serving chicken, steaks and chops since the year after I was born. How long ago was that? Don't ask me; ask Bruce.

IVY'S RESTAURANT • 398 Hayes (Gough) • 626-3930

California/American • $$

Lunch weekdays, Sunday brunch, dinners Monday-Saturday, service to 11:30 Friday and Saturday; reservations advised; casual to sport jacket; full bar; MC, VISA, AMEX • People who have fussed in the past about ordinary food at this trim little cafe near the Civic Center should give it another try. Under new owner Andrew Foxwell and Chef Rick Cunningham, it's serving rather fine California fare. A recent dinner of richly-seasoned seafood *fettucini* generous with shrimp and scallops, trimmed prettily in green and red pepper strips, and baby coho salmon with rice pilaf seasoned with pine nuts was excellent.

The establishment is eye-pleasing, too. It's a brightly-lit, cheerful place with large windows, off-white walls trimmed in green, and matching green chairs tucked under white-linen tables. "Great place to eat before the opera," offered a reviewer.

JACK'S RESTAURANT • 615 Sacramento (Montgomery) • 986-9854

French/Continental • $$$

Lunch weekdays, dinner nightly; reservations essential; dressy, ties required; full bar; AMEX only • Jack Redinger's restaurant is quintessential old San Francisco—a place of stern decor and straight up martinis where men (and women) of influence chew over business deals with their thick grilled steaks. The look, white walls with gold trim, brass greatcoat hooks and spartan wooden chairs, hasn't changed since the Gold Rush, although the menu is more contemporary. The hurriedly efficient service is neither stuffy nor fawning. Certainly, a worthy such as Herb Caen will get warmer smiles and a better table, but I've gone as a stranger and received good, if taciturn, service from the tuxedoed help. I'll take Jack's slightly detached waiters over gushing restaurant school grads ("Hi! My name is Bruce—") any day.

The place can get noisy despite its high ceilings, but if you're an authentic power broker, you'll do your dealing in a private dining room upstairs.

With the mortgage long paid, food and wine prices are

surprisingly moderate for an upscale restaurant; a five-course prix fixe dinner, for instance, is well under $20. Specialties from the huge menu include lightly done sole *Marguery* glazed with Hollandaise sauce, an alarmingly good chicken Jerusalem and a delicious curiosity called fried cream with rum.

The place has been serving the Financial District's culinary needs since 1864, so we assume Redinger isn't the original Jack.

JACKSON CAFE • 640 Jackson (Kearny) • 986-9717

Chinese/American • $

Lunch and dinner daily; casual; wine and beer; no credit cards • We've been curious to try American food at a "Chinese-American" cafe, so we selected the Jackson, which a cabbie had nominated as his "favorite cheap Chinatown restaurant for the last 25 years. The best won ton; great steamed clams." Opened just after World War II, it's a typical Formica/vinyl chow hall; the only adornment is a badly done mural that might be Yosemite Valley, several lighted beer signs and chrome coat racks beside vinyl booths.

Our American "ocean special" dinner consisted of soup, rolls, cooked vegetables and batter-fried shrimp, oysters and scallops, plus dessert. The soup was thin, flat and tasted canned; the oysters were mushy and strong-flavored and the shrimp was old and so over-cooked and rubbery that I could have used one as an eraser. The scallops were surprisingly good, as were crisp, lightly-done string beans. A large lump of boiled potato and a larger lump of white rice tasted just the way they looked. A generous wedge of custard pie was over-cooked and chewy, with a burned crust. All this largess came to $6.12, including tea and tax. Other choices include roast beef, pork chops and calves liver for about the same price, and a New York Steak for $7. Lunch versions, minus the soup and dessert, are 40 cents less.

Next time, we'll order the won ton.

JIL'S RESTAURANT • 242 O'Farrell (Mason) • 982-9353

American/Continental • $$$

Lunch and dinner daily; reservations accepted; casual to sport jacket; full bar; all major credit cards • New Dutch owner Jurgen Wondergem has transformed the old French Trianon into an informal yet stylish European country restaurant. Chef

Lucas Shoemacher has given the Continental menu some interesting American nouvelle accents.

A three-course prix fixe dinner appeals to pre-theater crowds and for $16.50, it appeals to pocketbooks as well. Re-opened under its new management in 1987, it received only a few votes but it certainly shows promise.

JOHN'S GRILL • 63 Ellis (Powell) • 986-0069

Continental • $$

Lunch and dinner Monday-Saturday; reservations accepted; casual to sport jacket; full bar; MC, VISA, AMEX • Both fiction and non-fiction permeate this 1908 San Francisco institution. It was the hangout of Sam Spade, America's first and most enduring poker-faced gumshoe, and his creator Dashiell Hammett, who worked at a nearby Pinkerton detective agency. John's is a mini-museum of Spade/Hammett lore, but it doesn't rest on literary laurels; the Continental kitchen is surprisingly good. It still serves simple and substantial food like steaks, an excellent chicken Girard and Spade's preferred pork chops with a baked potato. Only the prices have changed—but not as much as you might think.

The decor is what you'd expect of an early San Francisco museum-piece—masculine with dark, heavy woods and touches of brass.

JOVANELO'S • 840 Sansome (Pacific Avenue) • 986-8050

Northern Italian • $$

Lunch weekdays, dinner nightly; reservations advised; casual to sport jacket; full bar; major credit cards • "The book on veal dishes begins and ends here," reported a team member, so we checked it out. Indeed, more than half the entrees were veal; both our *picata* and *Marsala* were fresh, tender, lightly cooked and excellent. A chicken *cannelloni* was rather bland; *minestrone* made from scratch with fresh ingredients was first rate. By the way, Jovanelo's offers typical pastas and a few fresh fish entrees for non-veal fans.

The decor is pleasing—dropped ceilings with gold and black striped wallpaper busy with framed prints, brass plate and such. Romantics will like the dark woods, seductive subdued lighting and red-shaded sconces.

JUDY'S RESTAURANT • 2268 Chestnut (Scott) • 922-4588

American •

Breakfast and lunch daily; casual; wine and beer; no credit cards • "Outstanding breakfast!" exclaimed one of our crew members. We never get up that early, so we stopped by for lunch and confirmed that this quaint cafe with Early American decor is indeed a nice place to start the day, or to interrupt one with a lunch break. It's another of those rare restaurants that has doused the smoking lamp, as we used to say in the Marine Corps. It has two tiny dining rooms, one a balcony over the other, and both are off limits to puffing.

You could be dining in grandma's kitchen here. This store front cafe has been prettied up with old prints and mirrors on textured lemon walls, hanging and potted plants, blue-clothed tables with bentwood chairs and an antique or two. A large hutch is a nice focal point. The menu is essentially egg things for breakfast, which can be accompanied by pumpkin bread or blueberry muffins; and a couple of hot dishes plus sundry soups, salads, "waist watcher" fruit plates and sandwiches for lunch. Health enthusiasts will like this place; owners Charles and Mary China Bains use a lot of fresh vegetables in interesting combinations.

JULIE'S SUPPER CLUB • 1123 Folsom (Seventh) • 861-4084

American regional •

Dinner nightly except Sunday, service to midnight Friday and Saturday; reservations for six or more only; casual; full bar; MC, VISA • This boisterous new south of Market place with a quasi-Fifties look is much larger (and louder) than its narrow store front indicates. It expands into three separate dining rooms; one is entirely nonsmoking (thus the double symbol above) and another is an outdoor patio with tarp cover and gas heaters for chilly days.

This wasn't the Fifties I remember, but I spent that generation on an Idaho farm. I *did* recognize the sounds blasting over Julie's speaker system, from twanging Loretta Lynn and whining Bobby Vinton to someone wailing "I'll be ready, Eddie." The look is geometric Fifties drive-in shapes — beams with holes in them and a thick wedge-shaped, sparkly ceiling over the bar. Modern paintings on the walls look like a cross between Salvadore Dali and Hank Ketchum.

"Even though I liked the music they played, it was so loud

you could barely order dinner," one epicure complained. "Good atmosphere; wonderful drinks and appetizers," another said.

Here we go again with American nouvelle, and it was quite good, as was the service, considering the chaos. A pan-fried, corn meal and pecan breaded boneless Idaho trout had crisp and crunchy skin, with tender and flaky flesh. (Trout never tasted this good back home, but Idaho chefs confuse cooking with cremation.) Other menu items range from deep-fried tortillas and barbecued chicken wings for appetizers to chicken breasts in sweet garlic sauce and grilled lamb chops with oyster mushrooms as entrees.

When I arrived at 6:30 on a Friday, only Loretta Lynn was making much noise; by 7:30 the place was a standing-room-only bedlam. I finished my trout and got out of there just in time; I was beginning to enjoy the chaos.

JULIUS' CASTLE • 1541 Montgomery (Union) • 362-3042

Continental • $$$$

Lunch weekdays, dinner nightly; reservations advised; sport jacket to dressy; full bar; major credit cards • For generations, folks have been trouping up the side of Telegraph Hill (or riding the restaurant's limo) to enjoy the Victorian castle ambiance of this place, and its fine view of San Francisco Bay. Now, they can go for the food as well. "Excellent food; always get a good response from the guests I send there," reported one of our concierges. Owner Jeffrey Pollack has changed the ponderous tourist-oriented menu into a balance of more contemporary French and northern Italian dishes. Rack of lamb with rosemary, delicately done Dover sole and roast duck in ginger-chili sauce are among the offerings, along with one of the best Caesar salads in the city.

Pollack, who also owns the neighboring Shadows, has refurbished the dowager castle's interior as well as its menu. The dining areas, which had become rather scruffy, are a Victorian vision of chandeliers, dark paneling and high-backed Queen Anne chairs. The arrangement of tables and the large canted windows maximize the view of the busy bay below. For a really dazzling vista, attempt to talk your way into a turret table. The castle was built in 1922 by one Julius Roz, who used materials and craftsmen from the 1915 Panama-Pacific Exposition. (In case you're curious, the sole survivor of that expo is the Palace of Fine Arts in the Marina.)

KAN'S CHINESE RESTAURANT • 708 Grant Avenue (Sacramento) • 982-2388

Cantonese • $$$

Lunch Monday-Saturday, dinner nightly; casual to sport jacket; full bar; all major credit cards • One of our VIP critics, the owner of a notable local restaurant, praised Kan's "unsurpassed Cantonese cuisine," but he awarded the place six's, just above average. Perhaps this apparent contradiction tells the story of this landmark Chinatown establishment. When master chef and cookbook author Johnny Kan was alive, his was *the* Chinatown restaurant. Although Chinese family-style cafes date back to the early 1850s, it was the legendary Johnny who introduced upscale Asian cooking to this city. Celebrities, tourists and townspeople crowded in and were afforded excellent food and hospitality. Kan's sudden death several years ago was a major loss to the city and to Asian culinary arts.

He is survived by faded photos of the famous, the outdated but still sleek and attractive Chinese-modern dining room and well-prepared but ordinary Cantonese fare.

KHAN TOKE THAI HOUSE • 5937 Geary Boulevard (24th Avenue) • 668-6654

Thai • $$

Dinner nightly; reservations advised; casual; wine and beer; MC, VISA, AMEX • "An unintimidating way to discover Thai cuisine", "Outstanding food; very peaceful dining room", "Great atmosphere, decor excellent, service excellent, food excellent." Our cartel likes Khan Toke!

It's one of the best balanced restaurants in the city. The service is attentive and low key; the food is exotic yet wonderfully tasty and the room is charmingly decorated with Thai artifacts. Flickering candles and soft background music complete the mellow mood. As in finer Bankok restaurants, one sits on soft cushions at low tables (an improvement over Japanese tatami mats). Patient waitpersons explain the savory details and consequences of every dish. Khan Toke's offerings range from mouth-sizzling beef with home-made red curry, peanuts and coconut milk to a gentle pork and vegetable omelet. The large menu runs the gamut of the country's complex and spicy dishes.

A final ingredient—traditional Thai dancing is featured on Sundays, starting at 8:30 p.m.

KULETO'S ITALIAN RESTAURANT • 221 Powell (Geary) • 397-7720

California/Italian • $$

Breakfast, lunch and dinner daily; casual; full bar; all major credit cards • So new it hasn't made our phone book, this restaurant in the equally new Villa Florence Hotel is trying to be all things to all diners in a hurry. (It even honors the Discover card.) Serving continuously from 7 a.m. to 11 p.m., it catches hotel guests and early-bird stockbrokers with California omelets, entices the shopping and business crowd with light Italian and California nouvelle lunches, then settles in as an Italianate dinner restaurant.

Our associates indicate that it's succeeding very nicely. "Excellent food product; good menu variety; chocolate pecan torts to die for", "Voted best designed restaurant in S.F.; fun, high-energy crowd" and "Very good service; setting quite pleasing."

It is stylish indeed—a svelte composite of marble, copper, brass and mahogany, focused beautifully around a vaulted plaster ceiling and a refurbished bar from the (pre-Sheraton) Palace Hotel. It's yesterday and today in careful blend, just off the smart Italian designer lobby of the Villa Florence.

All this from the scruffy old Manx hotel? It's difficult to believe until you learn that the conversion was done by boutique hotelier Bill Kimpton and restaurant designer Pat (Fog City Diner, Corona Bar and Grill) Kuleto. Kimpton wisely painted Kuleto's name on the place.

KUM MOON • 2109 Clement (22nd Avenue) • 221-5656

Cantonese • $

Lunch and dinner daily; casual; wine and beer; MC, VISA • We didn't choose this place; our reviewers did. And we're pleased, for it gives us an excuse to mention the Richmond District's emerging Asian restaurant row, particularly along Clement Street. Some of the city's best inexpensive Chinese, Japanese, Korean, Vietnamese and Thai restaurants are cropping up out here like mushrooms in a rainforest. Kum Moon's decor is basic Formica, like that of most small Asian family cafes, but the food is excellent, and the place serves a fine dim sum assortment at lunch time.

Kum Moon runs counter to trends, focusing on the fresh, simple and lightly-sauced flavors of Cantonese dishes instead of adding red chili and hot oil and calling the food Mandarin, Szechuan, Nanking, Hunan or whatever. If you like the uncomplicated taste of fresh, crisp vegetables, try some of the stir fry. Excellent!

LA BARCA • 2036 Lombard (Fillmore) • 921-2221

Mexican • $

Dinner nightly, (from 2:30 Sunday), service to 11:30 Friday and Saturday; casual; full bar; MC, VISA, AMEX • La Barca is one of those wonderfully overdone examples of Mexican interior decor, with a fountain that pretends it's outdoors, lots of tropical plants and painted tiles, Mexican artifacts, copper pots and leather chairs. And the building, done up in stone and wrought iron, looks like a backdrop for a John Wayne taco western. The food is remarkably inexpensive for its Motel Row location: *Platos de combinaciones* with up to three items are under $10. For all you gordos out there, *El Grande de Gordo* with a *taco, enchilada, tamale*, chili *relleno*, twice-fried beans and rice is but $10.50. And catch this, gringos: Early-bird dinners (from 4 to 6) are 20 percent off. *Hola!*

You won't find any *grande* culinary surprises on the menu; it's mostly standard Cal-Mex fare. But prices that rival those of the scruffy Mission district places— that's surprise enough. After the dining room closes, the cocktail lounge functions as a popular pub for the surrounding Marina District.

LA FELCE • 1570 Stockton (Columbus) • 392-8321

Italian • $$

Lunch weekdays (except Tuesday), dinner Wednesday-Monday; reservations suggested on weekends; casual; full bar; major credit cards • La Felce is right where it belongs—near Columbus Avenue in the heart of Little Italy. Everything, the ambiance, the flowers on the tables, the family ownership, the *raffia* bottles, the menu, is quintessential southern Italian. The food is better than average for a neighborhood *trattoria*. The kitchen uses lots of fresh vegetables and pastas, like a small-town cafe in southern Italy.

The antipaso that begins each meal offers interesting variety (pearl onions, pickled pepperoni, *mortadella*) and the soup is hearty and homemade. We're *lasagna* aficionados, and La Felce serves some of the best baked pasta in the city. Traditional chicken and veal dishes are tasty, too.

"Excellent pastas, filet of sole and appetizers" says MC-78.

LA FUENTE • #2 Embarcadero Center (Sacramento and Front) • 982-3363

Mexican • $$

Lunch and dinner Monday-Saturday; reservations accepted; casual to sport jacket; full bar; major credit cards • To begin with, we like Embarcadero Center as a setting for restaurants; the environment is modern and airy and most places, including La Fuente, offer outdoor dining. And we're glad the cartel nominated La Fuente, for this cheerful restaurant with "upscale Mexican cuisine" has long been a favorite. Proprietor Vicente Aguilar draws from French and Spanish dishes for his tasty entrees. One can get the usual tortilla-wrapped things, but the heart of the menu is much more interesting. Our latest meal, grilled red snapper in cream of fish *velouete* with fresh tomatoes and cucumbers, was absolutely delicious; the fish was perfectly cooked and its delicate, smokey flavor managed somehow to come through the rich overlay of rich sauce and vegetables. Other menu items showing a strong Continental influence are *Ossobuco Bilbaina* (veal steak in demi-glass sauce) and lamb fillets with shallot sauce; La Fuente's version of *paella* is excellent.

The restaurant's orange and white color scheme isn't as garish as it sounds. Wrought-iron grillwork, modern cutout wall plaques with Mexican scenes and tile and parquet floors provide a pleasant setting; rows of colored ceiling lights add a touch of flash to the otherwise simple decor.

LA MEDITERRANEE • 2210 Fillmore (Sacramento) • 921-2956 • 288 Noe (24th) • 431-7210

Mideastern mix • $

Lunch and dinner Monday-Saturday; reservations for six or more; casual; wine and beer; MC, VISA • It's not exactly a franchise, but a simple idea that just grew. Ten years ago, Armenian Levon Der Bedrossian started the original Mediterranee on Fillmore. It served remarkably inexpensive Greek, Armenian and Lebanese food, such as *hummus* (ground chickpeas), *kibbeh* (ground lamb and spices), and a dish of chopped eggplant, garlic and other spices with the wonderful name of *baba ghanoush.* Sounds like a Turkish cussword.

Today, Las Mediterranee also are in the Noe Valley off upper Market, in San Rafael at 857 Fourth Street and in Berkeley at 2936 College Avenue (near Ashby). Most meals are well under $10, providing an inexpensive opportunity to sample the spicy fare from this part of the world. For a sampler, in fact, try the *meza,* an assortment of grapeleaf-wrapped *dolmas,* cheese *karni* in phyllo and other Middle Eastern specialties.

And save room for honey-rich *baklava.*

LA MERE DUQUESNE • 101 Shannon (off 500 block of Geary) • 776-7600

French • $$$

Lunch Monday-Saturday, dinner nightly; reservations accepted; sport jacket; full bar; MC, VISA, AMEX • The hand-painted billboard promises "French country dining in simple elegance." It delivers some of the elegance, but the food is French country ordinaire, say our critics. "Beautiful atmosphere but food mediocre," one comments, and our own experiences confirm this. In our opinion, there are better places around for the price, which averages over $20 for a typical dinner.

Its location does make it popular with the theater crowds. Although it offers no pre-show specials, it serves dinner early enough to get you to your seats on time.

LA PERGOLA RISTORANTE • 2060 Chestnut (Gough) • 563-4500

Northern Italian • $$

Dinner Monday-Saturday; informal; wine and beer; MC, VISA • Chef-owner Angelo Piccinini, a native of Lucca and former Amelio's proprietor, obviously likes atmosphere. His place is almost charming to a fault, with a lattice false ceiling from which hang simulated grapes and braided garlic, a wine rack wall and the requisite *raffia.* And the food in this Marina district cafe is nearly faultless, say our spies.

"The chef-owner and his son put out the best *carbonara* and *scampi* anywhere. Food is served very hot, right from the pan," says one reporter. "Fresh seafood and food is always served piping hot," says another. Yes, we *know* these sound like ringers, but one came from the owner of a coffee shop way out in the Richmond District, and the other from a downtown hotel employee (and the handwriting doesn't match). But just to be safe, we checked it out, anonymously, of course.

And you know what? The spaghetti *carbonara* was excellent, the veal *Parmigiana* was tender and tasty, and everything was hot, served right from the...

LA POSADA • 2298 Fillmore (Clay) • 922-1722

Mexican • $

Lunch and dinner daily; casual; full bar; MC, VISA, AMEX • "Excellent salsa and great margaritas, and after that, who cares?" confessed a critic, who then added: "But dinner was great, too!" We hope he stayed around (or awake) for the excellent *flan*. It has that rich, nutty flavor of real Mexican *flan*, instead of merely tasting like egg pudding.

Although the menu is Mexican, this stylish but modestly priced Pacific Heights place achieves a Victorian look with filigree and hanging plants. Photos and posters of Mexican film stars enliven the cocktail area.

LA VICTORIA • 1205 Alabama (24th) • 550-9309

Mexican/Spanish • $

Lunch and dinner daily; casual; no alcohol but it may be brought in; no credit cards • We move from Pacific Heights to the Mission District and from a few frills to no-frills. But the prices are even better, around $7 for dinner. "Nothing fancy, just great atmosphere, family-style," say owners Gabriel and Susan Maldonado. Our panel agrees: "Great food; cheap!"

The restaurant actually is part of a bakery and grocery store, and regulars often enter through the "front" (2937 24th Street), as they've been doing for a quarter of a century. In fact, a lot of Victoria's food goes out that door, since it's a popular take-out. Folks order a pot of *birria* (goat stew) to go, then pick up a bag of crisp, home-made tortilla chips and *cocadas* (macaroons) or sugar-dusted fried *churros* for dessert. Staying or going, you'll enjoy simple and thrifty Mexican specials like *tamales, burritos, rellenos, flautas* and pork in green salsa.

LAS MANANITAS • 850 Montgomery (Pacific Avenue) • 434-2088

Mexican • $$

Lunch weekdays, dinner nightly; reservations accepted; casual to sport jacket; full bar; major credit cards • You wouldn't hike up to Julius' Castle and order a hotdog; nor would you walk into any of Mexico's finer restaurants and request a taco. When you travel in Mexico, particularly in the coastal cities, you realize that Mexican *haute cuisine* is predominately seafood, grilled meats and fowl. Las Mananitas is upscale Mexico, both in menu and appearance. Brass sconces, wrought iron candle holders and cut flowers add nice highlights to the hand-hewn beams and antique Mexican furnishings. A gurgling fountain lures diners to an outdoor patio when the weather cooperates. Incidentally, we love the restaurant's name which, according to our *Universidad de Chicago Diccionario*, means "morning song."

Chilled lobster, garlic-spiced grilled prawns and petrale with sweet sauce and almonds are typical entrees, and one should try the *ceviche* as an appetizer. From the grill comes pork loin with avocado, and spiced sirloin tips. As you're enjoying dessert, you'll get something else not found in typical "Mexican" restaurants—a check averaging more than $20 a person.

MC-156 feels it's worth it: "You'll think you're in Mexico at an elegant villa."

LE CASTEL • 3235 Sacramento (Presidio Avenue) • 921-7115

French • $$$

Dinner Monday-Saturday; reservations essential; sport jacket to dressy; wine and beer; major credit cards • Everything about Le Castel suggests elegance; nothing suggests pretension. Three intimate dining rooms have been fashioned within a Victorian townhouse; each is carefully attired in rich colors and soft fabrics. *San Francisco Focus* magazine calls it the most romantic restaurant in the city.

There is no pretension here because creator-owner Fritz Frankel *is* Le Castel, and he welcomes you like a friend into his home. After training in European hotel kitchens, working for the legendary Claridge's in London and operating La Mirabelle in San Francisco, he created his personal castle of fine dining. To Fritz, that means classic French, *Alsatian* mostly, although the complex sauces have been lightened a bit. Calf's brain on spinach leaves, stuffed squab *Farci* and sweetbreads with wild mushrooms and champagne sauce are among the offerings.

"My favorite French restaurant in S.F.," said a waiter from another notable city cafe. "Owner Fritz Frankel welcomes you as a long lost friend," added one of our civilians.

LE DOMINO • 2742 17th (Florida) • 626-3095

French • $$$

Dinner nightly; reservations advised; sport jacket; full bar; major credit cards • Located on the south side of the tracks, Le Domino tries to bring a touch of elegance to the city's warehousing district. Some of our diners say that it succeeds; others say its floral curtains, gilt-edged portraits, Maria Teresa chandelier and formal staircase are a bit overdone.

Chef Erik Leroux' menu is French with California accents—coho with ginger and red bell pepper appetizers, rack of lamb with herbs and mint vinegar, things like that. Many of the faithful are from the nearby Galleria Design Center, who apparently like its opulence.

"Very good; steady quality", "Excellent ambiance" and "Very consistent, very amiable" were typical of the comments.

LE PETIT CAFE • 2164 Larkin (Green) • 776-5356

American • $

Breakfast and lunch daily, dinner Tuesday-Saturday; casual; wine and beer; MC, VISA ($20 credit card minimum) • Robert and Maria Drake recently abandoned their careers, which had nothing to do with food service, and took over this Russian Hill coffee house. They've created a homey little cafe that runs upstream to the nouvelle flow. The fare is simple and hearty with more emphasis on ample portions than on artistic presentations. They use only fresh ingredients and Maria creates all the dishes, breads and desserts in her busy kitchen while Robert runs things out front.

Prices are remarkably low. Breakfasts and lunches, usually egg dishes, quiches, salads and sandwiches, are around $5. The daily-changing dinner menu features a pasta or vegetarian dish, a chicken or veal and a fish course, from $7.50 to $10.50; lighter one-dish dinners are offered for even less. The Drakes pour a variety of beers, including several from little known "micro-breweries" and they offer a good yet inexpensive wine list.

The place retains its European coffee house atmosphere, with bentwood furniture, wooden tables and well-stocked bookshelves in case you feel like reading between courses. One of two dining rooms is smoke free, earning this listing the double no-smoking symbol.

"A fun place to go for a reasonably priced meal and a good bottle of wine with friends."

LE PIANO ZINC • 708 14th (Market and Church) • 431-5266

French • $$$

Open 6 p.m. to midnight daily except Monday; casual to sport jacket; wine and beer; MC, VISA, AMEX • Look not for zinc pianos (although the place does offer jazz piano and singers nightly) but for reasonably priced *cuisine de Francais.* Veteran restaurateurs Joel Coutre (out front) and Michel Laurent (in the kitchen) call it "a renaissance of classic French cooking." That translates as poached salmon with cream of tarragon, breast of duck with peaches and *sauce bigarrade* or grenadine of sauteed venison with *sauce Gran Veneur.* Four-course prix fixe dinners with dessert are offered nightly for $29.50.

The small, sleek Art Deco/modern dining room has peach wall fabric, forest green banquettes and tables set with hand-painted Villeroy and Boch china. And of course, *le piano.*

"Excellent presentation; quality", "Very cozy, romantic."

LEHR'S GREENHOUSE RESTAURANT AND FLORIST • 740 Sutter (adjacent to the Canterbury Hotel, near Taylor) • 474-6478

American • $$

Lunch Monday-Saturday, Sunday brunch, dinner nightly; reservations advised; casual to sport jacket; full bar; MC, VISA, AMEX • At least once in your life, take Mom to Lehr's. The place has carried the concept of garden dining to an adorable extreme; one sups under a hanging forest of Boston and assorted other ferns, and potted plants fill every corner. This place would make a rainforest turn greener with envy; one almost expects to hear monkeys in the forest canopy, discussing the banana crop.

A few years ago, we'd have given Lehr's a single spoon for ambiance and let it go at that. But the old tourist-and-ladies-teahouse menu has been improved and updated to include some interesting fresh fish and fowl dishes and something called the "Great American Soup and Salad Bar." The Greenhouse menu obviously has gone on a health kick. So just admire the plants; you don't have to eat them.

I believe something else has changed in this venerable novelty cafe; wasn't it originally called "Lehr's Greenhouse Restaurant and Potting Shed"? We liked that better. By the way, there *is* a florist shop up front.

When you make a reservation, arrive early and ask to be seated in the front dining room, which is particularly lush. The back room, while hardly a desert, is only about as bushy as a typical fern bar.

LEHR'S STEAKERY — see Phil Lehr's Steakery

L'ESCARGOT • 1809 Union (Octavia) • 567-0222

French • $$$

Dinner nightly; reservations advised; sport jacket; wine and beer; major credit cards • "Old fashioned country French cuisine," said one judge; another suggested that L'Escargot serves "the best rack of lamb in S.F." A third gushed so enthusiastically that we suspect he was a cousin. (Anyone who calls a place "adorable" must be a relative.) Although we've not dined there, we're convinced by our crew that this cafe is noteworthy; it's apparently elegant yet rather inexpensive for a first-cabin restaurant *Francais*. And it has the proper Old European decor—wood-paneled wainscoting, a chandelier and candle-lit tables.

Escargots are the feature here and "you can smell the garlic" exudes one phantom diner. Veal scallops with Dijon is highly rated; Pork *Normande* with apple slices and apple brandy sounds delicious and so does the chicken sauteed in a sauce of chicken liver puree and cognac.

We'll have to try this place. We may even find it to be adorable.

L'ETOILE • 1075 California (Taylor) • 771-1530

French • $$$$

Dinner nightly; reservations advised; dressy; full bar; all major credit cards • The French penchant for the capital "L" is creating an alphabetic string of Gallic eateries; L'Etoile is another of the San Francisco parade of opulent French restaurants with warm woods and cool crystal and all those innovative sauces. This one is more posh than those above and, predictably, more expensive.

It has been called the city's most beautiful restaurant, with its gilt mirrors, leather banquettes, crystal chandeliers and great bursts of potted flowers. Some critics say it's in a rut instead of a parade, but Chef Claude Bougard has lightened and brightened his classic French menu, trimming it from book-length to a short story with about fifteen entrees and some interesting new flavors. Things like lamb spiced with garlic and served with pasta; breast of duckling with pear, blueberry and orange sauce; and squab with *armagnac* sauce and liver pate.

The city's Beautiful People gather in the posh cocktail lounge to sip Bombay gin; they pause in their idly urgent talk to hear popular Peter Mintun at the piano.

"Excellent French cuisine" is the simple summation of one of our epicures, who is the owner of another worthy San Francisco restaurant.

LILIES ON MASON • 542 Mason (Sutter) • 391-2401

American • $

Daily from 7 a.m. to 3 p.m.; reservations accepted; casual; wine and beer; no credit cards • Lilies is the lilliputian of San Francisco cafes. It's probably the smallest in the city and it is definitely the cutest—a 14-seat jewel box with green walls and a green plaid carpet, accented by fawn tablecloths, burgundy nappery and even burgundy mattes around of some of the framed prints. Brass napkin rings and mini-gardens planted in ceramic pots occupy the tables.

Cuteness doesn't end with the decor. Butter appears in small scallop shells, accompanied by a delicious crusty white bread in baby wicker baskets. Salads arrived with flowered carrots and long coiled, paper-thin cucumber strips that are sometimes a challenge for your fork. The honey and lemon dressing is delicious, incidentally. A "Manly Quiche" comes with a tasty roof of ham and herbal diced potatoes. Although the menu is simple—omelets, sandwiches, salads and pastas—everything is prepared with originality and served with style.

Are we through being cute yet?

No way. This is the Chris and John show, folks. While owner Chris Bello creates in the kitchen, John Chambers pauses occasionally to tell patrons the joke of the day:

She: Excuse me, sir, but you look like my third husband.

He: Oh, really? How many times have you been married?

She: Two.

Now that's *cute.*

LINE-UP • 398 Seventh (Harrison) • 621-0442

Mexican • $$

Lunch and dinner daily; casual; full bar; MC, VISA, AMEX • "Very popular; just redecorated. Good food; large portions; slightly overpriced", "Exquisite sauces."

A slightly overpriced Mexican restaurant south of Market called the Line-Up, with exquisite sauces? This required checking out. Turns out that it's a noisily popular place that serves what we'd describe as Yuppie Mexican, a mix of standard enchilada and burrito things, plus some upscale innovations like *Enchilada Sonora* (chicken with guacamole, sour cream and onion rings) and *camarones con arroz* (prawns with onions, bell peppers and rice). My choice of *camarones Rancheros* was a good one—plump prawns with spicy veggies in a white wine sauce, served in a crisp tortilla shell. The more the sauce soaked into the shell, the better it tasted, and I ate every crumb.

Sad to report that the service is barely controlled chaos, the kind of galloping pace devised to maximize turnover; it's efficiency on a dead run. One gets dizzy watching waiters dash about in a bewildering relay—serving food, cleaning tables with great crashing thumps, shouting out the names of the next in line and seating them.

The interior is sort of austere Victorian, with ceiling beams, dropped table lamps and a handsome carved wooden bar. The only thing Mexican, other than the menu, is a wonderfully garish pink, yellow and red neon sign outside with a dancing senorita, bull, lobster and a convict (presumably a refugee from the line-up).

LITTLE CITY ANTIPASTI BAR • 673 Union (Powell) • 434-2900

American • $$

Lunch and dinner daily, service to midnight; casual; full bar; MC, VISA, AMEX • This is where you go when you can't squeeze into the Washington Square Bar and Grill. And what a neat, simple idea it is. In a neighborhood of crowded Italian restaurants and congested bars, Antipasti's owners created what is essentially an informal "little plates" cafe and a lively pub. This place is a cheerful blend of old brick, oak and brass, with windows on Washington Square.

Manager Vicki Fay calls the fare "American!" (the exclamation mark is hers), but it's more of an international brew of snacks, savories and salads of various origins. The changing menu runs the ethnic gamut from *baba ghanoush* to Thai barbecued ribs, and the place offers a selection of pasta. Yes, we know "antipasti" means "before pasta." We don't make the rules; we just write the material.

"Lively bistro; good bar; well-chosen wine list; fun", "Good place for several people to share a large variety of antipasto dishes."

LITTLE HENRY'S • 955 Larkin (Post) • 776-1757

Italian • $

Lunch and dinner daily except Sunday; casual; wine and beer; no credit cards • The only things Chinese about Little Henry's are chef-owner Henry Heng and his prices, well under $10 for full dinners. And we don't mean a plateful of spaghetti; we're talking about medallions of veal or calamari with soup and salad, veggies seared Italian-style in oil and garlic, and a glass of honest wine.

Henry opened his small, simply decorated place in 1980 after working at the old downtown Paoli and at Luisa's. "Great value! Popular with locals from the neighborhood", "Simple, good and inexpensive."

L'OLIVIER • 465 Davis Court (off Jackson) • 981-7824

French • $$$

Lunch weekdays, dinner Monday-Saturday; reservations accepted; casual to sport jacket; full bar; major credit cards • Located in a brick courtyard of the Golden Gateway near the Embarcadero, L'Olivier is one of the city's prettiest French country-style restaurants. Pretty is a better word than opulent; Christian and Guy Francoz have created a beguiling greenhouse vision, with a solarium entryway and a glassed-walled dining room. But this is no Lehr rainforest; brass chandeliers, French antiques, wainscoting and floor-length pink table linens create an inviting Gallic atmosphere.

Chef Jean Marc Cullsack brings his Strasbourg Culinary Academy training to the menu, which is more traditional than nouveau. Expect to find grilled veal chops with *shiitake* mushrooms, braised sweetbreads, rack of lamb with thyme and honey and several fresh fish dishes.

"Excellent food, service and decor," comments one of our waiter-agents (who is from a different restaurant, of course).

MAIN STEM — see Harvey's Main Stem

MAMA'S • 398 Geary (Mason) • 433-0113 • 1701 Stockton (Washington Square) • 362-6421

American • $$

GEARY: Breakfast, lunch and dinner daily, service to 1:30 a.m. Friday-Saturday and until 12:30 a.m. other days; casual; full bar; major credit cards; STOCKTON: Breakfast and lunch daily; casual; wine and beer; no credit cards • Every city has to have its Mama's and San Francisco's version was started nearly a quarter of a century ago by Frances (Mama) and Michael Sanchez. The original still functions at its Washington Square location, but other editions have moved around a bit, from Macy's Cellar to Nob Hill (both now closed) to the corner of Geary and Mason. Others are in Palo Alto and Greenbrae, and the family organization even has a corporate office. The cafes serve basic American breakfast-through-dinner fare, with some Continental dishes at the Geary outlet.

Sanchez family members are presumably enjoying their success, but most of our critics are sorry they left the kitchen. Once-excellent breakfasts at the Washington Square cafeteria-style original are now rather ordinary. The Geary Street version, with a full bar and longer hours, is a "better type of coffee shop" says one of our epicures, who is a hotel manager, but he feels there "is no supervision" and the service needs improving. Another hotel team member is more kind: "A nice place for family dining or a quick comfortable lunch; nothing fancy, but good."

MAMOUNIA • 4411 Balboa (45th Avenue) • 752-6566

Moroccan • $$

Dinner nightly; reservations accepted; casual to sport jacket; wine and beer; major credit cards • Think of Mamounia as a more affordable Marrakech. Mehdi Ziani, once chef at the more lavish and expensive downtown restaurant, retreated to the Richmond District to open this pleasant restaurant-within-a-tent twenty or so years ago. It serves spicy specialties such as *pastila*, (pasta stuffed with fowl and sundry spices), lamb with honey and almonds, and of course, the ubiquitous Middle Eastern grain dish called *couscous*. Dinners generous enough to sink a sheik are less than $20.

What sets Mamounia and similar Moroccan restaurants apart from other Mideastern cafes is the way you sit—cross-legged, on cushions on the floor. A wonderful Moroccan sopping bread is your only utensil and the more you sop, the better it tastes as it soaks up juices and spices. With a tent-like canopy overhead, silvery Moroccan music drifting from somewhere, attentive service and the sensual sensation of eating with your fingers, you become spoiled Moroccan royalty for an evening.

MANDALAY RESTAURANT • 4344 California (Sixth Avenue) • 386-3895

Burmese • $

Lunch and dinner daily; casual; wine and beer; MC, VISA • What, you ask, is Burmese food? It's similar to spicy Thai cuisine, with the addition of tea leaves as greens, an off-flavored fermented shrimp paste and stronger use of curries. (The paste is best avoided unless you're familiar with Asian fermented fish; when my wife and co-author cooks with a Chinese version of this stuff, I leave the kitchen.) Malodorous fish aside, you can sample a variety of tasty Burmese delicacies, seasoned and flavored with peanut, curry, coriander and coconut. Try the fish soup, chicken noodle curry or a curious concoction of fish, coconut milk, lentils and curry, and a very light touch of that shrimp paste. A salad using sesame, peanuts, fried coconut and green tea leaves is *very* Burmese and very tasty. The menu also has several Chinese dishes, some interestingly altered with Southeast Asian spices.

The decor is understated Oriental and uncluttered—light woods with Chinese lanterns and a few well-placed Asian artifacts. One of our epicures calls it her "ethnic favorite" and another said it was "very unusual and exciting." An overdose of curry, perhaps?

MANORA'S THAI RESTAURANT • 3226 Mission (Valencia) • 550-0856

Thai • $

Lunch and dinner daily; casual; wine and beer; MC, VISA • "Amazing use of herbs; unlike what passes for most Thai restaurants; not just hot, spicy food," says one. "Friendly service and wonderful flavors. Many of the dishes are spicy but not overwhelmingly so," agreės another.

Those curiously distinct Thailand flavors come into play here, including lemon grass, lime leaves and basil. Steamed prawns with herbs and coconut milk over a bed of lettuce and a delicious Thai version of a pot sticker (with spicy sausage, shrimp and crab, tofu and cucumber) number among Manora's interesting entrees. Like that of the Mandalay above, Manora's decor is nicely underdone—white-clothed tables over red carpet with Thailand accent pieces.

MARINA CAFE • 2417 Lombard (Scott) • 929-7241

Italian seafood • $$

Dinner nightly, service to 11:30; reservations accepted; casual; full bar; major credit cards • Mahogany and marble dress up Sal Salma's early San Francisco style restaurant; the tables are dressed with lamps and red carnations and the waiters are dressed in tuxedos. Yet there's a casual, neighborhood cafe ambiance about the place. Prices are reasonable, in the mid-teens for a full dinner, and they become even more modest during early bird hours from 4:30 to 6, when a daily selection with soup or salad is offered for $7.95.

Our agents liked the typical Italian dishes, particularly the veal *dore*, *piccata* and *parmigiana*. Sal calls his place an Italian seafood restaurant, so the menu is heavy with calamari, prawns *provencal*, fish of the day and a really fine *cioppino* with *marinara* and garlic.

MARTINELLI'S — see Festa Festa Festa

MARY GULLI'S • 3661 Sacramento (Spruce) • 931-5151

Australian • $$

Lunch and dinner Tuesday-Saturday; reservations accepted; sport jacket; wine and beer; MC, VISA, AMEX • This exquisite little restaurant is tucked into the garden setting of Mark Twain Court in a quiet area of Presidio Heights. Soft fawn colors, mirror strips, a tastefully displayed antique etched glass collection and comfortable banquettes provide an sensuous and romantic interior. Taped classical and modern music complete the effect.

Frank and Mary Gulli define their menu as Australian, but they don't just toss another shrimp onto the barbie or see what's in the tucker bag. They prepare full-course and rather inexpensive Continental dinners, featuring lamb, richly-flavored Australian seafoods and beef.

"One of my favorites," reports a restaurateur. "Fresh ingredients, good preparation, knowledgeable staff."

MASA'S • 648 Bush (Powell) • 989-7154

French • $$$$

Dinner Tuesday-Saturday; reservations absolutely essential; dressy; full bar; MC, VISA, AMEX, DISC • Groping for adjectives to describe the tasteful Burgundy and gray interior of Masa's, we sought manager John Cunin's aid and he offered "contemporary subdued elegance." We like that. Other adjectives have been invested in the carefully crafted French dishes and the attentive service that is never hovering. (Having nearly as many waitpersons and assistants as diners helps.) There is no mystery to the success of this experiment in dining elegance founded by the late Masataka Kobayashi: Obtain the best of everything and charge whatever is required.

Owner Bill Kimpton, manager Cunin and present chef Julian Serrano have done a remarkable job of maintaining Kobayashi's lofty level. Masa's is thus the most expensive and consistently one of the highest rated restaurants in the San Francisco Bay Area. The prices apparently have not been discouraging, for several days' advance notice is necessary for reservations. (It used to be weeks.)

"Beautiful food and presentation," offered an epicure, and he awarded Masa's a Bo Derek score. One of our women agents spoke for all when she also gave the restaurant straight tens and added this comment: "A real experience; glad I wasn't paying."

MAX'S DINER • 311 Third (Folsom) • 546-MAXS

American • $

Lunch and dinner daily, service to midnight Thursday, to 1 a.m. Friday and Saturday; casual; full bar; MC, VISA, AMEX • Managing partner Bob Gentile welcomes both truckers and BMW Yuppies to this campy bastion of 50s excess with slick chrome shapes, Frankie Avalon sounds and waitresses in bobby sox and poodle skirts. The look is more Eastern-style diner than our familiar California drive-in, so transplants from New Jersey will experience a better rush of *deja vu.* The menu offers such fare as White Castle style mini-hamburgers, Philadelphia cheese steak and Reuben sandwiches.

Both this Max and the one below were created by Dennis Berkowitz and friends, who have a knack for blending proper portions of campy nostalgia and nouvelle. The food is uneven, say our critics, but the prices are good and the ambiance packs them in; Max's serves up to a thousand people a day.

"Terribly greasy French fries but burgers are big and juicy; desserts are number one", "Busy noise and nostalgia", "Great diner food and atmosphere."

MAX'S OPERA CAFE • 601 Van Ness Avenue (Golden Gate) • 771-7300

American deli • $$

Lunch and dinner daily, service to 1 a.m. Friday and Saturday, to midnight Sunday to Thursday; casual; full bar; major credit cards • New Yorkers will smack their very lips over the thick pastrami and kosher style corned beef sandwiches with multiple mustard choices. But they'll blink in amazement at the marbled rye bread and what n'hell is a *pizelle*?

Max's Opera Cafe is what happens when you thrust a New York deli into a California space, with sleek brass and neon, tan colors and sunlight pouring in from greenhouse-style windows. The menu is a mix of Eastern deli items and trendy California croissants, guacamole and those *pizelles*, sort of but not quite tostadas in baked tortilla shells. It's the right cafe in the right place at the right time—an airy and cheerful expanse in Opera Plaza, providing lunches for nearby Civic Center bureaucrats, a lively happy hour bar and quick dinners before and after the opera, ballet or concert. It even offers a bit of show biz; waiters and waitresses take turns at the mike after 8:30 most evenings to croon a show tune or belt out a ballad.

We like the pert and cheerful decor and curious variety of foods, although not all the menu experiments succeed. And we particularly like the complete separation of smoking and non-smoking areas.

MAXWELL'S PLUM • Ghirardelli Square (North Point) • 441-4140

American/Continental • $$

Lunch and dinner daily; reservations; casual to sport jacket; full bar; major credit cards • "Superb view of the bay with great, lush bordello atmosphere."

Was a bordello ever this gaudy? Maxwell's Plum is a gimmick that survives on its wonderful outlandishness. It bursts with glitter and color—seven crystal chandeliers, splashy murals, Tiffany-style glass, carved woods and multi-colored leaded glass ceiling panels that would put Joseph's coat to shame. It's so gaudy it's pretty, like a giant bouquet of bedding plants. And when you take your eyes off the interior view, you can gaze through floor-to-ceiling windows at the bay beyond.

San Franciscans, accustomed to curiosities, were startled when this seven million dollar splash of garish excess opened more than a decade ago. They jammed the place for a few months, then moved on to other novelties. But a few regulars and the summer tourist trade keeps Maxwell's going. And the food isn't really that bad. The menu tries to do too much and is predictably uneven, but the steaks, chops and seafood are quite tasty. Desserts are as lush and extravagant as the decor—things like Grand Marnier souffles, Amaretto chocolate mousse cake and blueberry pie that's actually worth the $3 tab per wedge. And the place serves one of the city's more lavish Sunday brunches.

The Fantasia decor was done by Werner Leroy, son of film maker Mervyn Leroy. Are you sure it wasn't Cecil B. DeMille's kid?

MAY SUN RESTAURANT • 1740 Fillmore (Post) • 567-7789

Mandarin/Teriyaki • $

Lunch and dinner Monday-Saturday; casual; wine and beer; major credit cards • May Sun is what happens when you move a step up from Chinese family Formica, add Japanese teriyaki for variety and somehow keep the prices ridiculously low. It's one of our favorite small restaurants in the city. This isn't a place where stoic Chinese waiters thump down cups of lukewarm tea; the Jim Lam Ngo family members are friendly and communicative and the service is attentive. Food arrives piping hot, issuing wonderful aromas with flavors to match. Although the owners are Chinese, they have the proper touch for richly sauced, lightly done teriyaki dinners. Their Mandarin cooking is spicy, but it won't turn you into a fire-breathing dragon.

Ngo does the best *Kung Pao* shrimp in the city with lots of fresh, succulent shrimp, crisp bell pepper wedges, bamboo shoots and crunchy peanuts. And he does it for less than $4, as a filling luncheon special with a big dollop of rice and rich-tasting Japanese-style vegetable broth. His menu also lists multi-course Chinese dinners, a la carte dishes and even vegetarian plates.

The restaurant is tucked under a big bay window in an attractive pastel blue, gray, white and brown Victorian in the newly gentrified area of Fillmore Street. The interior, a simple rectangle, is prim and neat with white-clothed tables over a burgundy carpet. A seascape painting dominates one wall; the other is decorated mostly by cooler cases. A rack of newspapers at the door tempts you to linger over tea; it's a refreshing change of pace from the brisk and often brusque service of many small Asian cafes.

Secret Agent MC-6 says it perfectly: "Clean, friendly; fast service without the feeling of being rushed."

MAYE'S STEAK AND OYSTER HOUSE • 1233 Polk (Sutter) • 474-7674

Seafood/Italian •  $$

Lunch and dinner daily, service from 2 p.m. Sundays, holidays; reservations accepted; casual; full bar; MC, VISA, AMEX • Coincidence places two of our preferred cafes next to one another. May Sun is a new discovery; Maye's is an old favorite, which we selected as one of San Francisco's ten best seafood places in our earlier guide. Dating from 1867, it's one of the city's oldest eateries, three years younger than Jack's.

It has the early San Francisco look appropriate to its age—wainscoting, dark woods, white linens and deep booths. But new proprietors Bibi and Phyllis Fiorucci have brightened things up a bit. And they've modernized the kitchen, offering mesquite grilled seafood and steaks, as well as crab casserole, near-legendary steamed clams (in season) and assorted pasta dishes. They haven't modernized their prices, however; at around $12 for dinner, Maye's remains one of the city's least expensive seafood restaurants. Prices get even better on weekdays from 3:30 to 6, when $8.25 buys a full meal; the place also offers senior specials.

"Fresh seafood; friendly service," reports one of our civilian gourmands. We'll also quote from our other book: "With all the catchy new restaurants cropping up, don't neglect the old-timers like Maye's, that still give good service and a dollar's worth of fish for a dollar."

MAYKADEH • 470 Green (Grant) • 362-8286

Persian • $

Lunch and dinner daily; casual; wine and beer and you can bring your own; MC, VISA, AMEX • We're still on our economy kick. Persian dinners with their intriguingly complex spices and herbs are dished up for $6 to $9 at this informal, attractive little North Beach cafe. Entrees such as *khoresht bademjam* (lightly spiced eggplant and lamb shanks), *joojeh kebab* (grilled chicken on a skewer) or *ghorme sabzee* (lamb with lime, red beans and green veggies) with have your taste buds purring like Persian kittens. We like the still-warm *pita* bread and fresh-cut vegetable nibblies that arrive shortly after you do, but we'll pass on the chunk of *feta* that accompanies them. (Even after we wandered about Turkey for a month and had the stuff for nearly every meal, goat cheese still tasted like its source smelled.)

"Large portions, well prepared mesquite-broiled meats; dishes are served with very good (buttered) rice," says a bartender epicure.

MEL'S DRIVE-IN • 2165 Lombard (Fillmore) • 921-3039 • 3355 Geary Boulevard (Parker) • 387-2244

American diner • $

Breakfast, lunch and dinner daily, service to 3 a.m. Friday and Saturday, to 1 a.m. other days; casual; wine and beer; no credit cards • Is Agent HT-23 having fun yet? Her report reads: "Food is only OK; music good; a fun place; too noisy."

Unlike some of the new "old-style" diners, the two Mel's aren't garish examples of Fifties excess; they're more typical of the drive-ins of yesteryear, with juke box outlets on Formica-topped tables, plastic booths and waitresses in little doily-sized aprons. The legendary Mel's look was featured in the film *American Graffiti.*

The menu is predictably legendary, too—shakes and splits and root beer floats and Melburgers and, good grief, they've brought back the fried egg sandwich (which may have been a mistake). Both Mel's also serve all-day breakfasts, including a "'57 Ford Omelet" with fresh tomatoes, green onions, spinach and sour cream. That was the year of the rakish Ford Sunliner with a bold gold side stripe, so we don't get the connection, but it sounds interesting.

THE MELTING POT • 4063 18th (Castro) • 863-0484

American • $$

Dinner nightly, brunch Saturday and Sunday; wine and beer; MC, VISA, AMEX • This charming little bistro in the heart of San Francisco's Castro district changed hands recently and changed its name from The Neon Chicken to The Melting Pot. New owners Robert and Bonnie Ray say the comfy decor and simple menu won't change that much. The Neon Chicken we knew and liked served four or five homemade entrees each night, ranging from rabbit stews to *paella*. Ingredients were fresh, seasonings innovative and prices were fair. All of this happened amidst a cozy, country kitchen setting.

Although the cafe serves no hard liquor, it has a separate bar upstairs, offering a good selection of wines and beers. It's as intimate and relaxing as a living room; one can lounge on a comfortable couch with a fine glass of Mondavi red and thumb through its scatter of newspapers and magazines.

"Always consistent in every detail" and "Great every time," said regiment members of the old Chicken. Hopefully, the new owners won't pluck up a good thing.

MIFUNE • 1737 Post (West Building, Japan Center) • 922-0337

Japanese • $

Lunch and dinner daily; casual; wine and beer; MC, VISA, AMEX • When I was an underpaid Marine correspondent in Japan, I stretched my yen by frequenting inexpensive *o-soba* (noodle) houses. Since guidebook writing doesn't generate much more income than the military, I often visit Japantown's Mifune; it's part of a large Japanese chain of noodle parlors.

The best thing about Mifune, other than the price, is the availability of those wonderful buckwheat noodles I savored in the old country. Thick and tasty, they come in an excellent broth, with a choice of twenty or more ingredients ranging from tofu and pork to chicken and egg. The small place is *very* Japanese, from the simple slatted wood decor to the plastic replicas of menu items in the window.

MC-127 called the food "very mediocre," but we don't agree. Although not fancy, it's quite tasty and hearty. Maybe our critic was served one of the replicas.

MILANO — see Ristorante Milano

MIYAKO HOTEL RESTAURANT • 1625 Post (Japan Center) • 922-3200

Japanese/American •  $$

Breakfast, lunch and dinner daily; reservations accepted; casual to sport jacket; full bar; all major credit cards • Just across the Peace Pavilion from Mifune is one of the city's most under-rated restaurants. "Relaxing atmosphere, very good food", "Excellent food; atmosphere is very romantic at night; kimono-wearing ladies are delightful!"

Although it isn't trendy or upscale nouvelle, the mix of Japanese and American fare at the Miyako Hotel Restaurant is fresh, intelligently prepared and very tasty. The service begins Japanese-style, with the presentation of steaming, hot towels; then it switches accents with the arrival of crunchy-crusted sourdough bread. The menu wanders from sashimi to hamburgers to spinach *fettucini* to steaks and daily seafood specials. Try the Spicy Oriental Chicken—thick and lightly cooked chicken fillets in a teriyaki sauce with ginger, red and white bell pepper strips, *shiitake* mushrooms and cooked onions, topped by a scatter of fresh, thin-sliced scallions. Excellent!

The look of the place is curiously pleasant. Distinctive cushioned chairs made from polished tree limbs (not as rustic-looking as they sound) surround white-clothed tables. Anthuriums brighten the tables, Japanese artifacts are displayed about the large, high-ceiling room and old style Japanese prints in modern frames adorn the walls. One wall is a floor-to-ceiling window, bathing the restaurant in cheerful light. And it's quiet, the kind of place where you can carry on a hushed business conversation or an unbusinesslike bit of dallying.

MODESTO LANZONE'S • 601 Van Ness Avenue (in Opera Plaza, at Golden Gate Avenue) • 928-0400

Italian •

Lunch weekdays, dinner Monday-Saturday, service to midnight Saturday; dressy (jacket and tie suggested); full bar; major credit cards • We were startled when San Francisco's favorite debonair Italian restaurateur closed his long-time Ghirardelli Square restaurant (and in fact, we had to make a last-minute deletion from this tome). Perhaps now he can make his handsome, artistic showplace in Opera Plaza an even finer diner. We selected it as one of the city's ten best restaurants in our other guide, and recent meals there have reinforced our choice.

The fare is primarily Northern Italian and it rivals French nouvelle in its subtle yet creative use of sauces. The veals are tender and succulent. Pasta dishes are light, almost fluffy things, like delicate angel hair with mini-clams, scallops and shrimp; and puffy *guanciali* stuffed with ricotta, mushrooms and tomato. His fresh seafood dishes are, as Reporter MC-30 points out, "excellent."

The restaurant's subdued colors, tile floors and rather simple lines offer a properly neutral backdrop for Lanzone's excellent modern art collection; each of the three dining rooms is an intimate gallery, and one is smoke-free, earning the place a double smoke-free symbol. An artistic focal point is a bust of the never-modest Modesto, done by avant-garde artist Robert Arneson, whose impressionistic bust of slain Mayor George Moscone was evicted from Moscone Center.

With the closing of his Ghirardelli landmark, Modesto isn't down to his last restaurant; he recently opened his new Lanzone-Alexander Restaurant in Orinda.

MON KIANG • 683 Broadway (Stockton) • 421-2015

Hakka Chinese •

Lunch and dinner daily, service to midnight Friday and Saturday; casual; wine and beer; MC, VISA • The Hakka people are inland farmers who migrated from north China to Canton Province and their dishes have a simple earthiness, involving salted meats and fowl. It's actually rather rudimentary, since the Hakka in China are a rather poor farm labor group. The fare has been enhanced here to make it more suitable to local tastes. To sample the Hakka way, try Mon Kiang's steamed bacon with mustard greens, salted baked chicken, pan fried beef balls with greens or wine flavored chicken. Dinners are better than the special one-dish lunches here.

Are we having *funs* yet? Yes and no; a Hakka-style chow mein with shrimp, scraps of sugar-cured pork, calamari and *fun* (flat wheat noodles) was oily and not very interesting. Although it was a large serving for under $4, it was short on protein and long on noodles.

The look is a tad nicer than most Asian family cafes, with fake wood grain wainscoting, black and gold print wallpaper above and terrazzo floors. The effect is neat and clean, and a couple of silk embroidered pictures brighten the place.

NARAI RESTAURANT • 2229 Clement (23rd Avenue) • 751-6363

Thai/Chinese • $

Lunch and dinner daily except Monday; casual; wine and beer; MC, VISA, AMEX • Narai offers a cuisine combination rare in America but common in Thailand, a blend of delicately flavored rural Cantonese and spicy Thai cooking. Called *Chiu Chow* or *Chao Chow*, this Chinese fare consists of subtly flavored fish, fowl and fresh vegetable dishes of the Swatow region of south China. From Thailand come the lively curries and distinctive lemon grass, peanut and coconut flavors. And our judges report that all are well prepared and uniformly tasty. Examples are duck in soy with a light garlic and vinegar dip *(Chiu Chow)* and spiced chicken in a Thai-style *satay* sauce of peanut, coconut and chilies, served over spinach. Many of the dishes, such as a seafood hot pot, combine cooking styles and spices of both cultures.

It's a cheery place with bamboo print wallpaper, blonde furnishings and photos of Thai temple figures. And it's remarkably inexpensive, around $10 for a hearty and certainly creative meal.

NEIMAN-MARCUS ROTUNDA — see Rotunda at Neiman-Marcus

NEON CHICKEN — see Melting Pot

NEPTUNE'S PALACE • Pier 39 (The Embarcadero) • 434-2260

Seafood • $$

Lunch and dinner daily; reservations accepted; casual to sport jacket; full bar; major credit cards • Neptune's and Pier 39 have completed their first decade as part of the San Francisco waterfront scene. After ten years, folks don't bother giggling much about the tacky, awkward pier-piling decor of Warren Simmons' controversial shorefront development. And the early cafes that served ordinary tourist fare at startling prices have been filtered out.

The surviving restaurants have settled in, serving fair to middlin' vittles to visitors and residents. Although we're not Pier 39 aficionados, we do like the San Francisco-style opulence of Neptune's and it's impressive pier's-end views. We've gotten many a palatable meal there. And of course we like its well-defined non-smoking dining areas. The menu is predictable—marinated swordfish, petrale sole, abalone, crab in season and deep fried prawns, but at least it's predictably palatable.

"Excellent seafood; marvelous views of the bay (weather permitting)."

NEW JOE'S AT UNION SQUARE • 347 Geary (Powell) • 989-6733

Italian/American • $$

Breakfast, lunch and dinner daily; casual; full bar; major credit cards • Jeffrey Pollack found a need and filled it with the latest of the city's "Joe" restaurants. The need—an early-morning to late-night cafe near the city's shops and theaters. The look is basic San Francisco Joe formula—tables with starched linens; intimate booths, plus counter seats that stare into an open kitchen; and tux-clad waiters.

The menu offers a virtual department store of selections—from Italian pastas to American sandwiches to mesquite broiled fish to a New York style pizza. And of course Joe's serves Joe's Special—a spinach, ground chuck and onion omelet.

"Food was good; atmosphere was casual but nice", "Prices very reasonable; with exhibition (open kitchen) cooking.

NEW PISA • 550 Green (Stockton) • 362-4726

Italian • 🥄🥄 $

Lunch and dinner daily except Wednesday; casual; wine and beer; no credit cards • The New Pisa may be newer than it's namesake Italian city but it's one of North Beach's oldest cafes, dating back more than half a century. This is another of those venerable family-owned *trattorias* that forgets to keep pace with inflation; it offers tasty fare for tempting prices. Entrees such as chicken *cacciatore*, a memorable *osso bucco* and veal saute are centerpieces for five-course dinners for around $10. Sundry pastas and other dishes also are on the menu.

"Don't know how they do it for the price!" exclaims RE-55.

The place looks its age, which means it's pleasantly funky, with mahogany booths, family-sized tables, cafe curtains and memorabilia-cluttered walls. Dante Benedetti's father opened New Pisa in 1920 and Dante literally grew up in the kitchen. He's still there, planning tonight's feast on his daily-changing menu.

NIPPON SUSHI • 314 Church (Fifteenth) • no phone

Sushi • 🥄 $

Lunch and dinner daily; casual; no alcohol; no credit cards • Apparently the secret to Nippon Sushi's success is to keep it a secret, so perhaps we aren't doing the place a favor. No marquee or window sign betrays the location of this tiny storefront sushi parlor off upper Market. It's in a nondescript brown Victorian (that has curious Spanish roof trim) just beyond 15th, but you really have to *look* for it. You can't call and ask directions because, if it has a phone, it's unlisted. Once inside, you know it's a sushi parlor by looking at people's plates, and you finally discover the name when you're handed one of those plastic pictorial sushi menus. Ah hah! We're in Nippon Sushi!

But getting in is the trick. The place is so inexpensive (the cheapest in the city) that people often are lined up out the door and down the block. The place accepts no reservations, serves no booze nor allows any inside, takes no checks or credit cards and the service is hurried. The folks are nice enough, but the impression we receive is: "Eat your sushi, leave the money on the table and move along, please. Next!"

It's a good thing this place is a bargain.

NORTH BEACH RESTAURANT • 1512 Stockton (Columbus) • 392-1700

Italian • $$

Lunch and dinner daily, service to 11:45; casual; full bar; major credit cards • Another long-time trattoria in the Little City area, North Beach Restaurant drew both plaudits and protests from our panel. "Always fresh pasta", "Old Italian; great food; excellent ravioli", "Too expensive", "Dark and gloomy."

We've dined there, found it to be dimly lit (a.k.a. dark and gloomy if you've had a bad day) and we rated the food from average to below. Pasta dishes are generous, not inexpensive, sometimes tasty but frequently overdone; veals and fish can be ordinary or very good. There's little originality in the menu; this is old North Beach, not Italian nouveau. Service is invariably prompt and affable and the place is generally busy and lively (a.k.a. noisy if you've had a bad day).

OCEAN • 726 Clement (Eighth Avenue) • 221-3351
NEW OCEAN • 239 Clement (Fourth Avenue) • 668-1688

Cantonese • $

Lunch and dinner daily; casual; wine and beer; MC, VISA • This pair of Oceans, owned by the same family and separated by five blocks, serves traditional Cantonese fare—primarily fresh, lightly cooked, lightly seasoned seafood and vegetables. We recall having a rather good *gai lan* (Chinese broccoli in oyster sauce) and steamed whole rock cod. For the most part, Oceans' owners leave the chili peppers, heavy-handed gingers and Hunan hot oil to the dozens of Hunan/Szechuan/Beijing/Ping Pong/Ding How restaurants popping up these days.

Our agents like pair, too: "Excellent Chinese cuisine; fresh approach, unlike the usual MSG houses." That vote was cast for Ocean, but New Ocean is cast from the same mold, with an identical menu. Both offer ambiance typical of successful, small family-owned Chinese restaurants, which means there isn't much.

OCEAN CITY • 644 Broadway (Kearny) • 928-2328

Chinese dim sum • \\ $

Dim sum from 8 to 3 daily, then dinner to 10 p.m.; casual; wine and beer; MC, VISA • Ocean City is what happens when a big corporation instead of a small family builds a Chinese restaurant—it's vast, garish and rather institutionalized. As one of Chinatown's biggest dim sum houses, it offers a good variety of these "little hearts," which are hurried past your table in a dizzying parade of steam carts. Get there early for best selections, take a number and hope you get a seat in this crowded, noisy place before you faint from hunger.

Dim sum is served from 8 until mid-afternoon, then this two-story restaurant switches to conventional Chinese fare, with emphasis on Cantonese. It's also a take-out, and a couple of movie theaters occupy the same building.

"Great dim sum; loud; Hong Kong glitz."

OLD CLAM HOUSE • 299 Bayshore Boulevard (Oakdale) • 826-4880

Seafood • \\ $$

Lunch and dinner daily; casual; full bar; MC, VISA • Its roots go back to 1861 and possibly beyond, when it was a "mile house" and stage stop on the old El Camino Real. The Old Clam House retains the rustic look of those times—wood paneling, a rare hammered copper ceiling, a clutter of curios and (a harmless gimmick) tractor seats for bar stools. The place got its start not long after the Gold Rush, when clams were dug from the yet-to-be-polluted bay and served fresh in the restaurant. Other seafood dishes have since joined the bi-valve specialties here, and our agents like its "Fresh, wide selection", "Good sized portions" and "unpretentious" ambiance.

The Old Clam House celebrates its heritage in noisy camaraderie each night, but the establishment also has a second dining room that's quiet and peaceful.

ONE-UP • 345 Stockton (in Hyatt Union Square at Post) • 398-1234

Continental • $$$

Dinner nightly and Sunday brunch; reservations advised; sport jacket to dressy; full bar; all major credit cards • When critics start playing one-upsmanship with the city's skyroom restaurants and bars, the One-Up often is overlooked. Yet it offers one of the city's better dining views and while the food isn't all the nouvelle rage, it is quite good. The One-Up may not rival Victor's or the Carnelian Room, but neither do the prices. Its Continental menu is more affordable, with most entrees in the teens.

We like the clean, contemporary decor and we've enjoyed view luncheons there in the past. (My sister from Butte Falls, Oregon, was dazzled.) Unfortunately, the place currently serves dinner only, plus a rather elaborate Sunday brunch that critics rate as one of the best in the city.

"Very good," said MC-20; "Excellence in taste" chimed in MC-211.

ORCHID'S • 215 Church (Market) • 864-1601

Hunan • $

Lunch and dinner daily; reservations advised; casual; wine and beer; MC, VISA ($10 credit card minimum) • If there is such a thing as Hunan nouvelle, Orchid's has found it. Hardly an ordinary Formica Oriental chili parlor, Orchid's is a dramatic yet rather funky cafe in an old Victorian house on Church Street's growing restaurant row just off upper Market. It's decorated with a couple of beautifully ornate hand-carved screens, pots of blooming orchids, bentwood chairs (some starting to un-bend) and tables with pink nappery. Dining areas are segmented into several intimate spaces, each graced by ancient Oriental artifacts or oversized ceramic vase sprouting sprigs of orchids.

The peppery Hunan food is fresh, intelligently prepared and often innovative. Running counter to most Chinese restaurants, Orchid's offers a rather small yet creative menu. I lunched there recently on a hot and spicy chicken salad, with generous chunks of chilled chicken drenched in tasty peanut oil, over a bed of shredded lettuce. My friend ordered garlic chicken and was rewarded with a huge bowl of piping hot, perfectly cooked chicken bits over rice. Both were delicious, and both were less than $4, including bowls of excellent hot and sour soup. Other intrigues on the menu include garlic scallops with water chestnuts, lemon beef and spicy Hunan duck with snow peas, carrots and hot sauce. All of the ingredients are fresh and flawlessly prepared, and the menu declares that no MSG is used. After trying lunches and dinners in the original barn-like Hunan Restaurant on Sansome and a dozen or so smaller mom and pop places, Orchid's just became our favorite northern Chinese restaurant.

One of our reporters fussed that the service was slow (although was brisk during our three visits). But he rated the food at 7.5 and gave the ambiance a generous nine, so apparently it was worth the wait.

ORIGINAL JOE'S • 144 Taylor (Turk) • PRospect 5-4877

Italian/American • 

Lunch and dinner daily, service to 1:30 a.m.; casual; full bar; MC, VISA • We're glad the cartel voted Joe's into the book, because we might have bent our rules and listed it anyway. This dark-paneled piece of culinary history is the oldest survivor of the open-kitchen style cafe that was developed in San Francisco. It's strictly from yesterday—the kind of place where you can drop in, slide onto one of the big comfortable stools opposite the kitchen and sip a glass of wine while your dinner sizzles before you. Or you can disappear into the intimacy of a deep booth.

Although Joe's specialties are pastas, steaks, chops and fresh fish, we gave it a "Ten Best" rating in our earlier guide for its great hamburgers. They're formidable things—huge, spicy missile-shaped patties resting on thick slabs of French bread.

This is *almost* where the "Joe"-style restaurant began. In 1934, entrepreneur Frank Venturi went to nightclub owner Joe Morelio with a new idea—a restaurant with a long counter and an exposed kitchen where diners could watch the chefs at work. Morelio financed Venturi's venture, and he opened on Broadway, naming his place "New Joe's" for his benefactor. It was so successful that he sold out in 1937 and opened Original Joe's at its present site, with a dining room and tuxedo-clad waiters as well as the open kitchen. That first New Joe's is gone, so the Original survives as predecessor to dozens of Joe imitations around the country. It even survived the deterioration of its Tenderloin neighborhood; now that the area is rejuvenating, it should last another half century.

Some of Original Joe's crewmen have worked there more than 40 years and the average tenure is 20.

"We have the oldest waiters this side of Medicare," says co-owner Marie Rodin Duggan.

And, we'll add, some of the most likable.

OSOME RESTAURANT • 1923 Fillmore (Pine) • 346-2311

Japanese • $$

Dinner nightly; casual; wine and beer; major credit cards • A striking blend of modern American and restrained Oriental decor—glassed-in booths, clean wood-paneled walls and a curved glass sushi bar display case—provides a dramatic setting for one of San Francisco's finest Japanese restaurants. It was, in fact, voted the best Japanese place in the Bay Area by the *San Francisco Chronicle* in 1987.

Osome offers both a sushi bar and regular sit-down restaurant, and the quality of food matches the setting. The sushi is faultlessly fresh and artfully prepared; the typical Japanese entrees are generally excellent. The fare is served on exquisite Japanese ware, handsome pottery, laquerware and ceramics.

Prices are modest for such a harmonic setting, around $12 to $15 for a full dinner. A planned early bird special, whose details weren't available at press time, will be even less.

PACIFIC CAFE • 7000 Geary Boulevard (34th Avenue) • 387-7091
• Ghirardelli Square (Mustard Building) • 775-1173

Seafood • $$

GEARY: dinner nightly; casual; wine and beer; MC, VISA; GHIRARDELLI: lunch weekdays; dinner nightly; casual; full bar; MC, VISA • Pacific Cafe is a simple idea that works well: Serve a few fresh fish entrees at reasonable prices in a pleasantly funky atmosphere, and hand patrons a gratis glass of wine while they're waiting for a table. It works so well that five cafes Pacific have sprung up—two in San Francisco and others in Concord, South San Francisco and Kentfield. In the city, most of the votes were cast for the Geary Boulevard cafe; we're more familiar with the Ghirardelli place, where we've gotten consistently tasty fish.

While waiting and sipping gratis wine, one can admire the natural woods, nautical doo-dads and hanging plants. The menu is simple and straightforward seafood—red snapper, the omnipresent filet of sole, pan fried sand dabs and scallops. A steak is available for those who just won't dine on dishes from the deep.

PACIFIC HEIGHTS BAR AND GRILL • 2001 Fillmore (Pine) • 567-3337

Seafood/oyster bar • $$

Lunch weekdays, dinner nightly, Sunday brunch; reservations accepted; casual; full bar; MC, VISA, AMEX • Susan and Craig Bashel say they have the largest oyster bar on the West Coast, with "twelve to sixteen varieties daily." We didn't know that many species of the lumpy shellfish existed. The team likes the place: "Very, very creative sauces", "Great oysters, great selections." However, MC-5 complains that it's overpriced and bland. Perhaps he doesn't like oysters. (Not my favorite food either, but I'll go with the majority.)

You can plant yourself at the small oyster bar and slurp down Bluepoints, Golden Mantels, Quilcenes, Appalachicolas, Yaquina Bays or (take courage) New Zealand Green-Lipped Mussels. The assorted slippery things come with sundry sauces—sour cream dill, hot and sour sauce, tomato herb salsa and such. Or one can order from a generous seafood menu that features the typical mesquite-grilled catch of the day, plus less common items like peppered Louisiana redfish and Chilean sea bass. This flexible menu also lists pork medallions, steak and other meats for those who failed to note that Pacific Heights B&G was a seafood place.

All this happens in a chic restaurant tucked into a handsome pastel Victorian.

PANOS' RESTAURANT • 4000 24th (Noe) • 824-8000

Mediterranean/seafood • $$

Lunch daily (brunch on weekends), dinner nightly; casual; wine and beer; MC, VISA • Panos' looks like new because John and Vi Gianaras enjoyed such success with their decade-old restaurant that they remodeled it in early 1988. So it has gone from family funky to something a bit more sleek and romantic.

Perhaps the key to their success is their decision to feature not only Greek food but other savories as well, appealing to a broader range of palates. The menu offers Greek classics like *tsitsiki* (garlic, yogurt and *feta* appetizers) and assorted things with lamb. It also features fare from other Mediterranean lands, pastas and several fresh fish dishes. Ample dinners are about

$12, and the price drops 20 percent during a nightly 5 to 6 p.m. culinary happy hour.

"Small, clean artistic cafe; great Sunday brunch; slow service but great *gyros*; worth the trip." "Great neighborhood spot; romantic; simple fare; well-prepared and reasonable."

PASTA II • 381 South Van Ness Avenue (15th) • 864-4116

Italian •

Lunch Monday-Friday, dinner Monday-Saturday; casual; wine and beer and it can be brought in; MC, VISA • Tiny Pasta II needs a little color. The look is low-budget Ascot—black and white vinyl tile, black wainscoting with empty white walls above and straight-back black chairs tucked under white-clothed tables.

But the menu is also low-budget, which is the saving grace for this plain little place. Hearty Italian dinners, with emphasis on home-made pasta, are under $10 and several lunches are under $5. Chef-owner Peter Ciddio makes his pasta fresh daily, and he offers "a long list of fresh sauces." In addition to the *tortellini, fettucini* and *linguini* served with a variety of these sauces, the place offers a boneless chicken *tetrazzini* and daily specials that might include a veal *piccata* or savory eggplant dish.

In case you wondered, there is no Pasta I.

PASTARIA • 339 Taylor (in the Mark Twain Hotel, at O'Farrell) • 928-0999

American/Continental •

Breakfast and dinner daily, lunch weekdays; casual; full bar; all major credit cards (for purchases over $10) • This pleasant little cafe off the lobby of the moderately-priced Mark Twain Hotel offers diners a mix of freshly made pasta and a few of the standard fish, veal and meat dishes. Full dinners are $10, including pasta, veggies soup or salad; lunches go for around $5 to $8. With a drinkable house wine at $1.75 a glass, the place represents a good buy for downtown shoppers and theater crowds.

One of our agents says the "decor is clean, with simple, fresh linens." On the tables or the hotel beds?

PATIO CAFE • 531 Castro (18th) • 621-4640

American • $

Breakfast, lunch and dinner daily, service to 2 a.m. Friday and Saturday, until midnight other days; casual; full bar; all major credit cards • "A place to be seen and see," said one of our hidden diners about this mostly outdoor cafe that spreads its tables behind a pair of scruffy Victorians in the city's Castro district. "Champagne and orange juice, Eggs Benedict are only the beginning," says another, referring to the Sunday brunch; she likes the "dining in an outdoor atmosphere."

Although it's in the heart of the city's gay district, the clientele is mixed. Boy, is it mixed! This may be the best people-watching cafe in the city. (Check out the lady with the black eye patch and motorcycle helmet; and how did that nice old couple find their way back here?) The cafe is mostly patio; it's a split-level collection of sun-bleached wood, partly covered by corrugated plastic roofing and partly exposed to the Castro sun. Space heaters keep the place cozy through the seasons.

The food fits the funky feel of the place—light salads, omelets and sandwiches and some daily specials like chicken brochettes and deep-fried prawns. No miracles emerge from the kitchen but prices are good, portions are generous and service is friendly. The Patio specializes in breakfast fare, served from 8 to 5; we sampled Dutch eggs (a variation on Eggs Benedict with a generous swatch of lox instead of ham) and determined that it was tasty, although the sauce was a bit rich and heavy.

You're handed a menu on your way in, invited to find a seat, and you pay on the way out. It's generally busy, but there's usually a table available; dawdling over coffee or a glass of wine isn't discouraged. A juke box shouts out show tunes, but in the oversized patio's wide open spaces, the sound is not intrusive. These are lively, up-beat show tunes, incidentally; don't expect to hear "Climb Every Mountain" at the Patio Cafe.

PERRY'S • 1944 Union Street (Laguna) • 922-9022

American • $$

Late breakfast (from 9 a.m.), lunch and dinner daily, service to midnight; reservations advised; casual to sport jacket; full bar; MC, VISA, AMEX • Is Perry Butler the Ed Moose (Washington Square B&G) of the Marina District, or is Moose the Perry Butler of North Beach? Both restaurants have that special funky upscale ambiance, lively bar scenes and simple, hearty fare that appeal to the San Francisco business crowd. Perry's has been pulling in Marina District regulars and Marin-bound commuters since 1969. He sold part-interest in the place a few years ago and followed those commuters to Marin to open an annex, but he returned in early 1988 to devote full attention to the original.

Perry's, which Butler describes as an "atmospheric New York Third Avenue pub," serves pubbish staples such as a platter-filling steak, corned beef hash, excellent hamburgers and, of course, a fresh fish of the day or two. The Eggs Benedict and Eggs Blackstone are local legends.

Also legendary is the evening cocktail hour; Perry's is one of the city's quintessential after-office bird-watching and elbow-flexing pubs.

PHIL LEHR'S STEAKERY • **330 Taylor (in the Hilton Hotel, near Ellis)** • **673-6800**

Steaks/Continental • \$\$

Dinner nightly, service to midnight; reservations essential; casual to sport jacket; full bar; all major credit cards • This clubby, cozy restaurant is in the Hilton, but not *part* of the Hilton. Back in the 1950s, Lehr pioneered this American-style steakhouse concept. Premium steaks are displayed in a glassed-in cooler case where diners can make their selection, then pay by the ounce. Deep, plush booths, lots of brass and carved woods provide the proper Early Americana atmosphere for consuming the ideal cut of beef.

An assortment of European dishes has been added to the menu for balance, and some are prepared at tableside for added flair. However, our agents say they come here mostly for the steer.

"Great steaks and quite elegant", "Pick your own cut of steak; desserts great."

PIERRE-AT-MERIDIEN • **50 Third (at Hotel Meridien, near Market)** • **974-6400**

Contemporary French • \$\$\$\$

Dinner nightly; reservations essential; sport jacket to dressy; full bar; major credit cards • Pierre's is what one should expect in a modern, upscale French hotel dining room—a serene, almost severely elegant look, with calming gray and off-white walls, little bud vases on white-draped tables, exquisite crystal and hand-painted china. Service, as one would expect, is attentive and just comfortably short of haughty.

What one may not expect is an innovative menu with a strong California influence to lighten and broaden the French fare. Manager Gerard Hotelier defines it as "contemporary French." Hotelier and chef Sebastien Urbain (Can you believe these names?) have carried on, perhaps refined, a menu designed by Jean-Pierre Moulle, who was lured to the Meridien from now-legendary Chez Panisse in Berkeley. (Moulle is credited with teaching French cooking techniques to Alice Waters and Jeremiah Tower.)

Expect excellence in dishes like rack of lamb with baby California vegetables; filet of sea bass with fresh tomato fondue and snow peas; and grilled sirloin with coriander and sauteed artichoke hearts.

Expect the check to be over $100 per couple with wine and dessert, which isn't excessive for such elegance.

PIETRO'S RISTORANTE • 1851 Union (Laguna) • 563-4157

Italian • $$

Dinner nightly; casual; full bar; MC, VISA, AMEX • Chef-owner Pietro Bartolozzi brought his restaurant skills and his romantic Italian soul from the old country; both are evident in this quiet, intimate little enclave in the middle of bustling Union Street. Heavy beam rafters support a silent forest of overhead *raffia*, drop-lamps cast mellow light on white tables with fresh-cut flowers, and romantic music (probably Vivaldi) drifts from somewhere.

Secret agent MC-145, the regional director of a foreign government tourist office (not Italy) takes over from here: "Best for two or four; not more. Romantic. *Osso bucco* is excellent; *fettucini* Della Rosa with bacon and peas is sure to please casserole lovers. Herb butter with Italian bread is a meal in itself."

We've known MC-145 for years and she's not Pietro's cousin. Honestly.

PISCES SEAFOOD RESTAURANT • 2127 Polk (Broadway) • 771-0850

Seafood • $

Lunch Monday-Saturday, dinner nightly; reservations accepted; casual; wine and beer; all major credit cards • Pisces is a rarity; it's a small cafe serving excellent seafood, with attentive service and a cozy intimacy worthy of special occasions, yet with everyday prices. Now in its 10th year on Polk Street, it's owned by a Thai family, but the food and decor are more Continental, with slight Asian accents.

Flickering candles and cut flowers on white-clad tables provide a simple European setting for its extensive selection of fresh broiled fish, shellfish, calamari, lobster and a very tasty *cioppino* over rice. Dinners range from $8 to $10, and this includes chowder or salad, lightly cooked vegetables and French fries or rice. And would you believe the prices drop below $7 for early bird specials from 5 to 6:30? Pisces is simply the city's best inexpensive seafood restaurant, and one of its ten best fish cafes overall.

"I love the fresh fish and fresh salads, white tablecloths and fresh hors d'oeuvres," comments MC-210, a retired clerk who selected it as one of her five favorite restaurants.

PJ'S OYSTER BED • 2299 Van Ness Avenue (Vallejo) • 885-1155 • 737 Irving (Eighth Avenue) • 556-7775

Seafood • $$

Lunch weekdays, dinner nightly, Sunday brunch; casual; full bar; MC, VISA • You can't miss PJ's as you motor down Van Ness Avenue; it's that restaurant on the corner of Van Ness and Vallejo with the odd puffy, turquoise marquee. It looks much better inside, with oak chairs tucked under glass-topped tables, high ceilings, big windows and a small bar at one end that's a popular cocktail-hour gathering spot.

But this PJ's and its companion on Irving are more involved with seafood than decor, serving an abundance in a variety of ways: charcoal broiled, pan fried, blackened. A seafood combo with fish, scallops and prawns in wine sauce, shallots, garlic and *creme fraiche* is quite tasty. The two places offer an assortment of slippery things at their oyster stations.

The Van Ness version earned mixed reviews. "A very noisy place; too noisy for me," complained one, but others called the noise "cheerful camaraderie" and they liked the "good selection of fish and shellfish."

PORTMAN GRILL • 500 Post Street (in Portman Hotel at Mason) • 929-2087

California/Continental • $$$$

Breakfast, lunch and dinner daily; reservations advised; sport jacket to dressy, jacket required for dinner; full bar; major credit cards • After designing such stellar creations as the Hyatt Regency and the Los Angeles Bonaventure, architect John Portman opened his own hotel in San Francisco in 1987. It's a striking affair, with Portman's signature atrium lobby and carnival-missile elevators that look borrowed from the Regency. Twin fireplaces flank the large lobby; its centerpiece is a rose marble fountain and four bronze nude dancers with flying metal hair that add a nice touch of *joie de vivre* to this vestibule of subdued elegance.

The restaurant is essentially a continuation of the lobby. It's a handsome open space with circular rose marble columns, free-standing brass planters and comfortable modified captains' chairs around large, well-spaced tables. The daily changing menu is predictably innovative, offering grilled Sonoma quail, angel hair pasta with littleneck clams, calves liver with Bordelaise sauce and such.

Our only complaint is that the portions, while beautifully presented, are rather small—and they are not inexpensive. A grilled sea bass was perfectly seared, moist and flaky inside, accompanied by a wonderfully tart Pomeray sauce, with crisp baby vegetables. But the sauce was rather skimpy and there weren't enough veggies to keep a rabbit regular.

"They try, but it's too new," says one of our epicures. "It'll take time."

RAF CENTROGRIGLIA • 478 Green (Grant) • 362-1999

Northern Italian • $$$

Lunch weekdays, dinner nightly, service to 11:30 Friday and Saturday; reservations accepted; casual to sport jacket; full bar; major credit cards • Remember that funky mass of space called the Old Spaghetti Factory? This comfortable, barn-like stronghold of the Beat Generation has been reincarnated into the Upbeat Eighties, returning as RAF Centrogriglia. Brought to you by the designers of that strange bit of stucco and Reynolds wrap palm trees called Rosalie's, RAF is a free-form study in sculptured wall shapes, sofas with cubistic cushions and surrealistic light fixtures. The owners describe it as "an ancient

Tuscan villa" combining old European and modern funky forms.

The menu is northern Italian, and the upscale and up-priced *risotto, polenta*-based stews and sweetbreads are a distant cry from the spaghetti bowls of the earlier occupant.

This place drew a lot of votes, and not all of them were complimentary. "Pastas only fair; entree ordinary; not tempted to try the dessert", "Wonderful room! Food is great but it is so expensive. Fun place", "Moderately priced; somewhat pretentious", "Very interesting interior; food quite good", "Too open, therefore you can hear everything. Do not recommend for intimate dining."

And finally: "The service and food does not commensurate with the high prices."

RAFFLES • 1390 Market (in Fox Plaza, at Hayes) • 621-8601

Polynesian/Chinese • $

Lunch weekdays, dinner nightly; reservations accepted; casual; full bar; MC, VISA • We're a voice in the culinary wilderness, recommending this busy Polynesian-trimmed place on the ground floor of Fox Plaza; it's ignored by all other restaurant critics. However, a handful of our agents voted for its inexpensive fare and its handy location near Davies Hall, Civic Auditorium and the Opera House. It has been a fixture here for a couple of decades, and its age is beginning to show. The stuffed swordfish is getting a bit scruffy, the universally ignored big-screen video in the bar is generally out of focus and the wicker chairs in the two dining rooms creak a bit. But the food is ample, served briskly for the luncheon and pre-theater crowds and it's priced right. Listen, you want gourmet, you pay gourmet prices.

At lunch time, it's popular with Civic Center bureaucrats and auto club types. At 5 p.m., the same cast returns for fair-priced drinks and some of the best happy hour nibblies in the city—mini-drumsticks, sweet-cured Chinese pork and spiced meatballs. Later, the practiced wait staff will ensure that you get to your theater seats on time. (They know the routine; some have been there longer than the swordfish.)

REGINA'S • 490 Geary (in the St. Regis Hotel, at Taylor) • 885-1661

French Creole • $$$

Breakfast, lunch and dinner daily, service to midnight Sunday-Thursday and to 1 a.m. Friday-Saturday; reservations advised; sport jacket; full bar; MC, VISA, AMEX • Regina Charboneau came down from Alaska recently to swap climates and open an opulent Southern style restaurant in the new St. Regis Hotel. She's brought plenty of warmth, and early signs of success are evident.

The room itself would make a frost-bitten Sourdough head south. It has a refined old New Orleans feel with high ceilings, French chandeliers, flowered carpets and glossy black chairs drawn up to crisp white linens. Sketches of theatrical costumes bring bright touches to pink and cream walls.

The menu isn't faddish Cajun/Creole, but substantial New Orleans type fare such as *bouillabaisse*, sauteed chicken with a spinach crayfish sauce, peppery shrimp and a fair version of Oysters Rockefeller, which originated in the Crescent city. Flaming Bananas Foster is executed at tableside with a flair that will spirit you right back to Mardi Gras.

RINGS • 1131 Folsom (Eighth) • 621-2111

California nouvelle • $$

Lunch weekdays, dinner Tuesday-Saturday; reservations accepted; casual; wine and beer; MC, VISA • Recipe for San Francisco restaurant success: blend offbeat or upscale decor with innovative California cuisine and give the place a single-syllable name. In this case, however, Ring happens to be the family name of the owners; they've dropped the apostrophe to keep in trend.

Chef and co-owner Julie, late of Chicago, is an excellent student of California nouvelle, emphasizing fresh seafood, lightly cooked veggies and fresh pastas in her daily-changing menu. Among her specialties are *mariscos Mexicanos* (shellfish with cilantro and *jalapeno*); *linguini* with fresh tomatoes and pesta; and a humble American hot turkey pie. Desserts are excellent and her special French fries done in beer with a touch of vinegar are worth the trip across Market Street.

The Rings have transformed an old store front into a cheerfully earthy space, with pink and salmon walls trimmed in dark blue, and bentwood chairs or wooden benches on polished wood floors. "Fun restaurant; good variety of food; friendly personnel."

RISTORANTE FIRENZE — see Firenze Restaurant

RISTORANTE GRIFONE • 1609 Powell (Green) • 397-8458

Italian • $$$

Dinner nightly; casual; full bar; all major credit cards • North Beach suffers no shortage of trattorias, but Bruno Pella became bored with retirement and decided to open another one. After eight years, he's on the verge of becoming an institution in a neighborhood where most cafes count their seniority in decades. Although the menu is essentially northern Italian with its lightly-sauced veals and fish, Bruno has added some innovative pastas like *fettucini* flavored with smoked salmon. His *minestrone* is properly thick and hearty and the *cannelloni* caught columnist Herb Caen's attention, which helped ensure Pella's early success.

Decor is a romantic mix of modern and old Italian, with mirrored walls, banquettes, Portofino murals and Venetian style chandeliers for a touch of class.

"The best all-around Italian; service plus; food excellent."

RISTORANTE MILANO • 1448 Pacific Avenue (Hyde) • 673-2961

Northern Italian • $$

Dinner nightly; casual; wine and beer; MC, VISA • The city of Milan is Italy gone modern, with smart restaurants, the Galleria shopping center and high chic fashion. Tiny Ristorante Milano reflects its namesake city with sleek black and white decor, lattice ceiling and black and gray tile floors.

The food fits the pattern, lightly sauced chicken and veal dishes and pastas served with *gorgonzola* and assorted white sauces. *Pasta alla puttanesca*, with capers, olives, anchovies, fresh tomatoes, peppers and garlic, is a lively and tasty exception to the subtle Milanese flavors. Desserts receive special emphasis here; *zabaglione*, fresh strawberry custard and Italian cakes, all done in-house, are rich, tasty and probably fattening.

"Excellent atmosphere", "Good food; great ambiance; reasonable", "Authentic."

RODIN • 1779 Lombard (Laguna) • 563-8566

French • $$$$

Dinner Monday-Saturday; reservations advised; sport jacket; wine and beer; most major credit cards • Chef-owner Morgan Song has sculpted one of the city's most starkly beautiful restaurants, with smoothly-textured, sand-colored walls that display black and white photos of Rodin's works, and oil lamps on fawn-colored linens. Against this serenely austere backdrop, Song composes dishes that are themselves works of art, both in appearance and flavor.

Each night Song sculpts a complete prix fixe dinner for $37. Follow the French classics through oysters with bacon, garlic and shallots; a delicate limestone lettuce salad that is carefully assembled, not tossed; boneless quail with wild rice, mushrooms and black currant sauce; and a chocolate mousse with raspberry sauce.

A Korean, Song is hardly a typical French chef. He owned the Korean Palace in the city and became fascinated with classic French cooking through a customer who was a retired chef. The old mentor, in his seventies, spent several years teach his younger Korean student the French culinary classics. One of our epicures praises the results:

"The food and service are the best ever."

ROOSEVELT TAMALE PARLOR • 2817 24th (Bryant) • 550-9213

Mexican • \$

Lunch and dinner Tuesday-Sunday, open at 9 a.m. for take-out; casual; wine and beer; MC, VISA • Roosevelt Tamale Parlor has been serving San Francisco's best authentic corn husk tamales since 1922, and the affable, cluttered restaurant probably hasn't changed its decor much since then. Tamales are meat-filled, encased in a wonderfully rich *masa*, accompanied by a lively chili sauce. Why all our excitement about Roosevelt's tamales? Because they were selected as the best in the city during a taste-test for our previous guide.

Roosevelt's also serves the usual Mexican cafe fare—tacos, enchiladas, frequently-fried beans and such. White-collar gringos travel down Mission from the civic center to mingle with the locals, turning the place into a noisy, friendly lunch parlor.

ROSALIE'S RESTAURANT • 1415 Van Ness Avenue (Bush) • 928-7188

American regional • \\\ $$$

Lunch Monday-Saturday, dinner daily, service to 11:30 Friday and Saturday; reservations advised; casual; full bar; all major credit cards • The cement tent with tin furniture and Reynolds Wrap palm trees has settled in as one of the city's better upscale American regional restaurants (with touches of Southwest cuisine, says manager Robert Merryman). When Bill Belloli opened this restaurant a few years ago, he discarded all the rules in both decor and dishes, and the whole glitzy affair now works remarkably well.

Try such curiosities as a duck burrito, lamb sausage with *polenta* or grilled squab with fresh grapes and potato *galette.* You'll dine at an aluminum table, perhaps in a straw-upholstered booth, supping from an oversized clay platter. And around your head will swirl the chaotic camaraderie that typifies a trendy, popular restaurant. HT-79, a hotel musician, describes it all in a single word and therefore describes nothing: "Yuppie."

You'll just have to see for yourself. But call ahead first.

THE ROTUNDA AT NEIMAN-MARCUS • 150 Stockton (Geary) • 362-4777

American/California • $$

Daily from 11 to 5; casual; full bar; AMEX or Neiman-Marcus card • Attention, shoppers—slip off those shoes, kick back and relax in the "Baroque splendor" of a little cafe built around the landmark Rotunda of this upscale department store. It's the same space that annually sprouted a giant live Christmas tree during the days of the City of Paris. (Modernized by Neiman-Marcus into a striking glass silo, the Rotunda now houses a plastic tree at holiday time. It's still impressively huge.)

A stained glass dome bathes you in curious light as you peruse the menu in your role as the indecisive shopper. Chicken Georgia, papaya Oriental, scallops in sesame dressing or one of the daily specials?

The restaurant is dressed Neiman-Marcus style, with plush booths or well-spaced tables, damask napkins, leaded crystal and tasteful china. The food, say our spies, is uneven, but what an exquisite place in which to take a break from shopping!

"Nice place to browse," commented a panel member, but was she referring to the menu or the store's fur salon?

RUBY'S GOURMET PIZZA • 3249 Scott (Lombard) • 567-4488

Pizza • $

Lunch and dinner daily, service to 11:30 Friday and Saturday; casual; full bar; no credit cards • Forget those clever TV commercials about "one of the last honest pizzas." San Francisco is full of honest pizza parlors and Ruby's numbers among the better ones. Not afraid to experiment, owners Dan Rubinstein and Craig Cooper offer an amazingly tasty fennel and oregano-spiced sausage pizza with roasted red peppers, plus interesting variations such as smoked salmon, escargot and a pizza that even passes for Greek.

Pizzas are presented in a pleasant Italianate setting with an outdoor patio and (give that place two symbols) there's no smoking indoors. Obviously, Ruby's offers take-out pizzas, but with a difference; they're half-baked so you can finish them at home and fill your kitchen with those savory smells.

RUE LEPIC • 900 Pine (Mason) • 474-6070

French • $$$

Dinner nightly; reservations advised; casual to sport jacket; wine and beer; MC, VISA • "Nice restaurant, good service," reports one of our critics, "but I felt it was a little expensive for the quality." This tiny place turns out a rather simplified version of French fare, stressing broiled and sauteed meats, accompanied by perfectly done veggies and delicate, beautifully crafted salads. Some of the meat dishes can be excellent, say our agents, but the sauces are rather standard.

The dining room is intimate yet cheery, with an open kitchen and picture windows opening onto busy Pine Street. It's French in a casual mode.

RUSTY SCUPPER • 1800 Montgomery (Francisco) • 986-1180

American • $$

Lunch and dinner daily; reservations accepted; casual; full bar; major credit cards • Should we really include a pre-packaged franchise restaurant in the *ULTIMATE DINING GUIDE*? A place with formula open beams, glassworks and hanging plants and a formula menu? This Rusty Scupper near the waterfront received several votes (and it placed among the top ten in the cabbies' poll in our earlier guide), so we were moved to check it out.

And you know what? It's not a bad formula. The fresh sole was—well—fresh and lightly cooked and it arrived with a crisp salad and dollop of rice. The glass of house white was generous and quite good, and the service was restaurant-school attentive. No exciting culinary breakthroughs here, but it was a rather satisfactory dinner at a satisfactory price, around $13. During early-bird time, from 5 to 7, it drops to $9.95.

"Good, moderate and non- dressy fun spot."

RYAN'S • 4230 18th (Diamond) • 621-6131

California nouvelle • $$

Dinner Monday-Saturday, brunch Saturday and Sunday, deli lunch weekdays; reservations accepted; casual; wine bar; MC, VISA, AMEX • Built into an assortment of rooms in an old C neatest little cafe discoveries. A spiral stairway leads to several tiny dining rooms (one smoke-free) where people partake of California culinary experiments such as chicken *radiccio*, lamb with black pepper and pear butter and poached sea bass in blood orange sauce.

We ordered the bass and were rewarded with a huge, perfectly cooked filet. The sauce actually was more of a garnish with sugared bits of red orange, yet despite its sweetness, it didn't interfere with the flavor of the fish. An appetizer of sauteed chicken livers with chutney was large enough for a main course, and a dessert of mud pie with a caramel brown sugar crunch really put me through my chair.

Ryan's is both intimate and artistic; votive candles flicker on the tables, changing art exhibits enliven the walls and lively classic music filters through the place. A balcony dining area is popular for brunches and lunches. One awaits dinner at a tiny wine bar, where a dozen or so vintages are offered by the glass at reasonable prices. A *charcuterie* deli and gourmet take-out occupies the ground floor; folks can collect luncheon goodies there, including smoked meats and quiche specialties, and pack them up to the dining rooms or onto the balcony.

A non-smokers' advisory: get a table in a smoke-free area; the dining rooms are not well ventilated and the air can turn brown on a busy night.

"Delicious, inventive but not overly chic; Great service."

SABELLA'S — see A. Sabella's

SAM'S GRILL AND SEAFOOD RESTAURANT • 374 Bush (Kearny) • 421-0594

American • $$

Lunch and dinner weekdays; reservations for six or more only; casual to sport jacket; full bar; MC, VISA • Sam's is another slice of San Francisco yesterday; it's an earthy old grill dating back to 1867, with wood paneling, white-draped tables, deep booths and attentive service by tux-clad waiters. "Excellent food in an historic San Francisco landmark," says MC-221.

He said excellent, not innovative. The oversized menu is as historic as the cafe, with predictable local seafoods, chops, steaks and chicken. Our agents agreed that seafood is the best bet, and we recall a particularly tasty sand dab luncheon. As a matter of fact, Sam's is more of a luncheon place and by high noon, its small bar is crowded with business types, sipping through their table wait. The place closes at 8:30, when most San Francisco restaurants are just getting into the evening swing of things.

SAN FRANCISCO BREWING COMPANY • 155 Columbus Avenue (Pacific Avenue) • 434-3344

Pub fare • $

Lunch weekdays, dinner Monday-Saturday; casual; wine and beer; MC, VISA, AMEX • No, a microbrewery isn't a place where they ferment microbes. It's the latest bubble in boutique beer-making and this bubble isn't likely to burst. Several small breweries are emerging in California and some have merged with pubs to form "brew pubs." These are places where one can dine on light fare, sip home-made beer and sometimes watch the brewmaster putter around his copper kettles.

Enter Allan Paul and the San Francisco Brewing Company. This is the first and thus far the only brew pub in the city, opened in 1986. It occupies the former home of the Albatross, until recently a grand and rough old saloon. The building at 155 Columbus is rich in legend and probably exaggeration; it is said that Jack Dempsey was a bouncer here during the raunchy Barbary Coast days and that Baby Face Nelson was nabbed by the feds during a back room Prohibition bust in 1929.

Paul has preserved the 1907 mahogany bar and much of the character of the old Albatross; he's added the required copper kettles and light "pub fare" such as grilled sausage sandwiches, hot pastrami and assorted salads. Foods are designed around his beers, and he uses his suds as ingredients for fish and chips, chili and other dishes. And naturally, he serves his own brew by the glass or pint. Albatross Lager and Emperor Norton Lager, made from malted barley and whole leaf hops, have that hearty flavor of European beers. Other boutique brews are offered, including (of course) San Francisco's Anchor Steam. MC-57 calls the antique bar the prettiest in town and she gives the beer a ten.

SAN FRANCISCO BAR-B-Q • 1328 18th (Missouri) • 431-8956 • 730 Van Ness Avenue (Turk) • 441-1640

Thai barbecue • $

Lunch and dinner Tuesday-Saturday, 3 to 9 p.m. Sunday; casual; no credit cards • Mrs. Chittratun Kirdpirote emigrated from Thailand and somehow wound up running a barbecue joint in the south of Market industrial area. But it's not just another chicken-quick. She marinates a variety of meats, chicken, Thai sausages, lamb, scallops and even frogs legs in mystical Thai sauces that give them a distinctive herbal flavor. They're served with a salad, providing a filling meal for around $6. She does a brisk take-out business, so one can pack her savory creations back across Market Street.

"Best inexpensive non-Chinese food in town. Barbecue chicken comes with salad and fresh sourdough. Sweet and sour dipping sauce goes with everything."

SAN WANG • 1682 Post (Buchanan) • 921-1453 • 2239 Clement (23rd Avenue) • 221-1870

Northern Chinese • $

Lunch and dinner daily; reservations advised; casual; wine and beer at Post, full bar at Clement; MC, VISA • The six Wang brothers arrived from Hubei Province in northern China and promptly drew crowds to their restaurant opposite Japan Center. Folks came for the great variety of northern Chinese dishes like fish in wine sauce, stir-fried clams with red pepper and hot stir-fried pork and mung beans. One of their specialties from Hubei is a rather chewy hand-shaped noodle made by extruding, twisting and shaping the dough instead of cutting it. The versatile menu also features Cantonese-style whole braised fish and lobster, and it offers feverish *kim chee* to satisfy Korean palates.

Inundated by hungry crowds, the Wangs opened a larger annex in the Richmond District. It soon drew its own crowds, even with the competition of the dozens of other places along Clement Street's "Asian restaurant row."

Don't expect fancy decor but do expect lively Chinese fare at reasonable prices. Most of the cartel liked San Wang, but a catering coordinator fussed at the lack of coordination: "All courses taken out at the same time; rude waiter; pushy."

SCHROEDER'S CAFE • 240 Front (California) • 421-4778

Bavarian • $$

Lunch and dinner weekdays; casual to sport jacket; full bar; MC, VISA, AMEX • Some restaurants succeed by refusing to change. Schroeder's has been dishing out *sauerbraten*, potato pancakes and *wienerschnitzel* since 1893. While sleek glass towers of the financial district grew up around it, this friendly old barn of a place has remained rooted in the past as a clubby bastion of businessmen. In fact, lunches were "men only" until the women's lib movement got wind of it.

The menu is huge and almost exclusively German-Bavarian, with Teutonic standards like *bratwurst* with red cabbage, pigs' knuckles and roast duck with apple. Like its venerable brother Sam's Grill, Schroeder's is primarily a luncheon place. By 9 p.m., the last German chef is getting ready to hang up his cap and apron.

But at high noon, business types crowd into tables and booths, where a waiting plate of German potato salad or cole slaw functions as an appetizer. A big circular "bachelor's table" is set aside for loners who don't want to lunch alone.

"Good German food," comments one of our agents. Schroeder's is as simple as that.

SCOMA'S • Pier 47 (Fisherman's Wharf) • 771-4383

Seafood • $$

Lunch and dinner daily; casual; full bar; major credit cards • On any given day, any given tray of seafood at Fisherman's Wharf can be fresh and satisfactory or frozen and tasteless. These nautical but nice places share a similarity that makes them difficult to sort out. Tourists, lacking direction, will wander at will into one or the other; locals have their favorites. (More likely they're trying to get into Hayes Street Grill or Scott's or Yuet Lee.)

We've said before that there's nothing wrong with the Wharf's Italian seafood restaurants that careful ordering won't fix. A lot of locals prefer Scoma's, with its huge seafood menu and usually prompt service.

Frankly, we have trouble telling Wharf these places apart, although we lean slightly toward Tarantino's; perhaps it's because it's secretly owned by an Irishman. And it has a wonderfully quiet bar with a view of what's left of the fishing fleet; no one ever seems to use this lounge except us.

But this listing is supposed to be about Scoma's. "Huge portions; fast service; too loud", "Poor service", "All fish entrees excellent; selections varied to pocketbook", "Very fresh, well prepared."

SCOTT'S SEAFOOD • #3 Embarcadero Center (Drumm) • 981-0622
• 2400 Lombard (Scott) • 563-8988

Seafood • $$

Lunch and dinner daily; reservations accepted; casual to sport jacket; full bar; MC, VISA, AMEX at Lombard; major credit cards at Embarcadero • Scott's is what happens when you hide a good seafood restaurant from the tourists by locating it away from Fisherman's Wharf, raise the prices a bit and don't over-cook the fish. The original on the corner of Lombard and Scott is a traditional grill with warm woods, glass and brass inside a Cape Code Victorian. The Embarcadero version is light woods, glass and brass, open and airy. Clones also have emerged in Palo Alto, San Jose and at Oakland's Jack London Square, finally filling a need for an upscale fish place there.

The assorted Scott's try and generally succeed in serving very fresh fish and shellfish, and one doesn't have to remind the waiter to tell the chef when to pull it from the grill. The menu changes frequently, subject to what's been caught or flown in. A lone steak and single burger entry are available for those with a grudge against Friday.

Incidentally, the Embarcadero Scott's offers outside dining at lunch.

SEAL ROCK INN • 545 Point Lobos (48th Avenue) • 752-8000

American, mostly omelets • $

Breakfast and lunch daily; casual; no alcohol; major credit cards • This is the fun of writing a restaurant guide and leaving selections in the hands of others. You learn that the Seal Rock Inn serves excellent omelets in its pleasant little coffee shop with an ocean view. It even has a patio dining area for those few balmy days near the ocean. And all this time, we thought Seal Rock Inn was just a slightly upscale motel.

"Great breakfasts; nice view; pleasant service," and "A great place for Sunday brunch; omelets and Eggs Benedict."

We'll have to remember that.

THE SHADOWS • 1349 Montgomery (Union, on Telegraph Hill) • 982-5536

Contemporary French • $$$

Dinner nightly; reservations essential; sport jacket to dressy; full bar; major credit cards • Can Jeffrey Pollack make us forget the Shadows' past, when it was a vaguely German restaurant notched into the side of Telegraph hill, a "must" for visiting Kansas cousins? Jeffrey thinks he can. He now owns both the Shadows and Julius' Castle in a neighboring niche, and he has upgraded the look and the menu of these venerable hillside havens.

Gone are the grim, dark German woods; the Shadows is now a "French chalet" with soft pinks, blonde and wicker chairs, floral carpeting and enlarged windows to improve the view (although it's better from Julius' Castle). The Shadows' setting is certainly pleasant, tucked into a garden beside the Filbert Steps. Diners can go for the flown-in-fresh Maine lobster with spinach and Chardonnay, filet of sole with endives, breast of duck with fruit or other French dishes with light California touches. Brie soup can begin your evening, and rich French souffles are intended to send you back down the hill with a smile.

Can Pollack pull it off? Will Margo Lane find happiness? We had a clever answer ready, but another guidebook beat us to the punch line.

SOUTH PARK CAFE • 108 South Park (Bryant and Second) • 495-7275

French bistro • $$

Breakfast, lunch and dinner Monday-Friday, dinner Saturday; reservations accepted for dinner only; casual; wine and beer; MC, VISA • South Park is an oval enclave south of Market where architects and occasional attorneys have taken refuge in refurbished old brick warehouses. Robert Voorhees and Catherine Allswang opened a neat and charming little French style cafe here in 1985, serving the same sort of simple fare one would find on a side street of Paris.

The small menu lists some interesting main-course salads, fresh seafood including steamed mussels, and some grilled sandwiches. *Tapas,* hors d'oeuvres with Spanish accents, are featured appetizers.

SPARKY'S • 242 Church (Market) • 621-6001

American diner • $

Open 24 hours; casual; wine and beer; MC, VISA, AMEX • Say hello to the plastic kid on the pogo stick as you step into this 1950s American graffiti diner.

We'll admit an affinity for the Mels-Julie's-Sparky's Fifties fad, since that was our coming-of-age generation. Of course, none of these places quite capture the flaccid ambience of the Wilder Variety Store back in Idaho; we used to spend hours there, perched on a red plastic stool, sipping awful-looking green things called lime phosphates and listening to "I'll Walk the Line" on a jukebox that looked like a giant twin Noma Bubblelight. Wilder Variety is long gone, along with our youth, so it's nice to reminisce, even with inadequate imitations.

The plastic red-headed kid is the focal point of Sparky's decor, which is mostly black and white. Folding gym chairs (spray-painted black) take us back to noontime assemblies and basketball tryouts, and the glass brick partition dividing the counter and the dining room helps establish the Fifties look. Steaks, chops, soups and omelets on the menu are the sorts of things we might have eaten at Wilder Variety's lunch counter, except that we never had much more than a nickel for the phosphate and maybe another one for the jukebox.

"Inexpensive, good portions," says a member of the team.

SQUARE ONE RESTAURANT • 190 Pacific Avenue (Front) • 788- 1110

Mediterranean • $$$

Lunch weekdays, dinner nightly; casual; full bar; MC, VISA, AMEX • "The food is outstanding; make note of the breads", "Bread excellent; good dessert", "Delicious food from all over the world", "I always look forward to dining there."

Square One generated a lot of votes and most of them were complimentary. If popularity is a measure of success, it's one of the most successful new places in the city, serving around 500 meals a day from a very broad and complex menu. Chef-owner Joyce Goldstein, former Cafe at Chez Panisse manager, calls her fare "Mediterranean" but it gallops around a good part of the globe. There is no regional style, because she goes back to square one every day and designs her menu around what's available. It may be pork brochettes in Indonesian peanut sauce; Brazilian mixed grill with black beans and rice; grilled squab marinated in honey, bourbon and soy; or steak with a Korean-style ginger marinade. Joyce's kitchen prepares its own breads, ice creams and sorbets, and they are superb.

The global menu takes form under an expansive, modern space in one of the handsome new brick buildings near the Golden Gateway just off the Embarcadero. Set in the park-like environment of Pacific Avenue Mall, the restaurant is a pleasant study in brass, glass and and light autumn colors in the woods and upholstery of the plush, comfortable booths and chairs. Oversized windows draw in the green pleasantry of adjoining Walton Park, and a waffle ceiling helps absorb the pleasant clatter of the open kitchen and chatter of the diners.

"My favorite in San Francisco!" That came from an Oakland resident.

SQUIRE ROOM • 950 Mason (in the Fairmont Hotel, at California) • 772-5211

Continental •  $$$$

Lunch and dinner daily; reservations essential; dressy; full bar; all major credit cards • The American Automobile Association selects a handful of hotels and resorts for its prestigious Five Diamond Award. To earn it, every aspect of the place, including its restaurants, must be outstanding. Three of these hotels are in the city: the Westin St. Francis, Four Seasons Clift and the Fairmont. This gives us the excuse to point out that San Francisco is one of those rare American cities with some of its best restaurants in hotels, such as Pierre, Victor's and the Squire. Incidentally, AAA spies make their initial inspections anonymously, as we do. But they have an advantage; they can put the Squire's high prices on their expense account.

Our critics selected this place as one of their favorite celebration restaurants, and why not? It brims with elegance—chandeliers, plush carpeting, distinctive arched French-style windows and comfortable high-backed chairs. You've seen it all before, as the dining room setting for TV's *Hotel*. Chef Herve Le Biavant doesn't limit his menu to the French classics; his offerings vary from American spring lamb in zinfandel sauce to veal *aux morilles*.

"This is one of our favorite special restaurants, offering privacy, ambiance and luxury."

STARS • 150 Redwood (Van Ness Avenue and Golden Gate) • 861-7827

Contemporary American • $$$

Lunch weekdays, dinner nightly; reservations essential; casual to sport jacket; full bar; major credit cards • If Alice Waters of Chez Panisse invented American nouvelle cooking, her former partner and present Stars proprietor Jeremiah Tower invented the space in which to put it. He calls his big, high-ceiling restaurant an American brasserie. It's the consummate cafe: upscale yet casual, consistent yet innovative, with a great bar scene, an open kitchen, a genuinely likable wait-staff and generous servings of upbeat ambiance. Other than cost limitations (Stars isn't cheap) it's the kind of place that you enjoy repeating. If only we could afford to make it our regular hangout.

We won't go into Jeremiah's menu, because it changes frequently. Just call well ahead for reservations, order a pepper vodka, settle down to a table and let the restaurant start happening around you.

Since you've probably been leafing ahead in our book, you already know that Stars was voted the overall favorite among all our guest critics, the favorite cafe of our "civilian" voters (those not connected with the hotel-restaurant-travel trade), and it tied for first among our agents employed by other restaurants.

SUISSE ITALIA • 101 California Plaza (Drumm) • 434-3800

American deli • $

Open from 5:30 a.m. to 6 p.m. weekdays; casual; wine and beer; no credit cards • What's a deli doing in the *ULTIMATE DINING GUIDE*? It's here because it got a few votes, including one from us, as a slick, pretty deli in one of the most attractive spaces in the city. The 101 California plaza is a great wedge of open area with a monumental spillover fountain, planters and risers in the heart of the crowded, walled-in Financial District.

Suisse Italia serves a startling array of sandwiches, quiches, *frittatas,* salads, cold pastas, juices, wines and beers. Financial District regulars load up their trays and settle down at inside tables or distribute themselves outside, among the potted palms and multi-level granite slabs, which are spread with handy cushions.

SUSHI ON THE ROCK • 1475 Polk (California) • 549-9183 • 500 Broadway (Kearny) • 362-6434

Sushi • $

Lunch and dinner daily; casual; sake, wine and beer; no credit cards • The sushi craze hasn't wound down yet, so Sushi on the Rock jumped into the raw fish melee two years ago and has carved a comfortable niche with all-you-can-eat sushi lunches for $8.95 and dinner for $10.95. The sushi in these cozy, cleanly-decorated little places isn't awesome, but it's fresh and not all that bad for the price.

"Excellent value," says a Japanese crew member who works for a major city hotel. She should know her sushi.

SUTTER GARDEN • 562 Sutter (in the Orchard Hotel, near Mason) • 433-4434

American/Continental • $$

Breakfast, lunch and dinner daily; reservations accepted; casual to sport jacket; full bar; major credit cards • "Gentle elegance" is the term that comes to mind in describing this quiet place. It's done up in trendy hotel colors—salmons and pinks—with beveled mirror glass and potted plants. Piano music tinkles from somewhere. Sutter Garden has the kind of intimacy that makes you want to hold hands, so take someone with dry palms.

The food is beautifully presented and portions are generous for the modest prices. Unfortunately, some of the dishes just miss. Since we're Gold Country aficionados, we eagerly ordered the Hangtown Fry, but found this historic omelet to be a bit shy on oysters. Medallions of monkfish Madagascar with brandy and green peppercorn sauce were excellent, although accompanying veggies were slightly overdone. Desserts were exceptional and pretty enough to eat. The menu is an interesting mix of things American and European; entrees such as trout dumplings and veal in zinfandel sauce suggest an imaginative kitchen. The place opened in 1986; by the time we do a revision, it should be settled in and worthy of another spoon.

"Reasonably priced food in a very nice atmosphere," and "Service attentive; beautiful presentation," spoke the cartel.

TADICH GRILL • 240 California (Front) • 391-2373

American/mostly seafood • $$

Lunch and dinner Monday-Friday; casual; full bar; no credit cards • Tadich is the granddaddy of them all, a restaurant that literally dates back to the Gold Rush. Although it has been in its present spot only since the 1960s, the original opened its doors in 1849, not long after Sam Brannan galloped along Montgomery Street, yelling "Gold, gold on the American River!" Clever Sam then bought up every pick, shovel, biscuit pan and yard of tent canvas he could find and returned to the Gold Country to make his fortune.

Those who stayed in the city did well, too; some opened businesses—like Tadich—that have survived to this day. Present owners Bob and Steve Buich pack 'em in with modest prices on fresh, charcoal broiled fish and other simple dishes. This isn't nouvelle, but the Buich brothers, who are Yugoslavs, were practicing the art of lightly searing fish and serving it with simple sauces long before it became fashionable.

The place is always crowded, lunch or dinner, and advance reservations aren't accepted, but waiting is not unpleasant at the bar. Generally, you can get a seat at the serving counter if you haven't the time or patience to wait for one of the old fashioned booths. The Buichs have retained Tadich's old style look simply by not decorating it much. With its wainscoting and plain plaster ceiling, it could pass for a Gold Rush survivor.

"The best! Great ambiance; noisy but nice", "Fun atmosphere; only drawback—no credit cards."

TAI CHI • 2031 Polk (Broadway) • 441-6758

Northern Chinese • $

Lunch weekdays, dinner nightly; casual; wine and beer; MC, VISA, AMEX • "Nothing fancy, but the portions are generous and tasty; smoked pork is my favorite." Tai Chi is a cutely garish little place, about two tables wide with a clattering kitchen behind a screen along one wall. Bright orange plastic tablecloths clash nicely with red-tasseled Chinese lanterns above.

The food is quite tasty for the low prices. Some of its best bargains are luncheon specials; $3.46 (tax included) buys a delicious beef stock soup with ginger pork balls, a savory main dish heaped over a big mound of rice and a bottomless pot of tea. The chicken curry is exceptional—stir-fried with crisp zucchini and onions. And this is no wimpy curry shaken from a Shilling can; it's hearty and full-flavored, yet not mouth sizzling.

The tattered menu describes the fare as "Hunan, Szechuan, Peking and Shanghai." This small place offers remarkable variety, including several seafood dishes, the usual beef, pork and lamb, plus some vegetarian entrees. Four-course dinners are under $10, but it's more fun to go with a herd and sample widely from this interesting north China menu.

TAXI • 374 Eleventh (Harrison) • 558-TAXI

California cuisine • $$$

Lunch Monday-Saturday, dinner nightly; reservations essential; casual; all major credit cards • Call me a cab and take me away, please. Taxi is a stark, noisy, uncomfortable and overpriced south of Market restaurant that's cashing in on the nouvelle craze. The dishes sound and look innovative—grilled chicken with spaghetti squash and pink peppercorn butter, tomato fettucini with prawns and roasted peppers, stuff like that. Some are all right; others are ordinary to awful. A swordfish brochette was skimpy for the price and the delicate flavor of the fish was buried in a gloppy basil mayonnaise sauce. Accompanying carrots and zucchini were properly cooked, but for the $13, I could buy a lot of zucchini at Petrini's. An ordinary Clos Du Val cabernet was $5.25 for a modest-sized glass, close to the wholesale price of an entire bottle.

One has a choice between uncomfortable straight-backed chairs or hard, straight-backed bench seats. Tables along one wall are spaced about a foot apart and I suffered through a disjointed stereo of next-door conversations. Loud rock music and an open kitchen added to the cacophony. We don't mind lively sounds as part of the ambiance of a place, but this is just plain noise. The cafe is simply a blank space—a plain white-painted room with exposed rafters; there's nothing on the walls or floors to absorb the clatter and chatter.

I'd eaten at the Portman Grill the day before and was struck by the fact that my luncheon tabs were virtually the same at both places. So for a bit over $20, one can choose between stunning opulence or stark chaos.

"Inedible, greasy chicken; no flavor; overrated", "Pricy for what is offered overall", "Food is average; small portions; noisy room," and finally, "I can't figure out what everyone's raving about."

Neither can we; isn't that cab here yet?

TEDDY'S • 524 Sutter (in the Cartwright Hotel, at Powell) • 956-0493

California cuisine • $

Breakfast and lunch daily; reservations accepted; casual; wine and beer; no credit cards but checks accepted with ID • Tucked into the back of the recently refurbished Cartwright Hotel, Teddy's is a popular downtown breakfast and lunch cafe serving creations with cute names: Turkey Tango Salad, Quiche Your Cares Away and Teddy Bear Picnic (soup and sandwich). Our critics say they also taste good.

This medium-sized restaurant has the proper look of an old style hotel cafe with fans swirling from high ceilings, sculptured friezes, potted plants and pink-clothed wooden tables. With its lofty rafters and well-spaced tables, the place has a very open feeling. And of course, assorted teddy bears occupy various niches about the room.

TEN-ICHI RESTAURANT • 2235 Fillmore (Sacramento) • 346-3477

Japanese • $$

Lunch weekdays, dinner Monday-Saturday; casual; wine and beer; MC, VISA ($10 credit card minimum) • The owners have done a nice job of prettying up this small storefront cafe in the gentrified Fillmore district. Light bathes the place from an all-glass front, so it's bright and cheerful even with a dark wood beamed ceiling. Bentwood bamboo chairs are tucked under tables set with nice pottery ware, include cute, chubby little glazed earthenware bud vases with sprigs of fresh flowers. In contrast to the warmer woods up front, a back room sushi bar is a sleek design with blonde and natural textures.

The food is quite good, according to our spies, and we've confirmed that fact. A couple of interesting dishes have been added to the typical Japanese fare, such as "Butteryaki" (thin-sliced steak, pan fried in butter) and a seafood tempura that includes batter-fried fishcake and tofu as well as the usual prawns, fish filets, tofu and veggies. The tempura batter is crisp and grease-free, the measure of a good Japanese kitchen.

"Pleasant; good Japanese food," comments one of our epicures from the hotel industry.

THAI GARDEN • 3324 Steiner (Lombard) • 346-1689

Thai • $

Lunch Tuesday-Friday, dinner Tuesday-Sunday; casual; wine and beer; MC, VISA, AMEX • The Thais appear to be more style conscious about restaurant design than many other Asians. Even modest family operations are usually pretty little places, much more appealing than the family Formica look of many ethnic cafes. Thai Garden in the Marina district is a good example; it's a cute little storefront place with dusty blue walls, a stained oak frieze, bentwood chairs and glass-topped tables with burgundy covers. A Thai temple facade hang over the kitchen area.

The food is quite good overall. The owners need to liven up their basic veggie soup, but other dishes are quite tasty. We particularly liked spicy barbecued chicken served with a delicious peanut and coconut milk sauce. Again, the Thailand eye for prettiness was evident; entrees are accompanied by fresh salads with flowered carrot slices and carefully cut wedges of cucumber.

"Spicy food with subtly good use of fresh herbs. Very reasonable prices."

THEP-PHANOM RESTAURANT • 400 Waller (Fillmore) • 431-2526

Thai • $

Dinner nightly; casual; wine and beer; MC, VISA • The gentrification of Fillmore hasn't reached this far south but this prim little white-tablecloth cafe brims with business. People crowd into its small space for tasty, nicely presented and inexpensive cuisine.

The fare is typically Thai, with intriguing mixes of coconut, peanut, lemon grass, curry, basil and other flavors. Try the "Thai Five- Squid," a fiery concoction of squid stuffed with chili, citrus leaves, basil and green curry. For something a bit more tame, the place offers interesting chicken and duck dishes with coconut curry. "Small, sweet interior; delicious, consistent food; great appetizers."

TIA MARGARITA • 300 19th Avenue (Clement) • 752-9274

Mexican •

Dinner Tuesday-Sunday; reservations accepted; casual; full bar; VISA, MC, DC, DISC • "So dark you can't see the bones in your chicken enchilada. Refried beans have been refried too many times," reports a hotel concierge, who presumably doesn't send too many guests to this Richmond District taco palace.

Now, c'mon HT-18, we tried the chicken enchilada and didn't find any bones, but we agree with the rest of your analysis. The place is dim and the *refritos* have the consistency of mud. We also tried a *fajita* special, which is essentially a roll-your-own steak and chicken burrito; it was more fun to roll than to eat. The steak had a nice smoky flavor but the chicken was overcooked and tasteless and the guacamole was bland. Accompanying white rice had an unpleasant dampness.

It's a nice looking restaurant, sort of deliberately Mexican with arched doorways and windows, a bit of wrought iron, Latin doo-dads on small display shelves and some really pretty leaded glass windows. The prices are reasonable; the most expensive thing on the menu was $11.95 and most dinners were under $10. And we do like the fact that the non-smoking area is a separate dining room.

But Aunt Margaret, you've *got* to improve things in your kitchen.

TIEN FU • 3945 24th (Noe) • 282-9502 • 1395 Noriega (21st Avenue) • 665-1064

Chinese •

Lunch and dinner daily; casual; full bar; MC, VISA ($10 credit card minimum) • The Noriega Tien Fu is more conventional in appearance, but the Noe Valley branch is an intriguing blend of neighborhood bar and Chinese restaurant. The busy bar up front obviously came first; it's an attractive (although smoky) place with an unusual barrel-arch ceiling, rich laminated woods, stained glass insets along the walls and Spanish arches.

But it becomes very Asian when you sit at one of the tables in back and open the large Hunan-Szechuan-Cantonese menu with its appealing mix of curried shrimp, *Kung Pao* squid, steamed whole fish and various stir-fried veggie dishes. The places is particularly noted for its chewy green onion pancakes served with a savory peanut sauce. We were pleased (and overstuffed) by a generous serving of spicy garlic shrimp, with plump and perfectly cooked shrimp in a delicious red sauce with crunchy bits of water chestnuts. This is one of the city's better Mandarin-style restaurants; the Cantonese whole fish and vegetable dishes are excellent as well.

Smoking and non-smoking sections are clearly delineated, which is fortunate because the air around the popular neighborhood pub up front can get rather hazy.

"Green onion pancakes are excellent; waitresses seem confused," reported one of our epicures. By the green onion pancakes?

TOKYO SUKIYAKI • 225 Jefferson (Fisherman's Wharf, near Taylor) • 775-9030

Japanese • $$

Lunch weekends; dinner nightly; reservations accepted; casual to sport jacket; full bar; major credit cards • You mean it's still there? When I passed through San Francisco after Marine Corps basic training in 1951, I ventured timidly into this exotic place where (good grief) you sit on the floor, drink a funny-tasting warm wine out of little tiny cups and eat with chopsticks. It was a memorable night for a country bumpkin at fascinating Fisherman's Wharf. I probably ordered sukiyaki.

There's not much fascination left at the wharf, but Tokyo Sukiyaki survives, still ladling out its namesake dish to tourists and an occasional resident. Actually, our spies say the food is quite good under new chef Yasuhiko Okuyama; he does charcoal broiled salmon and charcoal barbecued scallops on a skewer, in addition to sukiyaki. And the place has an excellent sushi bar.

One still sits on the floor, although the tatami rooms have back rests for those of us whose spines aren't as supple as they were in 1951. Conventional tables also are available.

"Good sushi," says one; "Great selections; beautiful views (of the wharf)," adds another; "Best sake," offers a third.

That's the part I remember most.

TOMMASO • 1042 Kearny (Pacific Avenue) • 398-9696

Pizza/calzone • $$

Dinner Tuesday-Sunday; casual; wine and beer; MC, VISA • "Best pizza; warmest, friendliest restaurant in S.F."

Several places lay claim to the best pizza in the city and we all have our favorites. Tommaso, however, is unquestionably the best pizza *restaurant*. This is pizza cafe classico; it's a weathered, friendly old place where the decor probably hasn't been changed since it opened in 1935. Beneath the faded posters, faithful patrons enjoy outstanding, generously-topped pizzas baked to crusty perfection in an old-fashioned wood-fired oven. Owner Agostino Crotti frequently emerges from his kitchen (we have this vision of him wiping floured hands on his apron) to greet customers and bus tables. Tommaso is that kind of place. But you must sacrifice for Agostino's success; the waiting lines are invariably long and he doesn't take reservations.

His *calzone* (as we explained earlier, think of it as a giant Italian *flauta*) is at least as good as his pizza, maybe better. He also serves assorted pastas, but our agents say pizza and *calzone* are his forte.

Many other guidebooks point out that Frances Ford Coppola (whose Zoetrope studios are nearby in that wonderful wedge-shaped, copper green Victorian at Columbus and Kearny) drops by from time to time. He even takes his turn at the pizza oven. But there's no point in us mentioning this; Agostino is a much better pizza chef.

TOMMY TOY'S HAUTE CUISINE CHIONISE • 655 Montgomery (Washington) • 397-4888

Chinese/French • $$$$

Lunch weekdays; dinner Monday-Saturday; reservations advised; dressy, coat and ties required; full bar; major credit cards • The Chinese are wonderful extremists; they operate some of the most basic and some of the most ornate restaurants in the city. At the dazzling end of opulence is Tommy Toy's, a visage of elegance that stops just short of decorator excess. But then, Tommy has a background in interior decor, so he knew when to stop. Tommy opened this palatial place in the Financial District a couple of years ago, after catering to tourists, locals and occasional celebrities for fifteen years at his Imperial Palace in Chinatown.

He describes his new place as "an elegant 19th century Chinese palace." Specifically, says his brochure (printed in Japan), it was fashioned after a dowager empress' reading room. The restaurant is a vision of Chinese art and affluence with blue porcelains, wood carvings and rare paintings in sandalwood frames that would be the envy of any museum. Tables and brocaded silk booths are set with hand-painted vases and exquisite little porcelain Chinese bridal lamps.

The cuisine is a Mandarin-Szechuan mix with French touches. It's served European style; no dipping into a platter with chopsticks in Tommy's place! We've dined there twice, first at a dinner party hosted by long-time friend Ann Kailakona Holt of the Hawaii Visitors' Bureau, then later with a couple of friends. We anticipated excellence the first time, since Tommy came by to see how things were going. However, it was equally fine when we returned and dined anonymously. I recall a wonderfully crispy Peking duck, a spicy Szechuan lamb and a fresh Maine lobster in ginger sauce.

To sample the varied talents of Chef Ken Wu, we'd suggest the eight-course dinner at a $38 prix fixe.

TOMMY'S JOYNT • 1101 Geary (Van Ness Avenue) • 775-4216

Haufbrau • $

Lunch and dinner daily, service to 2 a.m.; casual; full bar; no credit cards • From the sublime, we go to the other Tommy's, a wonderfully garish fixture at the corner of Van Ness and Geary. Every few years, the cartoonish murals that have made this place a landmark are repainted. We recall that city officials once fussed that they were too gaudy, so Tommy had one side of his old structure painted to match the ugly brown and blue squares of the adjacent Jack Tar Hotel; in the right line of vision, the two blended together. Mercifully, that Texas excess hotel has become the more modest-looking Cathedral Hill, and Tommy's has wonderful new murals to brighten the corner. And one wall has been painted to match the demure Cathedral Hill Hotel.

Inside, it's the exemplary haufbrau, serving buffalo stew, good corned beef and cabbage, hot dipped pastrami on a roll, stuff like that. One dines amidst a friendly jungle of yesterday clutter. A bar filling one wall offers a hundred or so beers to help wash down Tommy's heavy, hearty steam table fare.

Tip for tourists—it's a bit less chaotic upstairs.

TRADER VIC'S • 20 Cosmo Place (between Post and Taylor) • 776-2232

Oriental/Continental • $$$$

Lunch weekdays; dinner Monday-Saturday, service to 12:30 a.m.; reservations essential; dressy, jacket and tie; full bar; major credit cards • No, history students, this isn't Victor

Bergeron's original restaurant; that was opened in Oakland in 1934 and is long gone. But this is the oldest of several "Vic's" and it's the flagship of the fleet. Vic invented the mai tai and he came up with the idea of creating an upscale Polynesian-Chinese restaurant. He spent a good part of his time clumping around in the kitchen (on his wooden leg), conjuring up new drinks and sauces. Vic went to his reward (where hopefully good rum is available) in 1984, but the family carries on, with son Lynn at the helm.

The restaurant's Boathouse Bar is a social focal point of old moneyed San Francisco. After a few rounds of gossip and gun club punch, the in-crowd adjourns to the elegantly austere Captain's Cabin. There, they order something from the Chinese barbecue ovens and a selection from the excellent California wine list to rinse away those three flavors of rum. As an ordinary mortal, you may be relegated to one of the more bambooish, tiki-trimmed dining rooms. But even if you're parked under a fish net, you'll do well to order from the Continental side of the menu. Try the scallops *meuniere*, Indonesian lamb roast or Parmesan prawns. The Chinese/Polynesian side of the menu offers tasty fare, too, but our spies say it's a bit dated.

"Dining here is an event; we select Vic's to celebrate special occasions," comments a local tour operator.

TRATTORIA CONTADINA • 1800 Mason (Union) • 982-5728

Italian •  $$

Dinner nightly; reservations accepted; casual; wine and beer (and you can bring your own); MC, VISA, AMEX • This friendly little family trattoria, operated with enthusiasm by brothers Vince and Dirk Correnti, serves the full range of diet-denting Italian pastas in man-sized portions. A *linguini pesto* or *rigatoni melanze* (with eggplant and *mozzarella*) with a house salad is more than enough for a hearty dinner, for $10. From the other side of the menu, you can pluck breast of chicken with *porcini* mushrooms, garlic-rich *calamari con conchiglie*, or maybe the catch of the day, written on a chalkboard. Should there be room for dessert, the place serves a fine *cannoli*.

Awnings, bentwood chairs and *raffia* provide the proper setting for warm culinary camaraderie.

"A small family-run operation with tasty sauces", "Authentic Italian, with great atmosphere."

TRE FRATELLI • 2101 Sutter (Steiner) • 931-0754

Italian • $

Dinner nightly; casual; wine and beer; MC, VISA • "Excellent pasta dishes and generous portions," says a hotelier, but a wine writer complained that he found shell bits as well as clams in his linguini with red clam sauce, and his "ravioli pasta was poorly cooked."

This is the third Fratelli, in both name and number, opened by Gianinni and Peter Huson. Each has a typically cozy trattoria atmosphere. The older two, I. Fratelli and Fratelli North, are on Hyde Street; Tre joined them in 1987. Are the Husons moving too fast and is quality suffering, or do we now have not two but three charming little Fratellis serving generous portions of excellent pasta? Whom do you trust: hotel men or writers?

TU LAN • #8 Sixth (Market) • 626-0927

Vietnamese • $

Breakfast, lunch and dinner Monday-Saturday; casual; wine and beer; no credit cards • You can get a lot of mileage out of a Julia Childs review. But newspaper clippings and their messages fade with time. We tried this ultra-scruffy place that Julie once praised, and were rewarded with awful service and mediocre food. A rice noodle, pork and shrimp dish was overcooked, spring rolls were greasy and requested tea never arrived. Perhaps management is living on Julia's 1981 praise.

On the other hand, many people give it high marks, including some other restaurant critics. Some of our agents like it as well. "Short on ambiance but the food is cheap and high quality," says one. So we've reluctantly granted it two spoons.

One thing we all agreed on: Everything about this little storefront cafe just off Market is scruffy—the neighborhood, the decor, and the tattered menu. One has to push past a bag lady or two and perhaps step over a derelict to reach the place.

Maybe the secret is to go for dinner, when life at Tu Lan is a bit more calm; at lunch time, the place is a frenzy of hungry white-collar types and Vietnamese from the nearby Tenderloin.

U.S. RESTAURANT • 431 Columbus Avenue (Green) • 362-6251

Italian • $$

Breakfast, lunch and dinner Tuesday-Saturday; casual; wine and beer; no credit cards • Never mind the name; U.S. Restaurant is as Italian as North Beach Italian can be. It's a homey little trattoria that has dished up inexpensive pastas to Little City dwellers and occasional tourists for more than half a century. "Great food and service; a very plain restaurant but very nice. You can't beat the quality of food for the price."

You may have to wait to get into this crowded wedge of a restaurant tucked into the Columbus, Stockton and Green intersection, but our agents say patience has its reward here. This is Old World cooking—spaghetti and *rigatoni* smothered with rich, homemade tomato sauce; veal *parmigiana*, and a spicy boiled *coteghino* Italian sausage. America does enter the menu, incidentally. The place serves an excellent beef roast and one of the city's largest French bread cheeseburgers.

Mangiamo!

VANNELLI'S FRESH SEAFOOD • Pier 39 (The Embarcadero) • 421-7261

Seafood • $$

Lunch and dinner daily; reservations accepted; casual; full bar; all major credit cards • Vannelli's is another of the early (1978) Pier 39 restaurants that has survived and settled in as a reliable local fishhaus. Perhaps the secret to its survival is simplicity; its rather small menu focuses on seafood dishes, with only a steak or two for beefeaters. And the chef likes to experiment with things like Salmon Wellington (stuffed with spinach) and baked bass with peppercorns and sour cream. Some of these experiments work; some don't quite. But at least they keep the menu interesting.

Early bird dinners from $8.95 to $9.95 are served weekdays from 4 to 6 p.m. and weekends from 3 to 6.

The decor, like neighboring Neptune's, is Old San Francisco and the restaurant also occupies a favored spot at the end of the pier, with views of Alcatraz, the Golden Gate and those other objects that tourists come all the way from New Jersey to see.

"Great seafood; nice view," says a hotelier.

VICOLO PIZZERIA • 201 Ivy (Franklin) • 863-2382 • 900 North Point (Ghirardelli Square) • 776-1331

Pizza • $

From 11:30 a.m. to 11:30 p.m. Monday-Friday, 3 to 11:30 weekends; casual; wine and beer; no credit cards • Is the world ready for pizza nouvelle? Perhaps not, but San Francisco is. These two popular parlors feature an unusual cornbread and olive oil crust under their deep-dish pizzas. Toppings get interesting, too—salsa, tomatoes and roasted red peppers (the Southwester) and spinach with *ricotta*. One might try the Grecian version—*feta, mozzarella*, roasted red peppers, Greek olives and rosemary. But don't panic, traditionalists. Pepperoni and sausage toppings are available, too.

Those curious toppings probably have them turning under their tombstones in old Napoli, but they love it in San Francisco. The original Vicolo, tucked into a corrugated shed in an alley, is so successful that it spawned a second one at Ghirardelli Square. We like the wonderful art nouveau funk of the Ivy place, done in pinks and blacks and decorated with modern artworks. The annex, in Ghirardelli's Rose Court, is similarly upbeat, with the advantage of a sunny patio and a bay view.

Obviously, Vicolo wasn't created by some cherubic little Italian pizza-maker with a spot of flour on his nose. Restaurant critic/restaurateur Patricia Unterman is part owner, along with others from her Hayes Street Grill crew.

"Great toppings, unique crust," and "Fresh salads, interesting pizza combinations" numbered among the team's comments. None indicated whether or not they were Italian.

VICTOR'S • 335 Powell (in the Westin St. Francis, near Geary) • 774-0253

California cuisine • $$$$

Breakfast, lunch and dinner daily; reservations advised; dressy; full bar, and wine may be brought in for a corkage fee; all major credit cards • Chef Joel Rambaud's cuisine changes with the seasons as he offers an intriguing variety of California nouvelle creations in this classy skyroom hotel restaurant in the St. Francis Tower. Examples are veal medallions in bourbon sauce with corn relish, lobster ragout with angel hair pasta and scallops with pink pimento sauce over a bed of spinach. The five-pound wine list offers an extensive selection of California and European varietals from a stock of 25,000 bottles.

When you've finished dinner and request coffee, a cart arrives bearing 14 blends of international beans, accompanied by a selection of complimenting brandies. This isn't bargain elegance, but one can lower the price with a $19.50 prix fixe dinner from 6 to 7 p.m.

The room—with its crystal chandeliers and plush Oriental carpeting—is as attractive as the view through its oversized windows.

The hotel restaurant just won the 1988 Travel Holiday Award, to go along with its AAA Five Diamond and a few others. In case you wondered, the place is named for Victor Hirtzler, the hotel's first chef, who ran the kitchen from 1904 to 1925.

Victor's received a lot of votes, all complimentary, some overdone: "A world apart", "Very elegant, beautiful", "The most romantic restaurant; for very special occasions" and (probably more realistic) "Very good scallops."

VILLA D'ESTE • 2623 Ocean Avenue (Junipero Serra) • 334-0580

Italian • $$

Lunch weekdays, dinner nightly; reservations accepted; casual; full bar; MC, VISA, AMEX • Who designed this place, Bill Belloli's grandmother? Belloli is the creator of the textured concrete and aluminum Rosalie's, and Villa D'Este looks like a 1930s version of this style of decorator overkill. It's a study in floriated plaster Art Deco excess with thick textured plaster draperies, the heavy curlicue chandeliers and doughy-appearing wall sconces. It looks like a Cecil B. DeMille set for an Italian remake of the dining scene from *David and Bathsheba.*

Now that we've kidded poor Villa D'Este, we'll point out that it's a pleasant and very friendly neighborhood Italian restaurant tucked among the 1930s row houses of the Ingleside District. The place opened in the 1940s; it's been under ownership of the Oropeza family for about a decade and most of the "hired help" are siblings, playing the role of tuxedoed waiters and prettily attired hostesses. In addition to Italian standards, the Oropezas bring forth tasties like rolled filet of sole with crab and shrimp in a light tomato sauce. My co-author's veal *scaloppine* was smothered in fresh mushrooms, lightly done and superior to similar dishes at many of the upscale downtown restaurants. Dinners for about $11 to $12 include a soup or salad, fresh pasta, entree and light dessert.

For that quality and those prices, we'll happily sit beside cement draperies.

"Good food; service okay for very leisurely dining; soup always hot", "Finest veal in the world."

VLASTA'S EUROPEAN RESTAURANT • 2420 Lombard (Scott) • 931-7533

Czechoslovakian/German/Hungarian • \\$$

Dinner Tuesday through Sunday; reservations accepted; casual; full bar; major credit cards • Vlasta Kucera originally called his place Vlasta's Czechoslovakian Restaurant, but his menu now includes other Eastern European delights like Bohemian duckling, a Germanic stuffed cabbage and *rouladin.* Prices are remarkable for these robust portions of hearty European fare, around $8 to $10 for a full dinner.

This is hearty old European homestyle cooking, with decor to match—dark woods and wainscoting. It's a warm, cheery family operation; Mrs. Kucera creates savories in the kitchen while he greets diners out front.

"Elegant and warm; personal service", "Roast duck is fabulous; order in advance to be sure to get some." The duck comment comes from the concierge of a major hotel.

WASHINGTON SQUARE BAR AND GRILL • 1701 Powell (Union) • 982-8123

Italian/American/seafood • \\\ ⊘ Y ☽ $$

Lunch and dinner daily, service to 11:30 Sunday-Thursday, until midnight Friday-Saturday; reservations essential; casual to sport jacket; full bar; major credit cards • Now, how can I write this review with a straight face? This is a media hangout, and sometimes a media event with its globe-hopping Savage Rabbits softball team. There's no way a former newsman can be unbiased about the Washbag. Not that I'm with the in-crowd here. I nod at Stan Delaplane at his "office table" and smile at Scott Beach in his favored spot by the window; they return my warmth with curious stares. I exchange brief greetings with Herb Caen, but I haven't convinced him to plug any of our three guidebooks. Proprietress Mary Etta Moose bought me a drink once when we discussed an autograph party for *The Best of San Francisco,* and I won't let her husband Ed buy me dinner, for fear of coloring my critique. (Not that he's ever offered.)

My review is biased because I can't help liking this place. It's the penultimate San Francisco hangout, with friendly and efficient bartenders and tuxedoed waiters, a crowded and noisy bar where no one ever seems to sit, an equally noisy dining room with white nappery and good contemporary Italian fare, fine fish and amazing hamburgers. Something is always happening here—the penny-pitching contests, the nightly live jazz, the Sunday brunch and Sunday piano. And by the way, noisy doesn't mean chaotic; the high ceilings in this old Victorian absorb an amazing amount of clamor.

It won our VIP popularity poll (thumb ahead to Chapter Six), but that didn't surprise us. If San Francisco is everybody's favorite city, the Washbag seems to be every San Franciscan's favorite hangout.

THE WATERFRONT • Pier 7 (The Embarcadero) • 391-2696

Seafood/Continental • $$

Lunch and dinner daily; reservations accepted; sport jacket; full bar; major credit cards • Restaurateur Al Falchi's formula for success is simple: Give the people a great bay view and consistently good food. His Waterfront is a handsome study in brass, oak woods, white linens and potted greenery, housed in a sturdy old Embarcadero structure with a glass wall to the bay. And he's terraced the dining area so folks don't have to fuss over who gets a view table. Our critics agree that the food is as good as the view.

"Established place; good for business entertainment," commented the manager of another waterfront restaurant; "A restaurant with real sole—amandine!!" added a local TV personality, who picked it as one of his five favorite cafes.

The kitchen does indeed lean heavily toward soul food from the sea; scampi, mixed grill, shellfish saute and assorted grilled fish are among its offerings. Falchi's Italian background emerges in the pasta selections and a couple of steaks are added for balance. He offers an excellent California wine list, with selections from more than a hundred vintners.

WHAT'S YOUR BEEF? • 759 Columbus Avenue (Greenwich) • 989-1852

Hamburgers • $

Daily from 11 a.m. to 3:30 p.m.; casual; wine and beer; no credit cards • The city's only restaurant that ends in a question mark is rarely queried about the quality of its hamburgers. This homey North Beach cafe specializes in thick patties with good cheese toppings on fresh buns, accompanied by properly rich milkshakes, or wine if you prefer. (We do, of course)

Co-owner George Erman left his post as maitre d' at Fournou's Ovens to open this cozy burger stand in 1982; he apparently prefers a fry-cook's apron to that stuffy suit.

Said one of our guest critics: "Perfect amount of beef for the best burger; homemade chips, mmmmm!"

WHITE ELEPHANT RESTAURANT • 480 Sutter (in the Holiday Inn, at Powell) • 398-1331

American/Continental • $$

Breakfast, lunch and dinner daily; reservations accepted; casual to sport jacket; full bar; all major credit cards • "Well prepared food in a quiet atmosphere."

The Union Square Holiday Inn's White Elephant is a charming little European style cafe with plate rails, fine print wallpaper, tulip chandeliers and high-backed booths and chairs. And it is indeed quiet, unless you're seated too close to the adjacent bar. No smoking areas are fairly well isolated from the puffing section, and you are given a choice upon entering the restaurant

A small American/Continental menu features the usual steaks, chops, fowl and fish of the day. A specialty is prime rib, which comes thick-cut and properly rare or medium or whatever, as you request it. We received a generous and tasty slice, although accompanying veggies were cooked beyond salvation. A zinfandel soup was intriguing and a cup of Manhattan clam chowder was excellent with thick and spicy broth and lots of clam bits.

Early bird dinners from 6 to 7 nightly are a thrifty buy; an entree, veggies and soup or salad are offered for $11.95, a good 30 to 40 percent off normal prices.

WHITE HORSE TAVERNE • 637 Sutter (Hotel Beresford, near Mason) • 771-1708

American/Continental • $$

Breakfast and lunch daily, dinner Tuesday- Saturday; casual; full bar; all major credit cards • This pleasant old English style restaurant has functioned for nearly thirty years as the dining room of Hotel Beresford, serving a traditional assortment of Continental dishes. It looks its role, with Tudor style cross timbered walls and rough-hewn ceiling beams.

At noon, the up front pub becomes a popular luncheon spot,

and it was the surprise winner in our search for San Francisco's best hamburger in our earlier guide. We liked its perfectly seared patty on a toasted sesame bun, accompanied by thick wedges of French fries.

Others of our cast like it at dinner time: "Limited menu with nightly specials. We enjoyed tournedos and prime rib with excellent watercress soup," reported one of our bartender agents.

YANK SING • 427 Battery (Clay) • 362-1640 • 53 Stevenson (Third) • 495-4510

Chinese/dim sum • $$

Dim sum lunch daily; reservations essential; casual to sport jacket; full bar; major credit cards • The Yank Sing version of dim sum has deserted Chinatown and gone upscale. Sleek decor and pastel colors, not tasseled Chinese lanterns, dominate the expansive Financial District restaurant on Battery Street. A second non- traditional dim sum parlor is housed in an old brick-walled warehouse with multi-colored banners just south of Market in Stevenson alley.

Our reporters say the little Chinese savories are quite good at Yank Sing, despite the Americanization of its restaurants, although the servings are a bit more expensive than at the noisier, more typical Chinatown places. Carefully crafted delicacies like seasoned shrimp dumplings, vegetarian black mushroom and noodle cachets and warm egg custard tarts are easily worth it.

YUET LEE • 1300 Stockton (Broadway) • 982-6020

Chinese seafood • $$

Wednesday-Monday from 11 a.m. to 3 a.m.; casual; no alcohol but it may be brought in; no credit cards • Two years ago, we picked Yuet Lee as one of the city's ten best seafood restaurants. But we've eaten there several times since and must reluctantly change our vote. Our disloyalty has been prompted by increasingly sloppy service, seafood that isn't always as fresh as it once was and (startling in a Chinese restaurant) fish that is occasionally overdone.

Yuet Lee has always been a scruffy, chaotic place with surly or at least stoic waiters, but that was to be forgiven because the seafood was exceptional and the prices were low. But prices are creeping up, service is slipping and—with all that money the owners must be making—you'd think they could do more than sweep the floor once in a while. This place has done nothing to keep pace with the more attractive and vibrant new Chinese seafood parlors that match its culinary accomplishments. Yuet Lee's complacency is showing.

YUN NAN • 832 Clement (Ninth Avenue) • 221-2699

Northern Chinese • $

Lunch and dinner Monday-Saturday; casual, wine and beer; no credit cards. • This is another of the dozens of places along Clement's Asian Restaurant Row. The fare, mostly Szechuan, Hunan and Peking, is good but not necessarily exceptional, and some dishes are just off target. Hot and sour soup, for instance, was generous and full of shrimp, chicken, pork and tofu bits, but it was a shade too vinegary; the pot stickers, while large and crisply fried, were a little bland with mushy filling.

We did like some of the more interesting items on the large menu, however, like hot pepper pork with cool napa cabbage and *Tung An* chicken with bamboo shoots, spicy sauce and a touch of vinegar. We also like the fact that menu items are clearly described and that non-smoking tables in this high-ceilinged restaurant are well-marked.

It's a basic storefront cafe, although it does offer oilcloth instead of Formica, pleasant fake woodgrain wainscoting and some attractive Oriental prints to remind you that you're in a Chinese restaurant.

ZEPHYR • 3643 Balboa (38th Avenue) • 221-6063

American • $

Lunch and dinner daily, service to midnight Monday-Saturday; casual; wine and beer; no credit cards (MC, VISA for purchases in the art gallery) • The Zephyr is a comfortable and contemporary espresso cafe and art gallery serving soups, salads, sandwiches, quiches and personalized pizzas, plus some interesting desserts. Owners Meg Kimura and Seth Mosgofian have put their cafe off-limits to puffers, earning this breezy place the double non-smoking symbol.

All of this pleasantry happens in a "modern deco" space of redwood, copper and beveled glass. Think of this Richmond District cafe as an "art take-out," since the artworks and graphics are for sale.

"Good coffees and lighter meals," comments one of our civilian correspondents.

ZOLA'S • 1722 Sacramento (Van Ness Avenue) • 775-3311

Contemporary Mediterranean • $$

Dinner Tuesday-Sunday; casual; wine and beer; major credit cards • There's obviously something special about Zola's, since two of our celebrity chefs selected it as one of their five favorite restaurants. Manager Nick Peyton of the Squire praised its "lovely, clean flavors and presentations" and Zuni Cafe's Vince Calcagno, who we'll join in a moment, commented: "Savory food; personal touches are satisfying."

With Larry Bain up front and former art student Catherine Pansios in the kitchen, Zola's serves some of the most artistic culinary creations in the city. Although they describe their fare as "contemporary Mediterranean," they draw from French, Italian and Japanese sources for their menu, which changes every few weeks. Some items are old world classics, like a *cassoulet* with beans, lamb, homemade sausage and duck; others suggest California nouvelle, such as breast of duck with *polenta* and wild mushrooms, or roast squab with spiced grapes. While Catherine fashions good flavors in the kitchen, partner Larry assembles an outstanding California wine list.

The pretty little restaurant with a vaulted ceiling and whitewashed walls, accented by a splashy flower display, offers a "romantic setting for dining," says one of our scouts. "Wonderful dining room; made for conversation," adds another.

ZUNI CAFE • 1658 Market (Franklin) • 552-2522

California/Mediterranean • $$$

Breakfast, lunch and dinner Tuesday-Sunday, service to midnight Tuesday-Saturday, closed Monday; casual; full bar (and wine can be brought in); MC, VISA, AMEX • Zuni is no stranger. Located just up the street from my former office at AAA's Motorland Magazine, it has been a routine lunch stop since it opened in 1979. But there's nothing routine about the food; we've never tired of eating there.

Originally, Zuni was a nouvelle Southwest cafe, and it still retains that look, with the odd Navajo blanket draped here and about. However, partners William West and Vincent Calcagno and Chef Judy Rodgers have expanded both the space and the menu; they've reached over the Atlantic to add *risotto* with *porcini* and leaks; pan fried confit of duck with lentils and swiss chard; and *linguini* with *gorgonzola* and walnut sauce. It's a curiously fascinating menu, wandering from nouvelle leg of lamb, from *polenta* to *guacamole.* Rodgers, who apprenticed with Alice Waters, never tires of experimenting.

This isn't the most comfortable restaurant in the city; its downstairs wall seats are straight-backed and cramped, although the new upstairs balcony is a major improvement. And we like the Southwestern motif and the spacious feel of its high ceilings and oversized windows.

Zuni was one of our biggest vote-getters, tying for second with Zola's and Stars in the celebrity chef and restaurant executive survey, and tying for fourth in overall scoring.

"Creative menu with Southwestern influence; great place to mingle at the bar", "Great menu; great cafe ambiance," said the troops. Among our celebrity chefs and restaurant execs, it won praise for "consistently excellent food and service" and "wonderful fresh food in a happy, artful environment." But there were a few negatives. A hotelier felt it "tried to cover too many areas" and Patricia Unterman complained that service can "sometimes be aggravating," although she named it as one of her five favorite restaurants.

Perhaps the manager of a San Jose restaurant said it best: "When they're on, they're on. Innovative."

Chapter Two
THE OUTSIDE GUIDE
Selected restaurants in other Bay Area communities

Culinary discoveries don't end at the San Francisco anchorages of the bridges or the San Mateo County line. Certainly, the city is the focal point of Bay Area dining (and nearly everything else in arts and entertainment) but neighboring communities have their share of savory dining salons as well.

You'll note that the spoon ratings tend to run high here; bear in mind that we received hundreds of out-of-city nominations, and we culled from these a rather elite list. A few that scored poorly are included because of their popularity, great views or other attributes that make them worth a visit despite unpredictable kitchens and/or service.

THE EAST BAY

"Anyway, what was the use of my having come from Oakland," Gertrude Stein wrote of her home town. "There is no there there." Well, Gertrude, there certainly is now. Oakland and neighboring Berkeley may not match rival San Francisco in restaurant numbers, but they certainly rival "the city" in cafe quality. Unless you're an out-of-towner, you know that Alice Waters and Jeremiah Tower originated the California nouvelle school of cooking at Berkeley's Chez Panisse.

BAY WOLF CAFE & RESTAURANT • 3853 Piedmont Avenue (Rio Vista), Oakland • 665-6004

California/Mediterranean • $$

Lunch weekdays, dinner nightly, Sunday brunch; reservations for dinner only; casual; wine and beer; MC, VISA • Oakland's Bay Wolf fits nicely into a restored turn-of-the-century house, but the ever-changing menu fits no particular mold. Proprietor-chef Michael Wild and Chef Carol Brendlinger decide a week or so in advance what culinary ventures they'll pursue in the kitchen, then they print their menus and go to work. The fare might include lemon-mint *fettucini, bouillabaisse,* rockfish and deep fried oysters with *remoulade* sauce or grilled filet mignon with artichoke and wild mushroom sauce. Two or three entrees are offered each night for several days, then the entire menu is changed. Mondays are "regional nights," when the fare highlights a particular country or cooking style, from Portugal to Cajun country.

These culinary adventures are served within a surprisingly sleek and sunny space, considering the yesterday look of the old tree-shaded mansion's exterior. Large windows allow sunshine to splash off the light natural woods of the roomy dining areas; a few select artworks highlight fawn-colored walls. Some windows offer a view of an attractive patio, where meals are served when the weather cooperates. Some of the vegetables and herbs used in the kitchen are grown in a garden just beyond.

Opened in 1974 by Wild and his childhood buddy Larry Goldman, Bay Wolf shares some limelight with neighboring Chez Panisse as one of the country's pioneering American nouvelle restaurants.

BROADWAY TERRACE CAFE • 5891 Broadway Terrace, Oakland • 652-4442

California grill • $$

Dinner Tuesday-Sunday; reservations essential; casual; wine and beer; no credit cards • Follow Broadway Terrace (not Broadway) about a mile into the Oakland hills from its junction with College Avenue, and you'll encounter an unassuming little cafe where amazing things are done with a mesquite grill. It's California nouvelle in a woodsy setting. Chef-owner Albert Katz specializes in lightly grilled fish, plus a few chops and birds, all served with innovative sauces. Katz' salads, pastas, soups and desserts are as creative as his entrees; examples are *gorgonzola* with romaine, fruit and nuts; a corn and pureed bell pepper custard *timbale* and for dessert, chocolate souffle cake with blood oranges, or brie cheesecake.

Prices are reasonable for such quality, in the mid-twenties for a full dinner. But bring a little money or your checkbook (if your bank is local), since the Terrace takes no credit cards. Although the woodsy setting is nice, the building's interior is rather plain, cheered a bit by fresh flowers.

Katz' show is almost a one-man operation; he spends evenings in the kitchen of his tiny 34-seat restaurant and his days shopping for the best meats, fish and veggies in the Bay Area. He even plans sojourns into California's vinelands to fill out his wine list.

CHEZ PANISSE • 1517 Shattuck Avenue (Vine), Berkeley • 548-5525

California nouvelle • $$$$

Lunch and dinner daily; reservations essential; casual to sport jacket; wine and beer; MC, VISA, AMEX • There's no marker out front, saying "This is where it all began," and such a thing likely would embarrass affable but somewhat modest Alice Waters. The history of Chez Panisse has been repeated before, earlier in this book and elsewhere, so we'll just move on to the specifics.

The main restaurant serves nightly prix fixe dinners for $45. Menus in a typical week could feature warm puff pastry with sweetbreads and artichokes; fennel, carrot and spinach soup; blood orange salad; a foil packet of sea bass filet with julienned carrots, scallions, thyme and lemon; and a simple strawberry tort. These are past menu items; you may see them next week or never again. Alice has conjured up literally thousands of intriguing recipes since she opened a modest neighborhood cafe here in 1971. It's now an elegant yet simple place with clean lines, wood paneling, diffused lighting and white-clothed tables. Chef Paul Bertolli does most of the cooking, but Ms. Waters is never far away, planning menus and conferring with her chef over some interesting new blend.

The Cafe at Chez Panisse is a less expensive and more informal version of the original, occupying an upper floor of this shingle-sided house where California nouvelle began. Prices here are more in the mid-twenties for a meal. The menu is sort of California-Mediterranean, featuring grilled fish, fresh garden salads and some excellent *calzone* and pizza from a wood-burning oven.

Our guest critics' comments were numerous and predictable: "Innovative use of fresh seasonal ingredients", "Best desserts in the Bay Area", "Creative!" Also not surprising, three of our celebrity chefs picked Chez Panisse as one of their five favorite restaurants, with comments such as "Constantly fine foods", "Wonderful light, fresh food" and "It feels like home!"

DAKOTA GRILL AND BAR • 2086 Allston Way (Shattuck Avenue), Berkeley • 841-3848

Southwestern • $$

Lunch weekdays, dinner Tuesday-Sunday; reservations advised; casual; full bar; MC, VISA, AMEX • It's no accident, except perhaps alphabetical, that our Oakland-Berkeley listings sound similar, since this is the home of California nouvelle and its close cousin, Southwestern cooking. But the newest member of this cult, opened in 1987 by Ellen Hyland and Jason Green, offers a strikingly different setting. Dakota Grill functions as the dining room of the venerable Shattuck Hotel, with lofty ceilings, Ionic columns and tall arched windows. But the setting is hardly stuffy. The wait staff wears neat khakis, and the place is done in warm desert browns and blues; an indoor garden with Southwestern flora is a striking focal point.

Chef Daniel Malzhan's Southwestern fare is intriguing and, say our agents, generally delicious. Ponder creations such as salmon with mango and chili sauce; buttermilk-cornmeal crepes with diced asparagus and zucchini in a goat cheese and red bell pepper sauce; or venison sausage served with salsa and a *couscous* style grain called *quinoa*.

"The food is outstanding and the room is beautiful," said the manager of a major San Francisco hotel restaurant. "Creative dishes," added another agent.

GERTIE'S CHESAPEAKE BAY CAFE • 1919 Addison (Martin Luther King Jr. Way), Berkeley • 841-2722

Seafood • $$

Lunch Monday-Saturday, dinner nightly; reservations accepted; casual; wine and beer; major credit cards • You mean it isn't California-Navajo-nouvelle? Gertie's takes us in the opposite direction, to the crabcakes and other regional seafoods of the East Coast's Chesapeake Bay. Our crew gives good grades to Maryland crab soup, steamed mussels and the like. Co-owner and chef John Shields also draws from the southeast for gumbo, pan-fried oysters and buttermilk-marinated southern fried chicken. He also does a nightly special that might draw inspiration from just about any culinary source.

Although the cooking is home style down east and down south, the look of the place is Art Deco modern. Diners can spill onto a sunny patio when it's sunny. Gertie, incidentally, was Shields' grandmother, who was a professional cook in Baltimore and taught him a lot of what he knows about crabcakes.

"Beautiful place, professional service; excellent food."

HUNAN • 366 Eighth (Webster), Oakland • 444-9255

Northern Chinese • $

Lunch and dinner daily except Wednesday; reservations accepted; casual; wine and beer; MC, VISA • Another of the growing herd of northern Chinese restaurants in the Bay Area, Hunan is a cut above the basic look of many Asian family cafes. It's not a decorator's dream, however; it's an incongruous blend of bentwood chairs and vinyl tables, bamboo wallpaper and the ubiquitous red-tassled lanterns.

But lanterns aren't on the menu; we go there for the excellent, fresh spicy seafood, Mongolian beef, hot and sour soup and pot stickers. The place also features more gentle Cantonese dishes, so one can balance a meal nicely between succulent and mild whole steamed fish with soy, spicy cold beef and any of a variety of stir frys enlivened with bits of chili pepper.

Our team's selection of Hunan gives us an excuse to point out an interesting fact: In all of northern California, Oakland's Chinatown is second only to San Francisco's for the number and variety of Asian restaurants. It's not a touristy place with souvenir shops and cutesy turned-up eves on fake temple facades; it's an ordinary living and working neighborhood that happens to be populated mostly by Chinese. The restaurants, almost always brimming with Asians, are generally less expensive than their counterparts in the older San Francisco Chinatown.

JUAN'S PLACE • 941 Carlton (Ninth), Berkeley • 845-6904

Mexican • $

Lunch and dinner daily (opens at 2 p.m. Sunday); casual; wine and beer; MC, VISA • This earthy little Mexican cafe is popular with locals. It draws them in with fresh, crisp tortilla chips, fills them up with hearty *rellenos, flautas* and similar fare, then sends them waddling happily down the street. Portions are huge; plates are weighted down with generous dollops of *refritos* and *arroz.* There's nothing innovative on the menu, but for an average of $6 for dinner and even less for lunch, we haven't heard anyone complain.

The place is a wonderful scatter of Mexican regalia; it looks like the morning after a post-revolution celebration.

"Crowded and noisy; good food; fast service; colorful atmosphere", "Good food, great beer list." *Hola!*

SKATES • 100 Seawall Drive (University Avenue), Berkeley • 549-1900

American regional • $$

Daily from 11 a.m. to 11 p.m., light snacks until 2 a.m.; reservations essential; casual; full bar; MC, VISA, AMEX • As we work alphabetically through the East Bay, we discover that the area does indeed have a variety of restaurants. We now come to the standard upscale, trendy palace of noise. It even has a single syllable name: Skates.

The formidable menu tries to cover it all: Southwest, California Nouvelle, Yuppie Nouveau, Cajun, sushi, mesquite grilled—or is it hickory smoked? No, as a matter of fact, it's *kiawe* wood from Hawaii. This luau of updated excess is extremely successful, despite an overly-ambitious kitchen that turns out more misses than hits.

Restaurants Unlimited of Seattle used its corporate millions and a detailed demographic study to create a guaranteed package of popularity. Built on piers over the bay, Skates offers great views through floor to ceiling windows, track lighting, beige walls and touches of brass. The attractive bar is Yuppie heaven, offering not only a good wine list but all the trendy international beers and an assortment of high-style whiskeys. The place is predictably noisy, but tall ceilings make the decibels tolerable, even on a Friday night. No wonder our panel says:

"Great bar, elegant atmosphere", "Nice ocean view", "Fun, upbeat, the place to be."

SORABOL • 372 Grand Avenue (Perkins), Oakland • 839-2288

Korean • $$

Lunch and dinner daily, Sunday brunch; reservations accepted; casual; full bar; major credit cards • Finally, our agents have nominated a Korean restaurant. They didn't select any of several now operating in San Francisco, but their pick is probably the best in the Bay Area. As you place your order at Sorabol, bear in mind that the Korean national dish is *kim chee*, a mouth-melting concoction of fermented cabbage, chili peppers, garlic and ginger. Spicy cooking gets Koreans through cold winters, but it might send you running for nearby Lake Merritt, unless you order selectively. And of course, all the dishes on the large menu aren't hot.

We balanced our meal with a mild and tasty *bul-gokee* (thin-sliced rib eye steak in a teriyaki-like sauce), fluffy egg pancakes called *beandu duk* and a spicy rock cod with hot sauce named *sengsun guyee.* Surprisingly, the sauce didn't bury the fresh, lightly cooked taste of the cod. Entrees are accompanied by rice, veggies and (of course) *kim chee.* Pass the ice water, please. Better yet, make that a tall beer, which is an excellent beverage for Korean food.

This spicy fare is served in a very temperate setting; Sorabol is a handsome place with carved wooden panels, Korean prints on the walls and a ceramic tile false roof to give it the look of a royal courtyard.

SPENGER'S FISH GROTTO • 1919 Fourth (University Avenue), Berkeley • 845-7771

Seafood •

Lunch weekdays, dinner nightly, service to 11:30 Friday-Saturday; reservations for six or more only; casual; full bar; major credit cards • Spenger-bashing is a favorite pastime of Bay Area restaurant critics, but we won't succumb to the temptation. It makes no pretense of being anything more than a mass-producing warehouse of a restaurant that churns out inexpensive seafood; some is fresh, a lot tastes frozen, most is overcooked. It's crowded, chaotic and noisy, yet it's one of the highest grossing restaurants in the country. So, what's the secret to its great appeal, when the Bay Area is full of better, quieter seafood restaurants? Apparently, it's a combination of very good prices and noisy ambiance that many find attractive.

Let our agents talk about Spenger's: "Good value; large place; long wait but great for young families with kids", "Hostess seemed very rude; mass dining experience", "Terribly noisy and crowded; not the place to go for an enjoyable Saturday night dinner."

We won't add any clever insults that would only contribute to the Spenger legend.

THORNHILL CAFE • 5761 Thornhill Drive (Grisborne; Thornhill exit from Warren Freeway), Oakland • 339-0646

French/Thai •

Lunch and dinner daily, weekend brunch; reservations advised; casual; wine and beer; MC, VISA • In location, appearance, food and service, the Thornhill is the best small cafe in the Bay

Area. It's in a woodsy area in the Monclair District of the Oakland hills, built into into a small 1930s California-Spanish style store front. Lots of mirrors expand and brighten the interior, although it can be a bit disconcerting to glance across the room and see yourself chewing. Walls are gleaming white, accented by gray tablecloths, green cushions on bench seats and forest green tile rimming distinctive round windows.

Thailand born chef-owner Diane Butsangde describes her fare as "French with Thailand accents," Our panel calls it delicious and after a recent lunch, we agree. Our entree was "Four-Flavor Fish," a perfectly cooked fillet in a lime, red onion, chili and palm sugar sauce; it was smothered in an overlay of stir-fried fresh tomatoes, string beans and snow peas. A pumpkin soup with roasted strips of red bell pepper was tasty enough for dessert; not sweet, just wonderfully rich. Chef Diane adds innovative touches to everything she serves; entrees are attractively presented and desserts are charming little artworks. Even the tea is a far cry from Lipton's; it's her own blend of Thailand black and jasmine, steeped with a vanilla bean.

To insure that one properly enjoys these subtle blends of East and West, the cafe forbids pipes and cigars and discourages all smoking, limiting it to "a few tables situated with prevailing winds." That's our kind of place. Meals are served on a tree-shaded patio in summer.

"Warm, enthusiastic staff", "Best food we have experienced in years; immaculate Art Deco", "Pleasant."

MARVELOUS MARIN

Demographic studies indicate that Marin is the most affluent county in the Bay Area; stand-up comics make jokes about its Yuppie consumerism and BMW mentality. Most of that affluence is drawn from San Francisco, for tens of thousands crowd across the Golden Gate Bridge each morning, and return in the evening. Obviously, many of them stay in their county for dinner, for Marin restaurants received strong support from our panel.

AVENUE GRILL • 44 East Blithedale (Sunnyside), Mill Valley • 388-6003

American • $$

Dinner nightly; reservations accepted; casual; wine and beer (and wine may be brought in for a $5 corkage fee); MC, VISA, AMEX • A comment from one of our epicures intrigued us: "Best diner concept in the Bay Area; wonderful ribs." We were further intrigued when owner Joe Leis described his fare as

"Norman Rockwell American." That reference came from the January, 1988, issue of Playboy. In selecting the best of assorted American passions, the magazine picked Avenue Grill for the "Best Norman Rockwell food," citing its inventive yet traditional 1950s *haute* diner cuisine.

A look at the menu reveals that this is indeed down-home Americana gone slightly gourmet—spicy meatloaf, gravy and mashed potatoes; rotisseried Tumbleweed Chicken with fries; pork chops with burnt onion gravy and garlic mashed potatoes. Grilled *polenta* with *marinara* and Louisiana crab fingers in sherry sauce number among the appetizers. The menu changes seasonally, to give Chef Philipe La Mancusa the opportunity to fiddle with new variations on American diner fare. Imagine what this place could do with Thanksgiving dinner!

The look, as you might expect, is sleek chic.

BUTLER'S • 625 Redwood Highway (Seminary Drive exit from 101), Mill Valley • 383-1900

American nouvelle • $$

Dinner nightly except Monday; reservations advised; casual to sport jacket; full bar; MC, VISA, AMEX • While many Marinites migrate to the city for both employment and dining, Perry Butler of San Francisco's Perry's pulled a reverse commute in 1986 and opened this handsome restaurant near the shore of Richardson's Bay. Actually, he owns twin restaurants here; somewhat of a clone of the San Francisco Perry's functions on the ground floor and the more sophisticated and sedate Butler's operates above. Oversized windows offer views of Richardson's Bay and Mount Tamalpais.

The menu follows American nouvelle trends, with some Continental accents—goat cheese chili relleno and fried *polenta* appetizers; Caesar salad with parmesan and garlic croutons; *tortellini* with *ricotta, pancetta* and sage; and entrees such as Grilled Tumbleweed Chicken with fried corn and biscuits and pork *scaloppine* with orange ginger cream and potato leek pancakes.

Chefs Laurie Newman and Heidi Krahling are the forces behind the menu; Perry peeks into the kitchen occasionally but our spies tell us he spends most of his time these days in his original hangout back in the city.

CASA MADRONA • 801 Bridgeway, Sausalito • 332-0502

American nouvelle • $$$$

Breakfast, lunch and dinner daily; reservations essential; sport jacket; wine and beer; major credit cards • It might be the most romantic dining spot in the Bay Area. Casa Madrona Hotel and Restaurant are housed in an 1885 historical landmark Victorian tucked into a brushy hillside above the Sausalito waterfront. Although the exterior of the carefully restored mansion retains its 19th century grace, the restaurant interior is more modern with light woods, glass walls to encourage the view, and subdued lights to enhance it. This sensual aerie is reached by a winding brick path from Bridgeway, Sausalito's waterfront street.

New chef Stephen Simmons, who honed his culinary skills in the Stanford Court and Campton Place, has created a seasonal American nouvelle menu. Offerings might include blue corn crepes, salmon and caviar or grilled bay scallops with sweet peppers and avocado for appetizers, and entrees such as lamb shank *ragout* with hominy and lemon thyme, or roast quail with *pancetta.*

This is the sort of place that inspires proposals, then tempts the couple to return for anniversaries.

"Great view; good variety; good service", "Romantic", "A hand-holding kind of place."

THE CHART HOUSE • 201 Bridgeway (Main), Sausalito • 332- 0804

American • $$

Dinner nightly; reservations accepted; casual; full bar; major credit cards • This is part of a chain of formula nautical restaurants, but it's a nice enough formula and our agents like the location, on a pier off Bridgeway, with a big-windowed view of the bay. Decor is seascape Victorian; some of it is left over from the days when this was Sally Stanford's glamorous Valhalla, some has been modernized by the franchise.

The menu is formula American—grilled seafood, steaks, chops and an occasional chicken.

"Beautiful view; generous and good salad bar; cheerful, easy service."

GUAYMAS RESTAURANT • #5 Main Street (Tiburon Boulevard), Tiburon • 435-6300

Contemporary Mexican • $$

Lunch and dinner daily; reservations accepted; casual; full bar; major credit cards • The spectacular view of the Marin fjords and distant San Francisco skyline from the flower-rimmed deck is reason enough to come to Guaymas. But this is no mere taco parlor with a buena vista. A Spectrum Foods creation, Guaymas features regional and upscale Latin specialties with American nouvelle accents, like breast of chicken in chili sauce, mesquite-grilled seafoods with Mexican spices, and veal with peanut-chili sauce. Banana leaf tamales with rich *masa* and stuffed with chicken, shredded pork or cactus strips and plantain are a specialty.

Probably no such upscale place exists in the real Guaymas, a small and rather disheveled fishing village in northern Mexico, and certainly no view across *Mar de Cortez* matches this sea, mountain and city panorama.

THE LARK CREEK INN • 234 Magnolia Avenue, Larkspur • 924- 7766

Continental • $$

Lunch and dinner Tuesday-Saturday, Sunday brunch; reservations essential; casual to sport jacket; full bar; major credit cards • Make it a point to call before you go, not just to ensure getting a table, but to make sure the Lark Creek Inn has reopened. It got in the way of a tree during a recent winter storm and owners Victor and Roland Gotti (of Ernie's fame) are having this century-old mansion tucked among Larkspur's redwoods completely remodeled.

Opening was set for spring of 1988 (appropriately, when it will be a century old) but we all know how construction schedules work. The polished woods of the cozy old bar will be retained, while the dining room, a modern extension of original the structure, will offer lots of glass, including a partial greenhouse roof to bring in the surrounding redwoods.

Brunch and lunch are served on a pretty patio when the Marin weather gods permit. The menu is essentially European, with stuff like beef Wellington, roast rack of lamb and a fish or two. One of our judges gave high marks for this "lovely little inn tucked away between the redwoods."

THE RICE TABLE • 1617 Fourth (G Street), San Rafael • 456-1808

Indonesian •

Dinner Thursday-Sunday; reservations essential; casual; wine and beer; MC, VISA, AMEX • We're amazed that Indonesian *rijstaffel* restaurants aren't more popular in the Bay Area, but we're pleased that San Rafael's Rice Table is within driving distance. Indonesian cuisine is a spicy, savory Southeast Asian blend, served in a style similar to the fare of colonial India, with a variety of condiments and dipping sauces on the side. This allows the diner to conjure up a great variety of flavors, with peanut sauces, shredded coconut, chili and fish sauces, dried banana flakes, shrimp chips and such. These are nibbled along with chicken *satay*, beef squares in soy sauce, fried rice noodles and other savories.

The Rice Table is the Bay Area's oldest Indonesian restaurant, dating from 1969, and our critics say it's the best. "Excellent all around; almost always packed", "Food more than excellent!" Despite its popularity, owners Leonie and Bill Hool resist the temptation to expand their small restaurant; they're open only four days a week and they take a month off every year. Leonie runs the kitchen, using recipes from her native Java; husband Bill and assorted offspring run things up front and publish a folksy newsletter for regular customers.

The multi-course *rijstaffel* (Dutch for "rice table") began under colonial rule in the former Dutch East Indies; it still thrives in both Indonesia and the Netherlands. We've had the opportunity to sample these multi-course feasts in both places, as well as the version in Marin; Leonie keeps things authentic.

SAM'S ANCHOR CAFE • 27 Main Street (Tiburon Boulevard), Tiburon • 435-4527

Seafood • $$

Lunch and dinner daily, weekend brunches; casual; full bar; MC, VISA, AMEX • Sam's is about as close as Marin gets to an historic landmark restaurant; it has been issuing simple seafood fare from its Tiburon waterfront location since 1920. The venerable storefront cafe resembles an ordinary neighborhood bar from the front, but step inside and it opens into the Blue Room, a large, busy and funkily-decorated restaurant. Go a few paces further, and it expands onto a large deck with a sterling view of the bay and distant San Francisco silhouette.

For all these decades, Marinites and other weekend mariners have boated over to Sam's dock to recover from Saturday night with a Ramos Fizz and Eggs Benedict breakfast. Some linger until lunch to watch the summer bikini parade; others return for golden sunsets and fresh, lightly-grilled seafood. I've been to Sam's numerous times and, like the locals, I get so comfortable I'm tempted to loll away a sunny summer day.

SAVANNAH GRILL • 55 Tamal Vista Boulevard (Madera), Corte Madera • 924-6774

American regional • $$

Lunch and dinner daily; casual; full bar; MC, VISA, AMEX • The Savannah is Marin's answer to American nouvelle; think of it as a Yuppie Broadway Terrace. Cherrywood paneling, brass and wrought iron give the place an old San Francisco look. Various smoked and broiled things emerge from the grill, notably smoked baby back ribs, grilled rabbit with *shiitake* mushrooms, grilled eggplant with red pepper pesto and similar nouvelle regional fare.

The place was established in 1985 and has quickly become a popular hangout for the BMW set, despite its rather un-Yuppie location in a shopping center. A second Savannah functions in Marin's upscale Southern California twin, Newport Beach.

One of our secret diners calls the food here "probably the best saloon-style cuisine outside the city."

THE PENINSULA

The predominately white collar San Mateo Peninsula fosters several fine dining spots; some of the most charming restaurants in the Bay Area are tucked into its woodsy hills.

ALPINE INN • 401 Primrose Road (Chapin), Burlingame • 347-5733

European • $$

Dinner Wednesday-Sunday; reservations advised; casual; wine and beer; MC, VISA, AMEX • Chef-owner Werner Bertram composes savory Swiss-German creations in the kitchen while his wife Heidi welcomes guests to this snug and charming little inn. Flickering candles and fresh flowers offer a romantic setting for a cozy, quiet and remarkably inexpensive dinner. Prices range from $10 to $13 for a hearty meal of *sauerbraten* (marinated in Werner's secret sauces for several days), pork (marinated in Werner's secret sauces for several days), pork tenderloin, Swiss veal in shallots and mushroom cream sauce, or chicken breast stuffed with veal.

A chef for 25 years, Werner cooked in Germany and Switzerland, then at Amelio's in San Francisco before opening this place in the late 1970s.

"Excellent food and service; personality plus", "Good food; pleasant Swiss-German style atmosphere."

BARBAROSSA RESTAURANT • 3003 El Camino Real (Selby Lane), Redwood City • 369-2626

French • $$$

Lunch Tuesday-Friday, dinner Monday-Saturday; reservations advised; sport jacket; full bar; all major credit cards • One of the Peninsula's better French restaurants, chef-owned Barbarossa earned a four-star Mobil rating for its *haute cuisine* and its elegant old European decor. Flower boxes ring this comely slate gray building off busy El Camino Real; the interior is divided into several warm wood-paneled dining rooms. Probably the best tables are in the bar, where dinners are served near the fireplace.

The cuisine is classic French, and our spies were unanimous in their praise. "Very romantic; old fashioned French food", "Expensive, elegant, intimate."

BELLA VISTA • 13451 Skyline Boulevard, Woodside • 851-1229

Continental • $$$

Dinner Tuesday-Sunday; reservations essential; sport jacket; full bar; all major credit cards • For more than half a century, this woodsy old house has looked down from its lofty perch, with a "bella vista" of the San Mateo Peninsula below. Legend says the owner sold bootleg hooch during prohibition, then began serving dinner. (The legend doesn't say what sort of fare went with bathtub gin.)

Today, it's a fashionable and properly elegant restaurant; Peninsulans wait days to get a window table. The fare is a Continental mix, tilted toward Italian and French. The list includes several veal dishes, duckling *l'orange flambe, Coquilles St. Jacques* and some Americanized steak and prawn entrees.

"The view is absolutely superb", "Unusual Continental food" and "Excellent service, food, view."

THE CASTAWAYS • Coyote Point County Park (take Poplar exit from U.S. 101), San Mateo • 347-1027

American • $$

Lunch and dinner daily; reservations accepted; casual; full bar; major credit cards • The Castaways occupies a large woodland bungalow on a point of land in Coyote Point County Park, with a sterling view of San Francisco Bay. Unfortunately, the management seems so pleased with the view that it pays little heed to food and service.

We received one favorable vote and several bad ones, so we decided to check it out ourselves. Our chicken stir fry was spoiled by too much salt and sugar and accompanying veggies were overdone. On another visit, we played it safe and stayed with an omelet and an ordinary BLT for lunch. The omelet was cooked to rubber and the sandwich was soggy, along with the French fries.

The service was slow and indifferent; a requested table change to escape from a squalling infant was greeted with sullen grumbling from the waitress.

"Excellent views; comfortable," said the lone advocate; he did not praise the food.

FONTANA'S • 1850 El Camino Real (Atherton Avenue), Menlo Park • 321-0601

California/Italian • $$

Lunch and dinner Monday-Saturday; casual; full bar; MC, VISA, AMEX • A former coffee shop has been remodeled into a sleek modern restaurant with lots of glass and earth tones that give it a contemporary Southwestern look. A nice touch on each of the white-clothed tables—a flower floating in a small goldfish bowl (sans fish).

The large menu lists California nouvelle offerings, ranging from baked goat cheese salads and chili-honey glazed duck to typical Italian pastas and veals. A roast section features chicken, ducks and ribs; fresh seafoods also are part of this lengthy list.

"I have been to this restaurant several times and have never been disappointed."

HONG KONG FLOWER LOUNGE • 1671 El Camino Real (Park Place), Millbrae • 878-8108

Cantonese • \\\ $

Lunch and dinner daily; reservations accepted; casual; wine and beer; MC, VISA, AMEX, DC • Despite the rather touristy name, Hong Kong Flower Lounge is one of the most attractive and accomplished Chinese restaurants on the Peninsula, perhaps in the Bay Area. This is no mom and pop diner; the decor is lavish and expensive, with hand-carved screens, silk tapestries and other Hong Kong opulence.

Owned by a group from Hong Kong, it offers a variety of excellent Cantonese dishes with their properly subtle seasonings, including the usual things stir-fried in oyster sauce, steamed whole fish and some interesting Hong Kong specialties such as baked crab with green onion, and clay pot spareribs simmered with wine. Several northern Chinese items are available on the huge, complex menu as well. The Flower Lounge is one of six branches owned by the group.

"Clean and nicely decorated; service is slow so it's the perfect place to dine at leisure."

IRON GATE RESTAURANT • 1360 El Camino Real (near Circle Star Center), Belmont • 592-7893

Italian/Continental • \\ Y $$

Lunch weekdays, dinner Monday-Saturday; reservations essential, particularly before the theater; casual; full bar; major credit cards • Iron Gate is the theater restaurant for the Circle Star crowd, starting dinner service at 5 p.m. and offering dancing music after the show. It's an opulent, candle-lit place featuring rather showy tableside service off fancy serving carts. The menu is predominately Italian, featuring a home-made *gnocchi* Neapolitan and a range of other pastas and chops. Curried lamb and poached salmon come from the Continental side of the menu.

"Good food; leisurely dining; service good. Personnel friendly and helpful."

MAHARAJA NORTH INDIAN CUISINE • 528 San Mateo Avenue (El Camino Real), San Bruno • 583-5226

Northern India • $$

Lunch and dinner daily; reservations accepted; casual; wine and beer; MC, AMEX, DISC • This small restaurant has a modern look, but the menu is strictly Northern India, with subtle spices and gentle curries typical of the more mild cuisine from this region. The place offers an assortment of richly flavored lamb and chicken dishes, plus hearty vegetarian specialties. An eggplant and rice creation is favored by one of our number, who is a catering coordinator for an airport hotel.

"Being a near-vegetarian, I appreciate a place that offers such good dishes of this type."

MAX'S OPERA CAFE OF BURLINGAME • 1250 Old Bayshore (Broadway) • 342-MAXS

New York/California deli • $$

Breakfast, lunch and dinner daily, service to midnight Friday-Saturday; casual; full bar (wine can be brought in for a $5 corkage fee); MC, VISA, AMEX • Dennis Berkowitz and crew have expanded their Maxy concept to the Peninsula. Like the other Max's, this one is sleekly modern with light woods and lots of glass and brass; think of it as a deli done by a decorator on a high budget. The food service crew pauses occasionally to clear their collective throats and sing a few Broadway show tunes and operatic arias, like the folks in the San Francisco Civic Center Max.

The food is an interesting mix of old New York deli and California nouvelle; the list wanders from hot pastrami and corned beef sandwiches to tostada-style *pizelles* in baked tortilla shells, interesting salads and croissant sandwiches. Portions are generous and so are the glasses of good house wine.

"Enjoyable for the entire family; great gathering place for Peninsula residents."

THE MOONRAKER • 105 Rockaway Beach Avenue, Pacifica • 359-0303

Continental • \ Y $$$

Dinner Tuesday-Sunday; reservations advised; casual to sport jacket; full bar; MC, VISA, AMEX • The Moonraker is similar to the Castaways, with a view of the ocean instead of the bay. Unfortunately, it's similar in more than one way.

These were typical of the comments received: "Extremely slow to poor service. Wrote to manager and returned to see if changes were made; still bad" and "Bad news." However, some praised the "great setting on the ocean" and "very pleasant people."

The consensus seems to be that the restaurant sells the view, hoping the folks won't notice the ordinary food and irregular service. Our own visit confirmed this. A roasted duckling certainly had been; even the raspberry sauce couldn't conceal its dryness.

PACIFIC CAFE • 3560 Callan Boulevard (Westborough Boulevard), South San Francisco • 952-0666

Seafood • \\ ⊘ Y $$

Dinner nightly; reservations accepted; casual; full bar; major credit cards • This is another of the pleasantly attractive cafes Pacific; the chain was started about a decade ago by Jim Thomason and Tom Hawker. The common denominator is a comfortable, warm wood setting and fresh broiled and pan fried seafood with reasonable prices that never come out even. (Petrale sole for $10.72, for instance.)

They keep things simple; the menu is small and almost exclusively seafood and shellfish except for a steak or two. Everything is fresh and either lightly broiled or pan-fried. A small but select wine list features mostly California whites. And if you have to wait for dinner, a glass is offered gratis.

We've eaten at cafes Pacific in San Francisco and Concord and can report that our experiences were always pleasant. "Excellent variety of seafood" and "Great fish, and bar also," spoke the troops, in confirmation.

PINE BROOK INN • 1015 Alameda de las Pulgas (Ralston), Belmont • 591-1735

German/American/seafood • $$

Lunch Monday-Saturday, dinner Tuesday-Saturday, Sunday brunch; casual to sport jacket; full bar; MC, VISA, AMEX • Belmont is a pretty little woodsy town in the central Peninsula and the Pine Brook Inn looks right at home there. It's popular with locals, both for the hearty and modestly priced food and the camaraderie of music and dancing in the lounge Thursday through Saturday. The decor is rustic; the place is even built around a redwood tree. Diners can look through big picture windows into a pretty garden.

Chef-owner Klaus Zander issues sundry German specialties from his kitchen, along with stuffed zucchini, breast of chicken and a few seafood dishes. Each dinner comes with a large salad, soup (often a *fladle* beef consomme laced with sherry squirted from a goatskin bag) and a basket of homemade breads, muffins and rolls. Nightly specials are served Sunday through Thursday, featuring an entree, soup, salad, dessert and coffee for a mere $9.95.

"Good basic food; excellent brunch; noisy."

SAN BENITO HOUSE • 356 Main Street (Mill), Half Moon Bay • 726-3425

American nouvelle • $$

Lunch Wednesday-Saturday, dinner nightly, Sunday brunch; reservations advised; casual; full bar; MC, VISA, AMEX • A former railroad hotel in Half Moon Bay's folksy downtown area has found new function as one of the San Mateo Coast's more pleasant restaurants. The yesterday look of the 1905 hostelry is carefully preserved, with wainscoting, green hurricane lamp chandeliers, cafe curtains, an old fashioned china cabinet and assorted other antiques.

We'll define the cuisine as "country American creative." A prix fixe dinner is offered nightly, with a choice of a seafood or meat entree. I inherited a thick and tender beef filet with *bearnaise* sauce and baby potatoes while Betty chose steamed crab with black bean, onion and butter sauce. *Fettucini* with smoked duck in a light cheese sauce functioned as a tasty appetizer. The hearty dinners also included a salad and loaf of warm, fresh-baked whole-wheat bread that tasted as good as it smelled.

This pleasant dining experience sometimes moves onto a patio when weather allows. Many of the veggies for the kitchen come from a nearby garden. Smoking isn't allowed in the dining room; to light up, one can seek refuge in a rather smoky good-old-boy bar across the hall. Incidentally, San Benito House also functions as a bed and breakfast inn. Chef-owner Carol Mickelsen restored the place in 1979, then educated herself in the ways of cuisine; she studied under some important European chefs, then completed her education with a brief apprenticeship in the kitchen of the late Masataka Kobayashi of Masa's.

THE SWEDISH PLACE • 2320 South Cabrillo Highway, Half Moon Bay • 726-7322

Scandinavian • $$

Lunch and dinner daily, Sunday brunch; reservations accepted; casual; wine and beer (and wine may be brought in); major credit cards • Two miles south of Half Moon Bay, the Swedish House offers rather inexpensive Scandinavian fare and a pretty view of the Pacific. In keeping with the menu of hearty Swedish and Norwegian fish dishes, the place has Old European decor, with wood wainscoting and antique furnishings.

"Comfortable family atmosphere," offers one of our restaurateur critics.

231 ELLSWORTH • 231 Ellsworth (Second), San Mateo • 347-7231

French • $$$

Lunch weekdays, dinner Monday-Saturday; reservations advised; casual to sport jacket; wine and beer (and wine can be brought in); all major credit cards • There's more to Peninsula dining than woodsy restaurants with good food, or great views with ordinary food. Our associates have uncovered a smart new French restaurant in downtown San Mateo. Chef-owner Kurt Grasing and his partner Ken Ottobuni modestly call their place with a street-address name an "affordable three-star restaurant." Lest you accuse them of excess enthusiasm, our critics seem to agree: "Superior; fine dining" and "Elegant atmosphere with great service" were among the comments.

Chef Grasing uses traditional French sauces and lots of butter, so don't expect light nouvelle. But the results, our agents affirm, are delicious and not heavy on the palate. And if the calorie-rich entrees aren't enough, the desserts are excellent.

The restaurant is roomy, yet it's divided into several smaller dining areas with well-spaced tables that permit intimate conversations. Soft tones of pink and gray and subdued lighting provide an atmosphere that might encourage such conversations.

CONTRA COSTA

It means the "opposite coast," but Contra Costa County touches only a brief strip of San Francisco Bay in Richmond. Mostly, it borders on San Pablo Bay and the Carquinez Strait, and its business and residential heart is in the Diablo Valley, tucked between the Oakland Hills and Mount Diablo. It's one of the fastest growing regions of the Bay Area. With growth comes hunger, and the result is obvious.

Although good restaurants are scattered throughout the county, all of our nominees are in the main growth corridor of Lafayette-Walnut Creek-Concord.

CALIFORNIA CAFE • 1540 N. California Boulevard (Bonanza), Walnut Creek • 938-9977

American nouvelle •  $$

Lunch weekdays, dinner nightly, Sunday brunch; reservations advised; full bar; major credit cards • California Cafes are nicely packaged versions of new American fare; about half a dozen are scattered around the Bay Area. Walnut Creek's version is located amidst the city's growing ranks of office buildings, so its future seems assured. The look is Contemporary American with aqua and peach colors, lots of rounded edges and regional posters. Tables are well spaced in two split-level dining areas, with a bar along one side.

The emphasis is seafood with a southern drawl; we came across our first blackened redfish here some years ago. The menu also features Sonoma duck breast, *fettucini* with veal, grilled chicken *paillard* and sundry grilled seafoods. True to its American nouvelle package, it's strong on fresh salads, and you're likely to find things with chutney and goat cheese (hopefully not in the same dish).

CRUCHON'S • 2599 North Main (Third Avenue), Walnut Creek • 937-0682

American • $

Lunch and dinner daily except Sunday; reservations accepted for dinner; casual; wine and beer; MC, VISA • "A sleeper! Excellent food, nice presentation; no atmosphere unless you like a hole-in-the-wall." It appears that someone decided to turn their living room into a cafe dining room, and brought the project in under budget. Cruchon's is the Diablo Valley's version of a funky Mom's Diner, but with more creative food. The small restaurant is housed in an old paint-peeling cottage, with dark woods, a tangle of climbing plants and fake Tiffany lamps.

The best things about Cruchon's are the prices; somehow the folks manage to turn out full dinners for under $8. And the food is better than the price suggests. It's essential American, mostly seafood, with some nice Continental touches. We tried the seafood grill on one occasion and were served a large plate of slightly overdone but fresh clams, scallops, some sort of fish filet and a large butterfly shrimp. We happened to be in the neighborhood later and experienced a sudden hunger pang, so we stopped by and ordered shrimp in garlic wine sauce. It would have been good at twice the price; at $7.45, it was outstanding.

FREDDIE'S PIZZA • 3598 Mount Diablo Boulevard (Dewing), Lafayette • 284-9110

Pizza/pastas • $$

Dinner nightly; casual; wine and beer; no credit cards • Freddie's is probably Contra Costa's oldest old fashioned pizza parlor, in business since 1946. It's situated in an attractive brick building, but it becomes pizza parlor funk inside. Walls are papered with hand-drawn signs and messages from customers, and the fanciest item of decor is a lighted Olympia beer sign. Diners can choose between a scatter of tables or a chipped Formica counter, where one can sit and stare into a big pizza oven. On a chilly winter's eve, this is the warmest corner of the cafe.

Freddie serves old style thin crust pizza with the usual variety of toppings and some interesting new ones, like artichoke hearts or chopped garlic and green chili strips. He also ladles up generous dishes of spaghetti and a couple of other pastas.

PACIFIC CAFE • 2151 Salvio (Grant), Concord • 678-3888

Seafood • $$

Lunch weekdays, dinner nightly; reservations advised; casual; full bar; MC, VISA, AMEX • We've ordered simple mesquite-grilled fish at other cafes Pacific and we've never been disappointed. For variety, we tried a couple of specials at the Concord branch, and we were pleased with the results. A Cajun snapper arrived not blackened but with a spicy, crusty coating that was crunchy and delicious, while the filet beneath was flaky and moist. A swordfish *piccata* was done in the style of the veal dish, with a lemon sauce and capers; the sauce wasn't too lemony and the fish, as we'd anticipated, was lightly grilled.

Prices are in the low teens for most dinners, and they drop to a bargain $7.95 for a 4 to 7 p.m. daily special that includes a cup of chowder, veggies and spuds or rice.

This cafe Pacific, incidentally, isn't open-rafter rustic like the original in San Francisco; the look is sort of country modern with French windows, beamed ceilings, wooden partitions between tables, hanging plants and cute little scalloped wall lamps. It's one of the most attractive of the chain. "Nice place; nice people; good fish."

SORRENTO'S • 2064 Treat Boulevard (Countrywood Shopping Center, at Bancroft), Walnut Creek • 938-3366

Italian • $$

Lunch Monday-Saturday, dinner nightly; reservations accepted; casual; wine and beer; VISA, MC • This family-run operation functioned for years in downtown Concord, then moved to an upscale neighborhood shopping center. It still retains the pleasant, friendly ambiance of a family trattoria and prices are very reasonable. Pizza ovens turn out tasty pies up front, while diners savor sundry pastas, veal specialties and similar Italian fare in comfortable wooden booths or roomy tables in the main dining room.

It's versatile for a small place, performing the chores of the local pizza take-out, an inexpensive family dinner restaurant and a busy lunch spot featuring cold pastas and sandwiches.

TOURELLE CAFE AND RESTAURANT • 3565 Mount Diablo Boulevard (Oak Hill Road), Lafayette • 284-3565

French • $$ and $$$$

CAFE: Lunch Tuesday-Saturday, dinner Tuesday-Sunday, Sunday brunch; casual; up to $20; RESTAURANT: lunch Tuesday-Friday, dinner Tuesday-Saturday, Sunday brunch; sport jacket; $40 prix fixe; reservations essential; full bar; MC, VISA, AMEX • Somehow, someone managed to drop a fully assembled brick, vine-covered French chateau in the middle of Lafayette. Within its walls, owner Annette Esser has assembled the Diablo Valley's most complete and stylish dining spot. La Tourelle offers both an elegantly formal old world restaurant and a lively bistro-style cafe with an open kitchen. French art enhances exposed brick walls, and the lounge becomes a lively jazz club from Thursday through Sunday evenings. During nice weather (most of the time in this valley) cocktails and snacks are served in a flower-trimmed courtyard.

Our reviewers admire the place: "The only 'city type' restaurant in the Lafayette area," wrote the co-owner of a San Francisco cafe. She complained about small portions and pricey wines but praised the food, particularly the "great fish and pasta." "Cafe is bright, with brick walls and mesquite grill, almost a clone of Cafe Chez Panisse," wrote our friend Carol Fowler, restaurant critic for the Contra Costa *Times*. "Restaurant is elegant, a French country room, one of the loveliest dining rooms in the Bay Area."

The prix fixe dinners in the fashionable, antique-furnished restaurant are French nouvelle, featuring delicacies such as Three Caviar Soup, smoked pepper *carpaccio* with peppers and red onions, medallions of veal in truffle oil with orange and Armagnac glace, or coho salmon with a scallop mousse. The smaller cafe across the courtyard issues lighter fare such as *cassoulet* and grilled meats. Both dining rooms serve ala carte lunches.

THE WINE COUNTRY

Ignore that subtitle. There is no longer a single California wine country; important wine-producing regions now range from Mendocino through Monterey to the valleys above Santa Barbara.

Of course, most of us think of the Napa and Sonoma valleys, assaulted by hundreds of thousands of visitors each year, as the Wine Country. Several notable restaurants have emerged there, providing a happy gustatorial wedding of good food with good, local wines and—in many cases—stunning vineyard settings. The opportunity to dine on fashionable French cuisine and sip a good cabernet while sitting within plucking distance of next year's harvest draws legions from the Bay Area. Think country elegance in most of these places, but think advance reservations as well.

AUBERGE DU SOLEIL, 180 Rutherford Hill Road (Silverado Trail) • Rutherford (Napa Valley) • (707) 963-1211

French nouvelle • $$$$

Lunch and dinner daily except Wednesday; reservations essential; casual for lunch, dressy for dinner; full bar (wine may be brought in for a corkage fee); MC, VISA • This exquisite hillside Mediterranean villa with an striking view of the Napa Valley is the one of the most dramatically situated restaurants in northern California. The interior look is rustic elegance—textured adobe walls, rough hewn beams, a fireplace and stone floors. Cocktails and lunches are served on a balcony, offering a panorama of olive groves, vineyards and the Mayacamus Mountains across the valley.

Our guest epicures gave the "Inn of the Sun" high marks although they did fuss a bit about small portions, an occasional off-dish and high wine prices. "Excellent but pricey", "Excellent food, beautifully presented in a lovely room with a sweeping view of the wine country."

This is where the legend of Masa Kobayashi began, before he moved on to create Masa's in San Francisco. Present Chef Michel Cornu continues the Masa movement with innovative translations of classic French fare. Dinners are prix fixe at $47, with two sittings. A menu sampler: Duck *foi gras*, lamb tenderloin stuffed with squash, and veal skirt marinated with soy and ginger; hors d'oeuvres include such curious delights as chicory and spinach salad with bacon, duck liver mousse and seafood sausage.

DOMAINE CHANDON • California Drive (off Highway 29), Yountville (Napa Valley) • (707) 944-2892

French/California • $$$$

Lunch and dinner Wednesday-Sunday; reservations essential; casual for lunch, sport jacket for dinner; wine and beer; major credit cards • A part of the winery complex owned by France's Moet and Chandon, this good-looking restaurant takes its architectural cues from a rather modern school. It features barrel vaulted ceilings, a simple green and white interior and glass walls to draw in the view of surrounding vineyards and beautifully landscaped winery gardens.

The fare is an interesting mix of French sauces and fresh California ingredients "to reflect California's openness to innovation," says Chef Philippe Jeanty's press release. The Reims Culinary Academy graduate also likes to style his foods for the crisp taste of Chandon's sparkling wines. (One does not call them champagnes in this French in-holding of the Napa Valley.)

We dined there recently on a designer chicken leg and breast (shaped like a d'anjou pear) over a fried Chinese noodle patty, with a tangy sauce of ginger, pimento and green pepper; and grilled shrimp with a reduced cabernet sauce. Both were delicious. A rich raspberry milkshake served in a dark chocolate bag (actually cast from a lunch sack) was an absolute delight.

EL DORADO INN • 405 First Street West (Spain), Sonoma • (707) 996-3030

California cuisine • $$

Lunch and dinner daily; Sunday brunch; reservations accepted; casual; full bar; MC, VISA, AMEX • Save the El Dorado for warm weather when you can dine in its charming old Spanish courtyard off the Sonoma Square. You can relax in the shade of a giant fig tree during lunch, or admire the stars at night. The indoor dining room is nice, too, offering a sort of modern Spanish look with leaded glass, polished light woods and lots of plants. Incidentally, the place still functions as a hotel, should you want to devote more than one day to Sonoma Valley vineyard sipping.

The fare is typical of the trend—prawns teriyaki, grilled breast of chicken with creole sauce, grilled Bodega Bay salmon with mustard herb butter, bow tie pasta with smoked duck and *marinara* sauce, things like that. This is probably one of the least expensive "nouvelle" restaurants in the wine country, with entrees in the low to middle teens.

LES ARCADES • 133 East Napa (First Street), Sonoma • (707) 938-3723

French • $$

Dinner nightly; reservations essential; casual to sport jacket; wine and beer; MC, VISA • "The Arcades" form a pretty brick pathway and patio leading into this handsome European style restaurant. Set back from Napa Street near the Sonoma Plaza, Les Arcades offers an exceptionally attractive alfresco dining environment, with a brick deck, giant olive tree, gurgling wine barrel fountain, brick-lined gas fire pit and heat lamps to keep things toasty on cool evenings. The chairs, surprisingly, are simple, rubber-covered Payless patio specials, but they're quite comfortable. The adjacent indoor dining room is of old European design, and no smoking is permitted therein.

The fare is country French and rather modestly priced, considering the quality of the food and the attractive setting. I recall that Betty and I enjoyed an excellent fluffy, rich *quenelle* with venison sauce, mussels with chablis sauce and a perfectly seared and wonderfully tender cut of beef. Veggies in the salad and side dishes were perfectly crisp. We departed happily, with the impression that owner Dominique Leiseing selects fresh ingredients with great care, and prepares them with a light hand.

MUSTARDS GRILL • 7399 St. Helena Highway (a mile north of Yountville), Napa • (707) 944-2424

American grill • $$

Lunch and dinner daily in summer, shorter hours in winter; reservations essential; casual; wine and beer; MC, VISA • In 1983, a band of young entrepreneurs opened Mustards (where several other restaurants had failed) and had an instant hit on their hands. Their solution for the previously jinxed site beside Highway 29 was simple. They provided an open "demonstration" kitchen, a wood burning grill and simple "new American" fare. And they dressed up this ordinary bungalow with black and white linoleum squares, lots of hanging plants and a front porch extension with large windows. The low ceiling here generates a rather high noise level and we wish they'd designate a non-smoking area. But a beefed-up ventilation system kept the air reasonably clear when we dined there.

The food was excellent. A chunk of good, crusty whole wheat bread hit the table about the time we did, but before we could completely spoil our appetites, other food began arriving. Our starter was delicious chilled melon-banana-grape soup with pistachios, followed by a perfectly grilled trout in bourbon almond butter; and quail with a jalapeno marinade, served with a spicy lime-papaya chutney. Accompanying veggies were fresh and crisply cooked, garnished with olives and pearl onions.

Taken with a bottle of excellent Burgess Cellars zinfandel, it was a nice finish to a day in the wine country.

On that upbeat note, we end our restaurant survey. And now, the various envelopes, please.

Chapter Three
WHERE THE ELITE MEET TO EAT
Favorite restaurants of personalities and community leaders

If you guessed that fitness enthusiast Joanie Greggains favors Greens for its vegetarian dishes, you'd be right. And we suspect that Stan Delaplane spends more time at the Washington Square Bar and Grill than at the San Francisco *Chronicle* that publishes his column.

But what restaurants do other community leaders, media types and personalities favor? Where do our supervisors and business leaders go for their power luncheons? What restaurants gain favor with members of wealthy families, who can afford the best? We sent questionnaires to some of these folks, asking them to list their five favorite restaurants. Their response was quite gratifying, and we feel it adds a fun dimension to our *ULTIMATE DINING GUIDE.* (Interestingly, our VIP panel gave us the highest response percentage of any of our groups.)

Please note that these are casual selections. They do not imply endorsements, but merely personal favorites. And you'll note that their selections are listed in alphabetical order; there is no numerical rating of their favorites.

Some of the restaurants named by our VIP corps aren't listed in our book. But a good many of them are, and we've marked them with an asterisk (*), so you can thumb back and find them.

We didn't ask that selections be limited to San Francisco (and a few went rather far afield); when their picks are outside the city, we say so.

Barbara Boxer, member of Congress, District Six
- Adriana's, San Rafael
- Butler's*, Mill Valley
- Donatello*
- Giramonte's, Mill Valley
- Modesto Lanzone's*

Mike Cleary, Radio Station KNBR
- Dakota Grill*, Berkeley: Never disappointed; wonderful!
- Graziano's: Monday through Friday lunch only.
- Mesa, Oakland: Innovative, consistent and friendly.
- Sumi's, Alamo: A Japanese treasure! Family-owned; great!

Victor's*: Elegant, romantic and classy!

John Curley, sports editor, San Francisco *Chronicle*

Khan Toke*: Beautiful, intimate surroundings; authentic Thai food.

Kuleto's*: Relatively new; they do everything well.

Stars*: Great for people-watching; meticulous staff.

The Swedish Place*, Half Moon Bay: Stashed away along the coast; a refreshing change of pace.

Washington Square Bar & Grill*: Real chummy place; great for late dinner after a game.

Stan Delaplane, columnist, San Francisco *Chronicle*

Amelio's Restaurant*: I went there as a young reporter. Chef Jacky Robert is a genius.

Bushati's: Splendid Italian; priced right and you can park!

Hotel Nikko restaurants: Les Celebrites for French traditional; Benkay for outstanding Japanese food.

Mulhern's: I go there for old fashioned mashed potatoes and gravy.

Washington Square Bar & Grill*: It's my office. Lively place. Good food; interesting folks.

Glenn Dickey, sports columnist, San Francisco *Chronicle*

Broadway Terrace Cafe*, Oakland: Chef/owner Albert Katz is an innovative chef who does marvelous things with pastas, fish grilled over mesquite and lamb, among others.

The Blue Fox*: This is my favorite of the grand old Continental style restaurants; a great place for a special occasion. I especially like the veal dishes and, of course, the pasta.

The Grotto, Jack London Square, Oakland: Owners Andy Franichevich, Tony Markovich and Mike Stipic have made this restaurant a more pleasant version of Tadich's. Good fish and other seafood and lots of it at very reasonable prices; can't beat the sand dabs.

Trader Vic's*: No place has ever been better at making regular customers feel like Very Special People than Trader Vic's, which is why it's long been known as the San Francisco Country Club.

Washington Square Bar & Grill*: The food is good (I love Mary Etta's pastas) and the atmosphere is unbeatable. Always noisy, but that just seems to add to the charm. It's a great place to go with friends and just kick back and enjoy.

Charles Dishman, division vice president, Tiffany & Company

Campton Place*: Elegant, great service; a southern touch on the menu.

Fog City Diner*: Great ambiance; lively and fun

Janot*: Gourmet cooking; wonderful

Kuleto's*: Lively bar; good Italian food; lively waiters. Fun!

Rings*: Casual; great fish and spicy.
Trader Vic's*: Personal, accommodating; a place to see friends.

Jerry DiVecchio, food and wine editor, *Sunset Magazine*
Balboa Cafe*: Small but changing and delightful menu; mad bar scene.
Butler's*, Mill Valley: Setting is fresh, bright and intriguing.
Jack's*: If you order the classics—roasts and grills—you'll never be disappointed; great history in this place.
MacArthur Park: In the wonderful old Veterans of Foreign Wars building. The food is simple, predictable and well-prepared.
Stars*: Eclectic, interesting food, lively room. I like the tiered offerings, from bar hotdogs to white-cloth grandeur.

M.F.K. Fisher, author
Ernie's*: I continue to like it because it's so completely old-fashioned.
Fournou's Ovens*: Excellent, and I think it is getting better all the time.
Jack's Restaurant*
Kan's Chinese Restaurant*
Yamato

Phil Frank, creator of "Farley"
Angelino's, Sausalito: Very local, very Italian and very good.
Caffe Sport*: An adventure for the eyes as well as the palate.
Squids: Don't go unless you love squid; I do.
Thai Village: Spicy cuisine from Thailand; yummy.
Washington Square Bar & Grill*: Everyone is treated the same; fun to see the folks.

Bill German, executive editor, San Francisco *Chronicle*
Brothers, Burlingame: Best kosher style; it deserves a vote.
Fabrizio, Larkspur: Consistently good and varied Italian dishes.
Harris'*: In the old tradition of food; ambiance still counts.
Hayes Street Grill*: Seafood, sausage, whatever.
Masa's*: For the big occasion.

Jim Gonzales, San Francisco Board of Supervisors
Don Ramon's: Great Mexican food; excellent service. Watch out: you may become an adopted member of the Ramirez family.
John's Grill*: The Malteze Falcon headquarters; every dish a treat.
Modesto Lanzone*: Masterpieces everywhere, especially the food.
Stars*: The best power luncheons for business, politics and the arts.
Washington Square Bar & Grill*: Ed Moose has great taste in food, sports and people.

Joanne Green, News Director, "Magic 61" KFRC
Broadway Terrace*, Oakland: Superb food, although rather pricey.
Cantina, Oakland and Mill Valley: Best fajitas; steak marinade is wonderful.
Four Star Restaurant: Great black bean soup and calamari salad.
Julius' Castle*: Great food; best sunset; romantic, fine service.
Yoshi's: Consistently great Japanese food and great jazz.

Joanie Greggains, fitness enthusiast, "Morning Stretch" show on KPIX Channel 5.
Ciao*: Ultimate fresh pasta and salads, vegetables.
Greens at Fort Mason*: Vegetarian dishes; delicious. Great bread, too!
Las Camelias, San Rafael: Healthy Mexican food; fresh and without a lot of grease.
Milly's, San Rafael: Excellent creative, healthy food; fresh with eye appeal.
Washington Square Bar & Grill*: A real San Franciscan restaurant; a feeling of old S.F.

Mrs. Walter A. Haas, Jr., community and cultural leader
Auberge de Soleil*, Rutherford: Nouvelle at its best, in a lovely setting.
Fleur de Lys*: Mixture of nouvelle and French; lovely atmosphere.
L'Etoile*: First class European cooking; restful setting.
Square One*: A variety of dishes; beautiful presentations.
Trader Vic's*: Nice atmosphere and warmth; interesting combinations of American and Chinese food, as well as good fish dishes.

Edward Hastings, artistic director, American Conservatory Theatre
Cafe Majestic*
Kuleto's*
Post Street Bar & Grill
Regina's*: Unusual menu.
Swiss Alps: Reliable; moderate prices.

Mike Hegedus, Channel Five, KPIX
Enrico's*: You can gain weight on the wings of his "Angels."
Fred's Sandwiches: The best of anywhere between two slices of bread.
Paprika's Fono: From one Hungarian (Fono) to another (Hegedus).
U.S. Restaurant*: All-American Italian.
The Waterfront*: A restaurant with real sole (Amandine)!

Art Hoppe, columnist, San Francisco *Chronicle*
Freddy's Hofbrau: Great sauerkraut
Hanno's: traditional turkey soup
Carlos 'n' Pancho's, San Anselmo: great daiquiris
Dominique's, Paris: Superb borsch
Duc Tho Bai, Bankok: Freshest fish in Asia
(Editor's note: It's always good to hear from an international gourmet.)

Larry Kramer, executive editor, San Francisco *Chronicle*
Butlers*, Mill Valley: A class restaurant.
Cafe Esprit: Great place for lunch; light and airy.
Fog City Diner*: The perfect San Francisco restaurant; first place to take out-of-towners.
Sam's Grill*, Tiburon: No better place for outside Sunday brunch.
Stars*: Always exciting; lots of action.

Ruth Asawa Lanier, artist/sculptor
Blanche's: A place in the sun, to visit with friends.
Diamond Street Restaurant: Quiet, always good, especially the calamari and freshly baked bread.
Hana Restaurant: Delicious, friendly, busy.
Heung Yuen Restaurant: Quick and reasonable.
Zaoh Restaurant: Intimate, great food.

Bill Maher, San Francisco Board of Supervisors
Bella Vista*, Woodside: Good food, great views.
La Triviata
North Beach Restaurant*: Great pasta
Tommy Toy's*
Washington Square Bar & Grill*: Great atmosphere

Charlotte "Tex" Mailliard, San Francisco's chief of protocol
Balboa Cafe*
Fleur de Lys*
L'Etoile*
Trader Vic's*
Washington Square Bar & Grill*

Fritz Maytag, proprietor, Anchor Brewing Company
Harris'*
Harry's Bar & American Grill*
Perry's, Mill Valley
Le Castel*
Stoyonof's, Corte Madera

Gerald Nachman, columnist, San Francisco *Chronicle*
Cafe for All Seasons: Yuppie fare, but hearty, good portions and a jolly place; inventive dishes and superb brunches.
Hick'ry Pit, Oakland: It's a "honky barbecue" but even the Blacks like the meaty ribs, pies and sauces. A bit mild for some. Best all-around ribs place, bite for bite, in the Bay Area.

La Traviata: The now-hard-to-find cozy little romantic Italian place; untrendy Italian, nice waiters, great basic pasta; great prices and atmosphere.

Nate's, Burlingame: Easily the best New York style Jewish deli in the Bay Area.

Sam's Grill*: Old San Francisco, totally unpretentious; fast service, good food, reasonable prices.

James A. Nassikas, president, Stanford Court

Harris'*: Superior quality beef in a comfortable, club-like atmosphere.

La Pergola Ristorante*: Northern Italian cuisine; small, intimate, chef-owned.

Le Castel*: Beautifully prepared French cuisine in a Victorian house.

Mandarin: Elegant Chinese food in a stunning setting

Scott's Seafood*: Fine, fresh seafood; popular, busy.

C.V. Nevius, sports columnist, San Francisco *Chronicle*

Cafe Riggio*: Our favorite "sleeper" restaurant. Start with sauteed cheese, have a fish and a pasta, and finish with a special dessert.

Christopher's, Berkeley: Small, pleasant; good specials on wine; varied menu.

Fresh Cream, Monterey: Maybe the best food in America; thankfully, the waiters aren't snooty.

Perry's, San Francisco* and Marin: Nothing fancy, but consistently good food; pick up a hamburger, not a date.

Washington Square Bar & Grill*: Great atmosphere, terrific bar and patrons—and food, too.

Rudy Nothenberg, chief administrative officer, City and County of San Francisco

Cafe Americain: Excellent kitchen; superb desserts; always fun.

Ivy's Restaurant*: Convenient to symphony and opera; very friendly; improved kitchen.

La Mediterranee*: Extremely friendly service; good good; very reasonable.

San Benito House*, Half Moon Bay: Superb country kitchen; quiet, warm.

Stars*: Always exciting; superb kitchen; fun.

Bea Pixa, writer, San Francisco *Examiner*

Carlo's, San Rafael: Terrific pasta; a "joint" but the food is served with heart.

Circolo*: Love this place for lunch; very California menu.

Le Piano Zinc*: Outstanding French fare.

Ristorante Milano*: Innovative Italian food.

Rodin*: Superb nouvelle French food.

Robert C. Pritikin, owner-developer, the Mansion Hotel
L'Etoile*: Love the piano bar before dinner.
Cafe Majestic*
Mansion Hotel Restaurant (Editor's note: we detect a bit of prejudice here.)
Stars*: Atmosphere great.

Mary Risley, Taute Marie's Cooking School
Balboa Cafe*
Chez Panisse*, Berkeley: Great food.
Fleur de Lys*
Stars*: Great food; great place.
Taxi*

Al Rosen, president and general manager, San Francisco Giants
The Blue Fox*: Elegant dining; food and service are outstanding.
La Pergola Ristorante*: Lovely, warm, intimate; food and service excellent.
Mulhern's: Lively, brassy, excellent food and service; an air of excitement.
Tadich Grill*: Best seafood in town; the wait is worth it.
Trader Vic's*: Service and food outstanding.

Joan Ryan, sports writer, San Francisco *Examiner*
Butler's*, Mill Valley: Unusual cuisine; good service.
Cafe Mozart: The best in SF; most romantic; perfect service and delicious food.
L'Escargot*: Consistent, great service, romantic.
Little City Antipasti Bar*: Variety, outrageous pasta, fun atmosphere.
The Mandarin: Great Peking duck.

Milton Salkind, president, San Francisco Conservatory of Music
Hong Kong Seafood (on Noriega): Favorite spot for Conservatory people to go to lunch; great dim sum.
Jackson Fillmore Trattoria: My favorite San Francisco restaurant.
Julie's Supper Club*: Great food; good place to take out-of-towners.
Le Piano Zinc*: Beautiful restaurant; fine food.
Zuni Cafe*: Perfect for Saturday lunch.

Carol Ruth Silver, San Francisco Board of Supervisors
Empress of China*
Harry's Bar and American Grill*
Hong Kong Cafe
Hunan Best (Golden Gate)
Stars*

Carter B. Smith, "Magic 61" KFRC
Greens*: In spite of its being "trendy" and "in," great food and a super view. Fort Mason is an important resource for the city.
Hunan* (Sansome): For those whose taste buds are blown by years of over-indulgence, this hot food will cut through anyone's dulled palate.
Monroe's: Elegance on Lombard Street? Yes.

Strange de Jim, mysterious contributor to Herb Caen's Column
China Court: Try the China Court chicken.
Gladwyns: International cuisine.
Orchid's*: Budget gourmet Chinese lunch.
Patio Cafe*: For the brunch bunch.
Left Coast Cafe: Julia Child would smack her very lips.

Martin Swig, owner-developer, San Francisco Auto Center
Ciao*: Milanese at its best.
Harry's Bar and American Grill: More great Italian food.
Il Fornaio, Corte Madera: The best Italian (in Marin)
Prego: Great Italian
Vanessi's: Friendly; great kitchen visible from counter seats.

Russ (The Moose) Syracuse, "Magic 61" KFRC
Harry's Bar and American Grill*
Scott's Seafood on Lombard*
Tommaso Famous Pizzeria*
Trattoria Contadina*
Vanessi's

Allan Temko, architectural critic, San Francisco *Chronicle*
Donatello*: The most classic cuisine; the most professional operators.
Christopher's, Berkeley: Our favorite neighborhood restaurant; wonderful when Christopher himself cooks; spotty otherwise.
Plearn, Berkeley: Fine, modestly-priced cuisine in a beautiful high-ceilinged room.
South Park Cafe-Restaurant*: Perfect modest French ambiance; sound, sensitive French cooking.
Square One* and Caffe Quatro: Very inventive; the Caffe is a great bargain. (Editor's note: Quatro is a lunchtime-only cafe at Square One.)

Anthony S. Tiano, president, KQED Channel 9
Prego
Yoshida-Ya
World Trade Club

Stephen Zellerbach, Zellerbach Vineyard
Cafe Mozart: Excellent French food; charming and warm setting.
Harris*': Best beef in town; well prepared.

Jacob Horner, Healdsburg: Unusual ever-changing menu; first rate food and a good wine list.
Monroe's: Classic cuisine; comfortable, good service.
Rodin*: Innovative French; light but satisfying.

Mel and Patricia Ziegler, founders of Banana Republic
Cactus Cafe, Mill Valley: A real Mexican joint run, of course, by gringos.
Island Cafe, Corte Madera: Spectacular salads and natural foods.
Olivetto, Oakland: Original Mediterranean fare, very imaginative.
Taxi*: Best restaurant south of Market.

Chapter Four
THE PROFESSIONALS' PICKS
Favorite cafes of celebrity chefs and restaurateurs

We were curious for our celebrity chef and restaurant executive ballots to start coming in. Who is better qualified to suggest restaurants than those who have made names for themselves in the dining business?

And what sorts of places did they choose? Quite often, our survey indicated, they choose one another's. In some instances, they literally (but probably accidentally) swap favorite places. F'rinstance, Barbara Tropp of China Moon listed Zuni Cafe as one of her five favorites. And Zuni's Vince Calcagno listed China Moon.

As with our VIP listings, the chef/restaurateur choices are shown in alphabetical order with no preference indicated within their lists. Their choices that appear up front in our book are marked with asterisks. And again, these are casual favorites, not endorsements.

Enrico Banducci, proprietor, Enrico's
Amelio's*: Italian "classico."
Fleur de Lys*: Very much the standards of olden days.
Romano's: An Italian "sleeper."
Stars*: Great food, businesslike atmosphere
Tommy Toy's*: Chinese with a modern twist.

Chef Paul Bermani, Doros Restaurant
Campton Place*: Excellent service, superb ambiance.
Carnelian Room*: Can't beat the view; outstanding service.
Fournou's Ovens*: Quality food preparation.
Julius' Castle*: Gorgeous view; friendly atmosphere
101 California: Trendy; excellent food.

Robert Buich, co-owner, Tadich Grill
Cafe Riggio*: Good Italian food, service and ambiance.
Gazziaro's: Great financial district lunch spot.
Gelco's*: Great lamb.
House of Prime Rib: New owner really does a fine job.
Le Marquis, Lafayette: French cuisine; nice atmosphere.

Vince Calcagno, proprietor, Zuni Cafe
Chez Panisse*, Berkeley: Always consistently good fine cooks and foods.
China Moon*: Great flavors; counter service a plus.
Square One*: Food always seems nourishing and excellent.
Stars*: The definitive Big City restaurant; bustling, exciting and great food.
Zola's*: Savory food; personal touches are very satisfying.

Vince & Dirk Correnti, Trattoria Contadina
Chic's Restaurant: Good food, well-run.
Cliff House*: Great brunch.
Chez Michel: Great French food.
Joe La CoCo's, Greenbrae: Good Italian food.
Mao's Palace, Millbrae: Very good Chinese food.

M. Laurance de Vries, restaurants manager, Ramada Renaissance
Hunan Homes*: Taiwanese specialties.
Little City Antipasti Bar*: Great food and atmosphere.
Mon Kiang*: Best Hakka cuisine.
Taiwan Restaurant: Taiwanese specialties.
Yun Nan*: Best northern Chinese.

Don A. Dianda, owner, Doros Restaurant
Campton Place*: Food and ambiance outstanding.
Del Boffo, Palo Alto: Excellent Northern Italian food.
La Felce*: Moderate prices; good, wholesome food.
Salutos, Burlingame: Excellent seafood.
Yamato: Best example of classic Japanese food.

Stanley Eichelbaum and **Tom Marshall**, co-owners, Cafe Majestic

Auberge du Soleil*, Rutherford: Best view in Napa Valley; great French cafe feeling.
Balboa Cafe*: Great lite fare; good salads.
Casa Madrona*, Sausalito: Romantic; good food; imaginative.
Fleur de Lys*: Very elegant; very expensive.
Matsuri Sushi: Clean; good quality sushi.

Chef Gabriel Elicethe, the Carnelian Room

Auberge du Soleil*, Rutherford
Brasserie Chambord
Fleur de Lys*
L'Etoile*
L'Olivier*

Guy Francoz, co-owner, L'Olivier

Ciao*: Pasta; Italian fun.
Le Piano Zinc*: Elegant casual atmosphere.
L'Entrecote de Paris: For salad, steak, fries.
Magic Flute: Comfortable dining, away from downtown.
Tommy Toy's*: Excellent food, superb service.

Chef-proprietor Joyce Goldstein, Square One

China Moon*: Good food.
Khan Toke Thai House*: Great Thai food.
Tong Kiang on Geary: Excellent Chinese food.
Zola's*: Good food, nice environment, good service.
Zuni Cafe*: Good food, but sometimes terrible service.

Marvin Israel, general manager, Carnelian Room

China Moon*: Brilliant.
Golden Turtle*: Great Vietnamese.
Le Piano Zinc*
Lupann: Excellent neighborhood restaurant.
Zuni Cafe*: Consistently excellent food and service.

Rich Jones, general manager, Greens

Chez Panisse*: Excellent food and atmosphere.
Masa's*: Excellent food.
Ratto's, Oakland: Best deli.
Ricardo's, San Anselmo: Great wines and inexpensive food.
Yuet Lee*: Best Chinese

Jacques Kadik, manager, Julius' Castle

Iron Horse*: Great contemporary Italian cuisine.
Izzy's: Great steaks.
New Joe's*: Great traditional San Francisco Italian cuisine.
The Shadows*: Great contemporary French cuisine.
Tommy's Joynt*: Great sandwiches and beer.

Chef Herve Lebiavant, Squire Restaurant, Fairmont Hotel
Amelio's Restaurant*: Continental: mixed French and Italian with Vietnamese.
Buca Giovanni: Authentic Italian country cuisine.
Fleur de Lys*: The best French restaurant in northern California.
Garden House: Vietnamese: Quality and price; the best in the city.
Tokyo Sukiyaki*: Japanese: Excellent sushi, sashimi.

Chef Nin-Fat Lo, Harbor Village Restaurant
Canton Tea House
Hing Lung Restaurant
Hong Kong Flower Lounge*, Millbrae
Hong Kong East Restaurant, Emeryville
Mao's Palace, San Carlos

Mary Etta Moose, co-proprietor, Washington Square Bar & Grill
Fleur de Lys*: Best food, all around classical, fine cooking; excellent service.
Monroe's: Food is good; room is very warmly cordial and comfortable. Unrushed, good service.
Yamato: Order through the owner (Joe), and you can get excellent Japanese delicacies. It's all there.
Cafe Majestic*: Excellent food, atmosphere and service.
Greens*: Healthy, flavorful food.

Chef Bradley Ogden, Campton Place
Casa Madrona*, Sausalito
Pat O'Shea's Mad Hatter
Square One*
Stars*
Zola's*

Nick Peyton, manager, Squire Restaurant, The Fairmont
Kuleto's*: Great ambiance and inexpensive.
Masa's*: Simply the best and most extravagant.
Rosalie's*: Adventuresome ambience and food.
Rue Lepic*: Cute and inexpensive.
Zola's*: Lovely clean flavors and presentations.

Chef Joel Rambaud, Victor's at the Westin St. Francis
Alejandro's*: Next to a trip to Spain, this is the only alternative.
Fleur de Lys*: Without doubt, the best, innovative, pure French cooking.
Janot's*: What French bistros are all about, and much more for the value.
L'Hermitage, Los Angeles: It has been the who's who restaurant for the past ten years; unsurpassed quality of food.

Square One*: Anyone who can prepare so many different varieties of food at such quality deserves a bow.

Jack P. Redinger, proprietor, Jack's Restaurant

Alexis*
Cafe Majestic*
Harris'*
Le Cyrano
Trader Vic's*

Claude Rouas, co-proprietor, L'Etoile

Balboa Cafe*: Good food, but mostly a fun place.
Fleur de Lys*: Top French cuisine in the city.
L'Entrecote de Paris: For a great *entrecote* and *sommes frites*.
Milano Restaurant: Great Italian food.
Stars*: Good food; a real brasserie.

Rahim Talai, proprietor, Elite Cafe

Campton Place*: Atmosphere great.
Donatello*: Great food and service.
Fleur de Lys*: Food presentation, quality, service and chef "number one."
Harris'*: Great food but snobby staff: too bad!
Harry's Bar (on Fillmore): Great cheeseburgers and fries.

Tommy Toy, proprietor, Tommy Toy's

Ernie's*: A complete, elegant restaurant.
Fleur de Lys*: The chef has a lot of imagination.
L'Etoile*: A great, traditional French restaurant.
Sherman House: A truly plush hotel and restaurant.
Trader Vic's*: An all-time reliable restaurant.

Chef-owner Barbara Tropp, China Moon Cafe

Chez Panisse*, Berkeley: Always good to wonderful light, fresh food in a happy, artful environment.
Jackson Fillmore Trattoria: My neighborhood Italian restaurant.
Vicolo Pizzeria*: Excellent salads, delicious fresh pizzas with hearty crusts.
Zuni Cafe*: Ditto as in Chez Panisse.

Patricia Unterman, co-owner, Hayes Street Grill and restaurant critic:

Caffe Roma: My son likes the strawberry ice cream; my husband likes the murals. I like Sergio, the owner.
Chez Panisse* and Cafe at Chez Panisse, Berkeley: It feels like home!
Vicolo Pizzeria*: It's mine, but I love the salads.
Yuet Lee*: I'm addicted to the fried squid.
Zuni Cafe*: Excellent, but sometimes the service can be very aggravating!

Pierre Vendroux, restaurants manager, Westin St. Francis

Baccarat, Redwood Shores: Beautiful brunch.

Benihana, Burlingame: Good food and excellent cooking show.

Gulliver's, Burlingame: Best prime rib.

Iron Gate*, Belmont: Good food and friendly service.

Pine Brook Inn*, Belmont: Excellent German food.

Chapter Five
THE BEST OF THE FINEST
The Bay Area's highest rated restaurants

When we sent out survey forms, we asked our guest epicures to assign numerical values to food, service and ambiance, with ten as a perfect score. From this, just for the fun of it, we've compiled lists of the highest scoring restaurants.

It's unrealistic to pit a tiny bistro with an excellent kitchen against the multi-million-dollar opulence of a first class French restaurant. Ambiance and service are part of a memorable dining experience, but so are sensational food and bargain prices.

So we've select the ten highest-rated places in each of four price ranges. That way, we're not comparing a *longe d'agneau a l'essence d'estragon* with a lamb chop in tarragon sauce. Restaurants are listed in order of finish. Prices indicate a normal meal with entree, veggies and soup or salad, not including wine or dessert.

THE TOP TEN EXPENSIVE RESTAURANTS ($30 and up)

1. DONATELLO, 501 Post (Donatello Hotel), 441-7182
2. AMELIO'S, 1630 Powell (Union), 397-4339
3. CAMPTON PLACE, 340 Stockton (Campton Place Hotel), 781-5555
4. FLEUR DE LYS, 777 Sutter (Jones), 673-7779
5. SQUIRE ROOM, 950 Mason (Fairmont Hotel), 772-5211
6. TOMMY TOY'S, 655 Montgomery (Washington), 397-4888
7. VICTOR'S, 335 Powell (Westin St. Francis), 774-0253
8. CARNELIAN ROOM, 555 Montgomery (Bank of America), 433-7500
9. PIERRE-AT-MERIDIEN, 50 Third (Hotel Meridien), 974-6400
10. CASA MADRONA, 801 Bridgeway, Sausalito, 332-0502

THE TOP TEN MODERATELY EXPENSIVE RESTAURANTS ($20 TO $29)

1. CHATEAU SUZANNE, 1449 Lombard (Van Ness Avenue), 771-9326
2. REGINA'S, 490 Geary (St. Regis Hotel), 885-1661
3. LE CASTEL, 3235 Sacramento (Presidio Avenue), 921-7115
4. JACK'S RESTAURANT, 615 Sacramento (Montgomery), 986-9854
5. BARBAROSSA, 3003 El Camino Real, Redwood City, 369-2626

6. GAYLORD INDIA RESTAURANT, Ghirardelli Square, 771-8822
7. LAS MANANITAS, 850 Montgomery (Pacific Avenue), 434-2088
8. CHRISTOPHE, 320 Mason (Geary), 433-7560
9. SQUARE ONE, 190 Pacific Avenue (Front), 788-1110
10. HARRIS', 2100 Van Ness Avenue (Pacific Avenue), 673-1888

THE TOP TEN MODERATELY-PRICED RESTAURANTS ($10 to $19)

1. JOVANELLO'S, 840 Sansome (Pacific Avenue), 986-8050
2. KHAN TOKE THAI HOUSE, 5937 Geary Blvd. (24th Ave.), 668-6654
3. DAKOTA GRILL, 2086 Allston Way (Shattuck Hotel), Berkeley, 841-3848
4. TADICH GRILL, 240 California (Front), 391-2373
5. ZOLA'S, 1722 Sacramento (Van Ness Avenue), 775- 3311
6. FIRENZE RESTAURANT, 1421 Stockton (Vallejo), 421-5813
7. KULETO'S ITALIAN RESTAURANT, 221 Powell (Geary), 397-7720
8. RINGS, 1131 Folsom (Eighth), 621-2111
9. BEETHOVEN, 1701 Powell (Union), 391-4488
10. LA PERGOLA RISTORANTE, 2060 Chestnut (Gough), 563-4500

THE TOP TEN INEXPENSIVE RESTAURANTS (less than $10)

1. PISCES SEAFOOD, 2127 Polk (Broadway), 771-0850
2. MANORA'S THAI RESTAURANT, 3226 Mission (Valencia), 550-0856
3. VICOLO PIZZERIA, 201 Ivy (Franklin), 863-2382; 900 Ghirardelli Square (900 North Point), 776-1331
4. MAYKADEH, 470 Green (Grant), 362-8286
5. CORDON BLEU VIETNAMESE RESTAURANT, 1575 Polk (California), 673-5637
6. ORCHIDS, 215 Church (Market), 864-1601
7. MAX'S DINER, 311 Third (Folsom), 546-MAX
8. MAY SUN RESTAURANT, 1740 Fillmore (Post), 567- 7789
9. LE PETIT CAFE, 2164 Larkin (Grant), 776-5356
10. LILIES ON MASON, 542 Mason (Sutter), 391-2401

Chapter Six
EVERYBODY'S FAVORITES
Top ten lists from various panel members

We now come to the popularity contests. On our survey forms, we asked our various panel members to name their favorite restaurants, as well as reporting on recent dining experiences. Since we like to make lists and most people like to skim them, we've compiled an assortment of "Top Tens." These are the restaurants most often named as favorites by our panelists.

They differ from the picks in the previous chapter, which were compiled by averaging scores used in rating the restaurants.

OVERALL TOP TEN
(Based on nominations from all participants in the survey)

1. Stars
2. Fleur de Lys
3. Harris'
4. Trader Vic's
5. Zuni Cafe
6. Fog City Diner
7. Washington Square Bar & Grill
8. Chez Panisse, Berkeley
9. Square One
10. Balboa Cafe
    Cafe Majestic (tied for tenth)

VIPs' TOP TEN
(Bay area personalities and community leaders)

The results hardly seem fair, since many of our VIP panelists are media types, who regard the Washbag as their second home. However, several others nominated it as well. Besides, we didn't say our popularity poll was fair; we only said it was fun to make lists.

1. Washington Square Bar & Grill
2. Stars
3. Trader Vic's
4. Butler's, Mill Valley
   Harris
   L'Etoile (three tied)
7. Fleur de Lys
   Harry's Bar
   Jack's
   Kuleto's (four tied)

CELEBRITY CHEFS AND RESTAURANT EXECUTIVES' TOP TEN

Now, if we were in the restaurant business, this is the list we'd *really* want to be on. (With few voters, we had several ties.

1. Fleur de Lys
2. Stars
   Zola's
   Zuni Cafe (three tied)
5. Balboa Cafe
   Chez Panisse, Berkeley
   China Moon
   Square One (four tied)
9. Auberge du Soleil, Rutherford
   Campton Place
   Casa Madrona, Sausalito
   Harris'
   Le Piano Zinc
   L'Entrecote de Paris
   L'Etoile
   Tommy Toy's
   Trader Vic's (eight tied)

RESTAURANT FOLKS' TOP TEN

(Panelists involved in various phases of the dining trade)

1. Fleur de Lys
   Stars (tied for first)
3. Zuni Cafe
4. Chez Panisse, Berkeley
5. Harris'
6. Zolas
7. Balboa Cafe
8. Campton Place
9. Auberge du Soleil, Rutherford
10. Cafe Majestic

BARTENDERS' TOP TEN

1. Fog City Diner
2. Gelco's
3. Beethoven
4. Zuni Cafe
5. Little City Antipasti Bar
6. Maykadeh
7. I Fratelli
8. Harris
9. L'Escargot
10. Vicolo Pizzeria

CABBIES' TOP TEN

(Also includes rental car agencies and tour bus operators)

1. Original Joe's
2. Alfred's
3. Gaylord
4. Tadich Grill
5. Zuni Cafe
6. Alejandro's
7. Scoma's
8. Beethoven
9. Neptune's
10. Fior d'Italia

CIVILIANS' TOP TEN

(Panelists not connected with the cafe, hotel or visitor trades)

1. Stars
2. Trader Vic's
3. Harris'
4. Fleur de Lys
5. Harry's Bar & American Grill
6. Kuleto's
7. Modesto Lanzone's
8. Cafe Majestic
9. Hayes Street Grill
10. Le Piano Zinc

Chapter Seven
DINING VARIETY
The selected restaurants listed by type

AMERICAN
(including California nouvelle)

Act IV (California French)
Avenue Grill, Mill Valley (American)
Bakers Square (American diner)
Balboa Cafe (California nouvelle)
Bay Wolf Cafe & Restaurant, Oakland (California/Mediterranean)
The Big Four (American/Continental)
The Billboard Cafe (Funky nouvelle)
Bill's Place (American, mostly hamburgers)
Bon Temps Louisiana Restaurant (Cajun/Creole)
Broadway Terrace Cafe, Oakland (California grill)
Bull's Texas Cafe (Texas Barbecue/Tex-Mex)
Butler's, Mill Valley ((American nouvelle)
Cafe d' Arts (California/Mediterranean)
Cafe Majestic (California nouvelle)
California Cafe, Walnut Creek (American nouvelle)
California Cafe Bar & Grill (American nouvelle)
Campton Place (American nouvelle)
Casa Madrona, Sausalito (American nouvelle)
The Castaways, San Mateo (American)
Cendrillon (American nouvelle)
The Chart House, Sausalito (American/seafood)
Chez Panisse, Berkeley (California nouvelle)
China Moon Cafe (California/Chinese)
Clement Street Bar and Grill (California nouvelle)
Cliff House Seafood and Beverage Co. (American)
Corona Bar & Grill (Southwestern/Mexican)
Cruchon's, Walnut Creek (American)
The Cultured Salad (salads and soups)
Dakota Grill and Bar, Berkeley (Southwestern)
Doidge's Kitchen (American)
Duffy's Tavern (American/Italian)
Eddie Jack's (California nouvelle)
El Dorado Inn, Sonoma (California nouvelle)
Enrico's Restaurant (American/Continental)
Equinox (American/Continental)

Faz (California nouvelle)
565 Clay Restaurant (American regional)
Fog City Diner (American regional)
Fontana's (American/Italian)
The Galleon Bar and Restaurant (American/Italian)
The Garden Court, Sheraton Palace (American/Continental)
Garibaldi Cafe (California nouvelle)
Greens at Fort Mason (vegetarian)
Grubstake II (American diner)
Hamburger Mary's (American, mostly hamburgers)
Hard Rock Cafe (American)
Harris' (American, mostly steak)
Harvey's Main Stem (haufbrau)
Hayes Garden Cafe (American/Continental)
The Hillcrest Bar and Cafe (American regional)
The Holding Company (American)
Hornblower Dining Cruises (American/Continental)
Hot and Hunky (American, mostly hamburgers)
House of Prime Rib (American, mostly beef)
Ironwood Cafe (American)
It's Tops Coffee Shop (American diner)
Ivy's Restaurant (California/American)
Jil's Restaurant (American/Continental)
Judy's Restaurant (American)
Julie's Supper Club (American regional)
Kuleto's (California/Italian)
Le Petit Cafe (American)
Lehr's Greenhouse Restaurant and Florist (American)
Lilies on Mason (American)
Little City Antipasti Bar (American/Italian)
Mama's (American)
Max's Diner (American diner)
Max's Opera Cafe (American deli)
Max's Opera Cafe, Burlingame (American deli)
Maxwell's Plum (American/Continental)
Mel's Drive-in (American diner)
The Melting Pot (American)
Miyako Hotel Restaurant (Japanese/American)
Mustards Grill (American grill)
New Joe's at Union Square (Italian/American)
Original Joe's (Italian/American)
Pastaria (American/Continental)
Perry's (American)
Phil Lehr's Steakery (American, mostly steaks)
Portman Grill (California/Continental)
Regina's (Creole/French)
Rings (California nouvelle)
Rosalie's Restaurant (American regional)

The Rotunda at Neiman-Marcus (American/California)
Rusty Scupper (American)
Ryan's (California nouvelle)
Sam's Grill and Seafood Restaurant (American)
San Benito House (American nouvelle)
San Francisco Brewing Company (pub fare)
Savannah Grill, Corte Madera (American regional)
Seal Rock Inn (American, most omelets)
Skates, Berkeley (American regional)
Sparky's (American diner)
Square One (American/Mediterranean)
Stars (American Regional)
Suisse Italia (American deli)
Sutter Garden (American/Continental)
Tadich Grill (American, mostly seafood)
Taxi (California nouvelle)
Teddy's (California nouvelle)
Tommy's Joint (haufbrau)
Victor's (California nouvelle)
What's Your Beef? (hamburgers)
White Elephant Restaurant (American/Continental)
White Horse Taverne (American/Continental)
Zephyr (American)
Zuni Cafe (California/Mediterranean)

CHINESE

Brandy Ho's (Hunan)
China Moon Cafe (California/Chinese/dim sum)
Empress of China (mostly Cantonese)
Four Seas (mostly Cantonese)
Hang Ah Tea Room (Chinese/dim sum)
Happy Valley Restaurant (Cantonese/Mandarin)
Harbor Village (Chinese/dim sum)
Hong Kong Flower Lounge, Millbrae (Cantonese)
Hunan (Hunan/northern Chinese)
Hunan, Oakland (northern Chinese)
Hunan Home's (Hunan/Taiwanese)
Jackson Cafe (Chinese/American)
Kan's Chinese Restaurant (Cantonese)
Kum Moon (Cantonese)
May Sun (Mandarin/teriyaki)
Mon Kiang (Hakka)
Narai Restaurant (Thai/Chinese)
New Ocean (Cantonese)
Ocean (Cantonese)
Ocean City (Chinese/dim sum)
Raffles (Polynesian/Chinese)
San Wang (northern Chinese)

Tai Chi (northern Chinese)
Tien Fu (northern Chinese/Cantonese)
Tommy Toy's (Chinese/French)
Yank Sing (dim sum)
Yuet Lee (Chinese seafood)
Yun Nan (northern Chinese)

CONTINENTAL/EUROPEAN
(French and Italian are listed separately)

Alexis (Continental/French)
Alpine Inn, Burlingame (European)
Amelio's Restaurant (Continental/French)
Beethoven (German)
Bella Vista, Woodside
The Big Four (American/Continental)
The Blue Fox
The Carnelian Room
Chateau Suzanne
Compass Rose (Continental/Oriental)
Des Alpes (Basque)
Doros
English Grill (Continental/seafood)
Enrico's (American/Continental)
Equinox (American/Continental)
Fournou's Ovens
Gelco's (Yugoslavian, lamb specialties)
Hayes Garden Cafe (American/Continental)
Hornblower Dining Cruises (American/Continental)
Iron Gate Restaurant (Italian/Continental)
Jack's Restaurant (French/Continental)
Jil's Restaurant (American/Continental)
John's Grill
Julius' Castle
Lark Creek Inn, Larkspur
La Mediterranee (Mediterranean)
Maxwell's Plum (American/Continental)
The Moonraker, Pacifica
One-Up
Panos' Restaurant (Mediterranean/seafood)
Pastaria (American/Continental)
Phil Lehr's Steakery (steaks/Continental)
Pine Brook Inn, Belmont (German/American)
Schroeder's Cafe (German/Bavarian)
Square One Restaurant (American/Mediterranean)
Squire Room
Sutter Garden (American/Continental)
The Swedish Place, Half Moon Bay (Scandinavian)
Trader Vic's (Oriental/Continental)

Vlasta's (Czechoslovakian/German/Hungarian)
The Waterfront (Seafood/Continental)
White Elephant Restaurant (American/Continental)
Zola's (contemporary Mediterranean)
Zuni Cafe (California/Mediterranean

FRENCH

Adriatic (seafood/French)
Alexis (French/Continental)
Amelio's Restaurant (French/Continental)
Auberge du Soleil, Rutherford (French nouvelle)
Barbarossa Restaurant, Redwood City
Christophe
Domaine Chandon, Yountville (French/California
Ernie's Restaurant
Fleur de Lys
Jack's Restaurant (French/Continental)
Janot
La Mere Duquesne
Le Castel
Le Domino
Le Piano Zinc
L'Escargot
L'Etoile
L'Olivier
Les Arcades, Sonoma
Masa's
Pierre-at-Meridien
Rodin
Rue Lepic
The Shadows
South Park Cafe (French bistro)
Thornhill Cafe, Oakland (French/Thai)
231 Ellsworth, San Mateo
Tourelle Cafe and Restaurant, Lafayette

INDIA AND MIDDLE EAST

Bombay Palace (Northern Indian)
Gaylord India Restaurant (Northern Indian)
The Grapeleaf (Lebanese)
Maharaja, San Bruno (Northern Indian)
Mamounia (Moroccan)
Maykadeh (Persian)

ITALIAN (and pizza parlors)

Adolph's
Alioto's Restaurant (seafood/Italian)
Allegro
Bardelli's Restaurant (Italian/Continental)

Basta Pasta (Italian/seafood)
Caesar's
Cafe Riggio
Caffe Sport (southern Italian)
Calzone's Pizza Cucina (pizza, pasta)
Circolo
De Sandro
Donatello (northern Italian)
Duffy's Tavern (American/Italian)
E'Angelo Restaurant (northern Italian)
Enzo's
Ernesto's Restaurant
Festa Festa Festa (Italian buffet)
Fettucini Brothers (pastas and salads)
Fior d'Italia
Firenze Restaurant
Fontana's, Menlo Park (California/Italian)
Freddie's Pizza, Lafayette (pizza/pastas)
The Galleon Bar and Restaurant (American/Italian)
Harry's Bar and American Grill
I Fratelli, I Fratelli North
Il Pirata
Il Pollaio (Italian/Argentinian)
Iron Gate, Belmont (Italian/Continental)
Iron Pot
Jovanelo's (northern Italian)
Kuleto's (California/Italian)
La Felce
La Pergola Ristorante (northern Italian)
Little Henry's
Marina Cafe (Italian/seafood)
Modesto Lanzone's (northern Italian)
New Joe's at Union Square (American/Italian)
New Pisa
North Beach Restaurant
Original Joe's (Italian/American)
Pasta II
Pietro's Ristorante
RAF Centrogriglia (northern Italian)
Ristorante Grifone
Ristorante Milano (northern Italian)
Ruby's Gourmet Pizza (pizza)
Sorrento's, Walnut Creek
Tommaso (pizza, calzone)
Trattoria Contadina
Tre Fratelli
U.S. Restaurant (Italian/American)
Vicolo Pizzeria (pizza)

Villa d'Este

JAPANESE

Goemon Japanese Restaurant
Isobune Sushi Restaurant (sushi)
Kamon
May Sun Restaurant (teriyaki/Mandarin)
Mifune
Miyako Hotel Restaurant (Japanese/American)
Nippon Sushi (sushi)
Osome Restaurant
Sushi on the Rock (sushi)
Ten-Ichi Restaurant
Tokyo Sukiyaki

MEXICAN
(and other Latin)

Alejandro's Sociedad Gastronimica (Latin mix)
Bull's Texas Cafe (Tex-Mex)
Cadillac Bar & Grill (Mexican/seafood)
Carlos Goldstein's (Gringo Mexican)
Compadres Mexican Bar & Grill (Mexican/American)
Corona Bar & Grill (Mexican/Southwestern)
El Sombrero
El Tazumal Restaurant (Mexican/Salvadorean)
El Toreador Fonda Mejicana
Guaymas Restaurant, Tiburon (contemporary Mexican)
Juan's Place, Berkeley
La Barca
La Fuente
La Posada
La Victoria (Mexican/Spanish)
Las Mananitas
Roosevelt Tamale Parlor
Tia Margarita

SEAFOOD

A. Sabella's
Adriatic (seafood/French)
Alioto's Seafood Restaurant
Cadillac Bar and Grill (Mexican/seafood)
Cafe San Marcos (Cajun/seafood)
The Elite Cafe (Cajun/Creole/seafood)
English Grill (Continental/seafood)
Gertie's Chesapeake Bay Cafe, Berkeley
Hayes Street Grill
Marina Cafe (Italian/seafood)
Maye's Steak and Oyster House (Seafood/Italian)

Neptune's Palace
Old Clam House
Pacific Cafe
Pacific Cafe, Concord
Pacific Cafe, South San Francisco
Pacific Heights Bar and Grill (seafood/oyster bar)
Pisces Seafood Restaurant
PJ's Oyster Bed (seafood/oyster bar)
Sam's Anchor Cafe, Tiburon
Scoma's
Scott's Seafood
Spenger's Fish Grotto, Berkeley
Tadich Grill (American/seafood)
Vannelli's Fresh Seafood
The Waterfront (seafood/Continental)
Yuet Lee (Chinese seafood)

SOUTHEAST ASIAN
(and other Oriental)

Angkor Wat (Cambodian)
Bankok Express (Thai)
Cordon Bleu (Vietnamese)
Emerald Garden (Vietnamese)
Golden Turtle (Vietnamese)
Khan Toke Thai House (Thai)
Mandalay Restaurant (Burmese)
Manora's Thai Restaurant (Thai)
Narai Restaurant (Thai/Chinese)
The Rice Table, San Rafael (Indonesian)
San Francisco Bar-B-Q (Thai barbecue)
Sorobol, Oakland (Korean)
Thai Garden (Thai)
Thep-Phanom Restaurant (Thai)
Tu Lan (Vietnamese)

Chapter Eight
WHAT PRICE GUMBO?
Budget restaurants and early-bird specials

ECONOMY RESTAURANTS

To assist you when you're caught between paydays and tired of raiding the refrigerator, here's a list of selected restaurants that can offer you a full meal for under $10.

BAKER'S SQUARE, 2353 Lombard (Scott), American diner
BANKOK EXPRESS, 907 Irving (10th Avenue), Thai
THE BILLBOARD CAFE, 299 Ninth (Folsom), funky nouvelle
BILL'S PLACE, 2315 Clement (24th Avenue), hamburgers
BRANDY HO'S, 217 Columbus Avenue (Pacific), Hunan
BULL'S TEXAS CAFE, 25 Van Ness (Market), Tex-Mex
CAFFE SPORT, 574 Green (Front), southern Italian
CARLOS GOLDSTEIN'S, 282 O'Farrell (Mason), Gringo Mexican
CHA CHA CHA, 1805 Haight (Shrader), Caribbean
CORDON BLEU, 1574 California (Polk), Vietnamese
CRUCHON'S, 2599 North Main, Walnut Creek, American
THE CULTURED SALAD, #3 Embarcadero Center, salads/soups
DES ALPES, 732 Broadway (Stockton), family-style Basque
DUFFY'S TAVERN, 451 Pine (Montgomery), American/Italian
EL SOMBRERO, 5800 Geary Blvd. (22nd Avenue), Mexican
EL TAZUMAL, 3522 20th (Mission), Mexican/Salvadorean
EL TOREADOR, 50 West Portal (Vicente), Mexican
EMERALD GARDEN, 1550 California (Larkin), Vietnamese
FESTA FESTA FESTA, 532 Columbus (Green), Italian buffet
FETTUCINI BROTHERS, 2100 Larkin (Vallejo), pastas/salads
FOUR SEAS, 731 Grant Avenue (Sacramento), Chinese
GRUBSTAKE II, 1525 Pine (Polk), American
HAMBURGER MARY'S, 1582 Folsom (12th)
HANG AH TEA ROOM, #1 Pagoda Place (Sacramento), Chinese/dim sum
HAPPY VALLEY RESTAURANT, 2346 Lombard (Scott), Chinese
HARD ROCK CAFE, 1699 Van Ness (Sacramento), American
HARVEY'S MAIN STEM, #2 Turk (Market), haufbrau

HOT AND HUNKY, 4039 18th (Noe)
1946 Market (Duboce), hamburgers
IL PIRATA, 2007 16th (Potrero), Italian
IL POLLAIO, 555 Columbus Avenue (Union), Italian
IT'S TOPS COFFEE SHOP, 1801 Market (McCoppin), American
JACKSON CAFE, 640 Jackson (Kearny), Chinese
JUAN'S PLACE, 941 Carlton, Berkeley, Mexican
JUDY'S RESTAURANT, 2268 Chestnut (Scott), American
KAMON, 1655 Market (Gough), Japanese
KUM MOON, 2019 Clement (22nd Avenue), Chinese
LA BARCA, 2036 Lombard (Fillmore), Mexican
LA MEDITERRANEE, 2210 Fillmore (Sacramento)
288 Noe (24th), Mideastern
LA POSADA, 2298 Fillmore (Clay), Mexican
LA VICTORIA, 1205 Alabama (24th), Mexican/Spanish
LE PETIT CAFE, 2164 Larkin (Green), American
LILIES ON MASON, 542 Mason (Sutter), American
LITTLE HENRY'S, 955 Larkin (Post), Italian
MANDALAY, 4344 California (Sixth Ave.), Burmese
MANORA'S THAI RESTAURANT, 3226 Mission (Valencia), Thai
MAX'S DINER, 311 Third (Folsom), American
MAY SUN, 1740 Fillmore (Post), Mandarin/teriyaki
MAYKADEH, 470 Green (Grant), Persian
MEL'S DRIVE-IN, 2165 Lombard (Fillmore)
3355 Geary Boulevard (Parker), American
MIFUNE, 1737 Post (Japan Center), Japanese
MON KIANG, 683 Broadway (Stockton), Hakka Chinese
NARAI, 2229 Clement (23rd Avenue), Thai/Chinese
NIPPON SUSHI, 314 Church (Fifteenth), sushi
ORCHID'S, 215 Church (Market), Hunan
PASTA II, 381 South Van Ness Avenue (15th), Italian
PASTARIA, 339 Taylor (O'Farrell), American
PATIO CAFE, 531 Castro (18th), American
THE RICE TABLE, 1617 Fourth (G Street), Indonesian
ROOSEVELT TAMALE PARLOR, 2817 24th (Bryant), Mexican
RUBY'S GOURMET PIZZA, 3249 Scott (Lombard), pizza
SAN FRANCISCO BREWING COMPANY, 155 Columbus (Kearny), American
SAN FRANCISCO B-B-Q, 1328 18th (Missouri), Thai barbecue
SEAL ROCK INN, 545 Point Lobos (48th Avenue), American
SPARKY'S, 242 Church (Market), American
SPENGER'S FISH GROTTO, Berkeley, seafood
SUISSE ITALIA, 101 California (Drum), American deli

SUSHI ON THE ROCK, 1475 Polk (California)
500 Broadway (Kearny), sushi
TAI CHI, 2031 Polk (Broadway), northern Chinese
TEDDY'S, 524 Sutter (Powell), California cuisine
THEP-PHANOM, 400 Waller (Fillmore), Thai
TOMMY'S JOYNT, 1101 Geary (Van Ness Avenue), haufbrau
TU LAN, #8 Sixth (Market), Vietnamese
VICOLO PIZZERIA, 201 Ivy (Franklin)
900 North Point (Ghirardelli Square), pizza
WHAT'S YOUR BEEF?, 759 Columbus Ave. (Greenwich), hamburgers
ZEPHYR, 3643 Balboa (38th Avenue), American

EARLY BIRD DINNERS

Several restaurants in our survey offer special dinner prices during the early evening hours to fill their empty tables. The happy result: you can fill your empty tummy for less. Most early bird specials are offered nightly, but some aren't available on weekends, so it's best to call ahead. And since they can be popular (which is the whole idea), make reservations.

BARDELLI'S RESTAURANT, 243 O'Farrell (Mason), 982-0243; Italian/Continental: An early bird special dinner is offered for $11.95, starting at 5 p.m.

BOMBAY PALACE, 600 Beach (in the Cannery), 776- 3666; northern Indian: Special dinners are served from 5 to 6:30 for $10.95.

CAESAR'S, 2299 Powell (Bay), 989-6000; Italian: A Tuesday-Friday dinner special from 4:30 to 6 is priced at $7.95.

THE CARNELIAN ROOM, 555 California (atop the Bank of America building), 433-7500; Continental: You can get that stunning 52nd floor panorama and the Carnelian Room's opulence with a "Sunset Dinner" from 6 to 7 p.m. for $23.

CHRISTOPHE, 320 Mason (Geary), 433-7560; French/California: A special dinner is served from 5:30 to 10:30 for $16.95, with a choice of three entrees, soup, salad and dessert.

CLEMENT STREET BAR & GRILL, 708 Clement (Eighth Avenue); California nouvelle: Entree prices drop by 15 percent from 5 to 6 p.m.

GAYLORD INDIA RESTAURANT, Ghirardelli Square (North Point); northern Indian: Full dinners are discounted around $5 from 5 to 6:30.

IRON POT, 441 Washington (Sansome), 392-2100; Italian: Early-bird hour is 4:30 to 5:30, when special dinners range from $5.75 to $7.75.

JIL'S RESTAURANT, 242 O'Farrell (Mason), 982- 9353; American/Continental: A three-course pre-theatre dinner with coffee is priced at $16.50, from 5 to 8 p.m.

LA BARCA, 2036 Lombard (Fillmore), 921-2221; Mexican: Early-bird dinners from 4 to 6 p.m. are 20 percent off regular menu prices.

MARINA CAFE, 2417 Lombard (Scott), 929-7241; Italian/seafood: A daily special is $7.95 from 4:30 to 6 p.m.; it includes an entree and soup or salad.

MAYE'S STEAK AND OYSTER HOUSE, 1233 Polk (Sutter), 474-7674; seafood/Italian: You can get a full meal for $8.25 from 3:30 to 6 p.m.; Senior Specials are $6.50 for a Saturday lunch (11:30 to 4:30) and $7.95 for Sunday and holiday dinners (2 to 4:30). Early bird and senior specials include a choice of four entrees, soup and salad.

OSOME RESTAURANT, 1923 Fillmore (Pine), 346- 2311; Japanese: A special early dinner is available, but details weren't set as we went to press.

PACIFIC CAFE, 2151 Salvio (Grant), Concord, 678- 3888; seafood: Several specials are served from 4 to 7 p.m. for $7.95, including entree, chowder and veggies.

PANOS' RESTAURANT, 4000 24th (Noe), 824-8000; Mediterranean/seafood: All entrees are discounted 20 percent nightly from 5 to 6 p.m.

PINE BROOK INN, 1015 Alameda de las Pulgas (Ralston), Belmont, 591-1735; German/American: A $9.95 special, available throughout the dinner hour Sunday through Thursday, includes entree, salad, soup, dessert and coffee.

VANELLI'S FRESH SEAFOOD, Pier 39 (The Embarcadero), 421-7261; seafood: Special dinners are priced from $8.95 to $9.95 from 4 to 6 weekdays and 3 to 6 weekends.

VICTOR'S, 335 Powell (Westin St. Francis, at Geary); 774-0253; California nouvelle: The Continental elegance of Victor's is yours for $19.50 for a three-course prix fixe dinner from 6 to 7 p.m.; the great city view from the St. Francis tower is thrown in at no extra charge.

WHITE ELEPHANT RESTAURANT, 480 Sutter (in the Holiday Inn, at Powell), 398-1331; American/Continental: A nightly special, including an entree, soup or salad, is $11.95 from 6 to 7 p.m.

Chapter Nine
MIDNIGHT DINERS
For prowling night owls: places that serve after 11 p.m.

When your tummy growl puts you on a late-night prowl, always call ahead. Late hours are very vulnerable to change; hours are usually the first thing to be trimmed when business slows. Also, some of the late-nighters listed below may be seasonal.

ACT IV, 333 Fulton (Inn at the Opera, near Franklin), 863-8400: to 1 a.m. nightly.

ADOLPH'S, 641 Vallejo (Columbus), 392-6333: Tuesday-Sunday to 11:30.

BAKERS SQUARE, 2353 Lombard (Scott), 931-1174: to 1 a.m. Friday and Saturday.

BASTA PASTA, 1268 Grant Avenue (Vallejo), 434-2248: to 2 a.m. nightly.

THE BILLBOARD CAFE, 299 Ninth (Folsom), 558-9500: to midnight Friday and Saturday.

BRANDY HO'S, 217 Columbus Avenue (Pacific), 788-7527: to midnight Friday and Saturday.

CADILLAC BAR AND GRILL, 1 Holland Court (off Howard, between Fourth and Fifth), 543-8226: to midnight Friday and Saturday.

CAFE SAN MARCOS, 2367 Market (Castro), 861-3846: nightly to midnight.

CALIFORNIA CAFE BAR & GRILL, 900 Bush (Taylor), 775-2233: to 11:30 Friday and Saturday.

CALZONE'S PIZZA CUCINA, 430 Columbus (Vallejo), 397-3600: to 1 a.m. nightly.

CIAO, 230 Jackson (Battery), 982-9500: to midnight Monday-Saturday.

CIRCOLO, 161 Sutter (off Kearny, in Crocker Galleria), 362-0404: to 11:30 nightly.

ENRICO'S RESTAURANT, 504 Broadway (Columbus), 392-6220: nightly until 3 a.m.

ERNESTO'S RESTAURANT, 2311 Clement (24th Avenue), 342-3932: to midnight Friday and Saturday.

FESTA FESTA FESTA, 532 Columbus (Green), 391-3800: nightly to midnight.

FOG CITY DINER, 1300 Battery (Greenwich), 982- 2000: to midnight Friday and Saturday.

GRUBSTAKE II, 1525 Pine (Polk), 673-8268: to 5 a.m. daily.
HAMBURGER MARY'S, 1582 Folsom (12th Street), 626-1985: until 2 a.m. nightly.
HARD ROCK CAFE, 1699 Van Ness Avenue (Sacramento), 885-1699: until 11:30 nightly.
HARRY'S BAR AND AMERICAN GRILL, 500 Van Ness Avenue (McAllister), 864-2779: to midnight Friday and Saturday.
THE HILLCREST BAR AND CAFE, 2201 Fillmore (Sacramento), 563-8400: light "pub menu" until 3 a.m. daily.
HOT AND HUNKY, 4039 18th (Noe), 621-6365: to midnight Sunday-Thursday and until 1 a.m. Friday and Saturday.
HOT AND HUNKY, 1946 Market (Duboce), 621-3622: to midnight Friday and Saturday.
IVY'S RESTAURANT, 398 Hayes (Gough), 626-3930: to 11:30 Friday and Saturday.
JULIE'S SUPPER CLUB, 1123 Folsom (Seventh), 861-4084: to midnight Friday and Saturday.
LA BARCA, 2036 Lombard (Fillmore), 921-2221: to 11:30 Friday and Saturday.
LE PIANO ZINC, 708 14th (Market and Church), 431-5266: to midnight daily except Monday.
LITTLE CITY ANTIPASTI BAR, 673 Union (Powell), 434-2900: nightly to midnight.
MAMA'S, 398 Geary (Mason), 433-0113: to 1:30 a.m. Friday and Saturday and until 12:30 a.m. Sunday to Thursday.
MARINA CAFE, 2417 Lombard (Scott), 929-7241: nightly to 11:30.
MAX'S DINER, 311 Third (Folsom), 546-MAXS: to midnight Thursday and until 1 a.m. Friday and Saturday.
MAX'S OPERA CAFE, 601 Van Ness Avenue (Golden Gate), 771-7300: to midnight Sunday-Thursday and until 1 a.m. Friday and Saturday.
MAX'S OPERA CAFE, 1250 Old Bayshore (Broadway), Burlingame, 342-MAXS: to midnight Friday-Saturday
MEL'S DRIVE-IN, 2165 Lombard (Fillmore), 921-3039; also at 3355 Geary Boulevard (Parker), 387-2244: to 1 a.m. Sunday-Thursday and to 3 a.m. Friday-Saturday.
MODESTO LANZONE'S, 601 Van Ness Avenue (in Opera Plaza, at Golden Gate Avenue), 928-0400: to midnight Saturday.
MON KIANG, 683 Broadway (Stockton), 421-2015: to midnight Friday and Saturday.
NORTH BEACH RESTAURANT, 1512 Stockton (Columbus), 392-1700: to 11:45 nightly.
ORIGINAL JOE'S, 144 Taylor (Turk), PRospect 5-4877: to 1 a.m. nightly.

PATIO CAFE, 531 Castro (18th), 621-4640: to midnight Sunday-Thursday and until 2 a.m. Friday and Saturday.

PERRY'S, 1944 Union Street (Laguna), 922-9022: nightly until midnight.

PHIL LEHR'S STEAKERY, 330 Taylor (in the Hilton Hotel, near Ellis), 673-6800: nightly until midnight.

RAF CENTROGRIGLIA, 478 Green (Grant), 362-1999: to 11:30 Friday and Saturday.

REGINA'S, 490 Geary (in the St. Regis Hotel, at Taylor), 885-1661: to midnight Sunday-Thursday and until 1 a.m. Friday and Saturday.

ROSALIE'S RESTAURANT, 1415 Van Ness Avenue (Bush), 928-7188: to 11:30 Friday and Saturday.

RUBY'S GOURMET PIZZA, 3249 Scott (Lombard), 567-4488: to 11:30 Friday and Saturday.

SKATES, 100 Seawall Drive (University Avenue), Berkeley, 549-1900: light fare until 2 a.m. nightly.

SPARKY'S, 242 Church (Market), 621-6001: the ultimate night-owl roost; it's open 24 hours.

SPENGER'S FISH GROTTO, 1919 Fourth (University Avenue), Berkeley, 845-7771: to 11:30 Friday and Saturday.

TOMMY'S JOYNT, 1101 Geary (Van Ness Avenue), 775-4216: until 2 a.m. nightly.

TRADER VIC'S, 20 Cosmo Place (between Post and Taylor), 776-2232: to 12:30 a.m. Monday-Saturday.

VICOLO PIZZERIA, 201 Ivy (Franklin), 863-2382; also at 900 North Point (Ghirardelli Square), 776-1331: until 11:30 nightly.

WASHINGTON SQUARE BAR AND GRILL, 1701 Powell (Union), 982-8123: to 11:30 Sunday-Thursday and until midnight Friday and Saturday.

YUET LEE, 1300 Stockton (Broadway), 982-6020: Wednesday to Monday until 3 a.m.

ZEPHYR, 3643 Balboa (38th Avenue), 221-6063: to midnight Monday through Saturday.

ZUNI CAFE, 1658 Market (Franklin), 552-2522: to midnight Tuesday-Saturday.

Chapter Ten
SPECIAL PLACES FOR SPECIAL FACES
Romantic, special occasion & view restaurants; outside dining

RESTAURANTS FOR CELEBRATIONS AND ROMANCE

About the time we were putting finishing touches on this book, a friend (and one of our civilian panel members) called and asked us to recommend a romantic restaurant for a special occasion.

After skimming our list and suggesting several for her, an idea struck: Why not list them separately in the book? Certainly, there have been times when you wanted to get cozy with someone, or perhaps celebrate a birthday or some such event.

Herewith, our list of special occasion restaurants. Just for fun, we've given those which are particularly suited to romantic encounters a "heart rating" from one to four. Avoid four-heart places unless you're ready for a commitment.

ALEXIS, 1001 California (Mason), 885-6400; French/Continental: Byzantine-French opulence; intimate little cellar bar for after-dinner drinks. ♥♥

AMELIO'S RESTAURANT, 1630 Powell (Union), 397-4339; French/Continental: Brims with Old San Francisco elegance; get cozy in plush banquettes. ♥♥

AUBERGE DU SOLEIL, 180 Rutherford Hill Road (Silverado Trail), Rutherford (Napa Valley); French nouvelle: The perfect spot for a run-away weekend; the look is rustic elegance, the food is wonderful and the hillside setting above the vineyards is dazzling. Rooms are available, starting around $200. Pack a suitcase with filmy little things and hope they never find you. ♥♥♥♥

BEETHOVEN, 1701 Powell (Union), 391-4488; German: Warm Black Forest look, likable staff, good place to gather with friends.

BELLA VISTA, 13451 Skyline Boulevard, Woodside, 851-1229; Continental: A woodsy hilltop retreat with a view of the San Mateo Peninsula; pleasant for intimate conversations or significant celebrations. ♥♥

THE BLUE FOX, 659 Merchant (off Montgomery), 981-1177; Continental: Luxurious old restaurant, recently redecorated; nice for special occasions. ♥

CAMPTON PLACE, 340 Stockton (Campton Place Hotel, near Sutter), 781-5555; American nouvelle: More sleek than intimate; excellent service. Fine environment for quiet power meetings. ♥

THE CARNELIAN ROOM, 555 California (at Montgomery, atop Bank of America Building), 433-7500; Continental: Beautiful decor and view, great place to impress someone special. ♥♥

CASA MADRONA, 801 Bridgeway, Sausalito, 332- 0502; American nouvelle: Wonderfully sensual environment. With an elegant Victorian setting, excellent food and dreamy night vistas of Sausalito and the Bay, you're guaranteed results — whether you want them or not.♥♥♥♥

CHATEAU SUZANNE, 1449 Lombard (Van Ness Avenue) 771-9326; Continental with Chinese accent: Pretty interior but bright; it's better for celebrations than for amour. ♥

CHEZ PANISSE, 1517 Shattuck Avenue (Vine), Berkeley, 548-5525; California nouvelle: Dine where culinary history was made; but it's more suitable for special events. With Alice Waters' wonderful food, romance would be a distraction. ♥

DONATELLO, 501 Post (at Mason, in the Donatello hotel), 441-7182; Northern Italian: Our critics called it San Francisco's best restaurant. Its "light elegance" is better for milestone events than for hand-holding. ♥

DOROS, 714 Montgomery (Washington), 397-6822; Continental: Snuggle with someone special in a red leather banquette in this luxurious old San Francisco restaurant. ♥♥

ERNIE'S RESTAURANT, 847 Montgomery (Pacific), 397-5971; French: Plush Victorian grandeur provides a romantic setting for getting the right answer (depending, of course, on the question). ♥♥♥

FLEUR DE LYS, 777 Sutter (Jones), 673-7779; French: She or he will believe anything you say under the lush, sensual canopied ceiling. ♥♥♥

GAYLORD INDIA RESTAURANT, Ghirardelli Square (North Point and Polk), 771-8822; northern India: Lavish colonial India setting is great for special events; the food's too spicy for flirtation.

THE GRAPELEAF, 4031 Balboa (41st Avenue), 668- 1515; Lebanese: After watching the belly dancer, he may forget who he came with, so forget amour. But it's a wonderful and affordable place to gather with friends for a special celebration.

JULIUS' CASTLE, 1541 Montgomery (Union), 362- 3042; Continental: The new lighter look isn't quite as earthy as before but the view and improved food make up the difference. ♥

THE LARK CREEK INN, 234 Magnolia Avenue, Larkspur, 924-7766; Continental: After the fallen tree has been pried loose and the renovations completed in the spring of 1988, Lark Creek will offer a quiet retreat among the redwoods for quiet moments. ♥♥

LAS MANANITAS, 850 Montgomery (Pacific Avenue), 434-2088; Mexican: A place that's both stylish and festive; plan a party there.

LEHR'S GREENHOUSE RESTAURANT AND FLORIST, 740 Sutter (adjacent to the Canterbury Hotel, near Taylor), 474-6478; American: Dine under a canopy of plants; bring Mom to lunch here before telling her what you did to her car.

L'ETOILE, 1075 California (Taylor), 771-1530; French: If this comely restaurant with its guilt mirrors, leather banquettes and potted flowers doesn't impress her, stop making payments on the ring. ♥♥♥

L'OLIVIER, 465 Davis Court (off Jackson), 981- 7824; French: It's bright and pretty, sort of a cheerfully elegant greenhouse; great for special events. ♥

MAMOUNIA, 4411 Balboa (45th Avenue), 752-6566; Moroccan: There's something sensual about sitting on sateen pillows and eating with your fingers. With luck, this place will get you into trouble. ♥♥♥

MASA'S, 648 Bush (Powell), 989-7154; French: The impeccable food and service are too much of a distraction; it's better for a very special occasion than a very romantic evening. ♥

PIERRE-AT-MERIDIEN, 50 Third (at Hotel Meridien, near Market), 974-6400; Contemporary French: It's more serene than cozy; celebrate birthdays and business deals here, not amour. ♥

THE SHADOWS, 1349 Montgomery (Union, on Telegraph Hill), 982-5536; Contemporary French: It has been brightened and lightened, but it's still in a sensual setting. There's a view but it isn't awesome; focus on the person next to you. ♥♥

SQUIRE ROOM, 950 Mason (Fairmont Hotel, at California), 772-5211; Continental: It's the dining room setting for TV's *Hotel*, a lush, sophisticated place for a power conference or promotion party. ♥

SUTTER GARDEN, 562 Sutter (Orchard Hotel, near Mason), 433-4434; American/Continental: Understated elegance, quiet intimacy and pretty food presentations add up to a romantic scene. And it's even affordable. ♥♥

TOMMY TOY'S HAUTE CUISINE CHIONISE, 655 Montgomery (Washington), 397-4888; Chinese/French: This imperial Chinese palace is the ideal place to relax and celebrate; it's a bit too pretty and busy for coziness. ♥

TOURELLE CAFE AND RESTAURANT, 3565 Mount Diablo Boulevard (Oak Hill Road), Lafayette, 284-3565; French: The sunny courtyard of this French chateau is a perfect retreat for afternoon dalliance, followed, with luck, by a quiet dinner. ♥♥

TRADER VIC'S, 20 Cosmo Place (between Post and Taylor), 776-2232; Oriental/Continental: Impress that key business client with lunch in the Captain's Cabin; the trick is to get reservations.

VICTOR'S, 335 Powell (Westin St. Francis Hotel, near Geary); California cuisine: It's beautiful and refined, with an awesome view. The sky's the limit in this St. Francis Tower restaurant; if romance doesn't work, dance your partner's fanny off at Oz next door. ♥♥♥♥

VIEW RESTAURANTS

The better the view, the more "V's" we place at the end of the listing, again with a range of **V** (fair) to **VVVV** (awesome).

A. SABELLA'S, 2766 Taylor (Fisherman's Wharf), 771-6775; Seafood: A nice view of the Wharf. **VV**

ALIOTO'S RESTAURANT, #8 Fisherman's Wharf, 673- 0183; Italian/seafood: Similar to Sabella's. **VV**

AUBERGE DU SOLEIL, 180 Rutherford Hill Road (Silverado Trail), Rutherford (Napa Valley), (707) 963-1211; French nouvelle: A bucolic vista to remember, through the olive groves, into the vineyards and across to the Mayacamas Mountains. **VVV**

BELLA VISTA, 13451 Skyline Boulevard, Woodside, 851-1229; Continental: A pretty panorama of the San Mateo Peninsula from a woodsy perch. **VVV**

THE CARNELIAN ROOM, 555 California (at Montgomery, atop Bank of America Building), 433-7500; Continental: The ultimate restaurant aerie—a 52-story view of the entire city; it's narrow with terraced tables to maximize the panorama. **VVVV**

CASA MADRONA, 801 Bridgeway, Sausalito, 332- 0502; American nouvelle: An elegant vantage point from which to admire Sausalito and the bay. **VVV**

THE CASTAWAYS, Coyote Point County Park (take Poplar exit from U.S. 101), San Mateo, 347-1027; American: The bayside vista from a forested peninsula is probably the best thing about this place. **VV**

THE CHART HOUSE, 201 Bridgeway (Main), Sausalito, 332-0804; American: Occupying Sally Stanford's old Valhalla pier, the Chart House opens its big windows to the north bay. **VV**

CLIFF HOUSE SEAFOOD AND BEVERAGE CO., 1090 Point Lobos (Great Highway), 386-3330; American/Continental: Drink in this grand postcard panorama of Seal Rocks and the restless Pacific. In fact, the drinks are probably better than the food here. **VVV**

DOMAINE CHANDON, California Drive (off Highway 29), Yountville (Napa Valley), (707) 944-2892; French/California: Glass walls open onto a landscaped garden and nearby vineyards. **VV**.

EQUINOX, #5 Embarcadero Center (in the Hyatt Regency), 788-1234; American/Continental: The structure is rather low and you see mostly waistlines of adjacent buildings. But the revolving restaurant eventually swings over the bay, so eat slowly. **VV**

EMPRESS OF CHINA, 838 Grant Avenue (Clay), 434-1345; Chinese: Lay your chopsticks aside and admire picture-window glimpses of the waterfront and bay. **VV**.

GREENS AT FORT MASON, Fort Mason Building A (Marina Boulevard), 771-6222; Vegetarian: It's a nice low-level view of the bay and Golden Gate Bridge beyond. **VV**

GUAYMAS RESTAURANT, #5 Main Street (Tiburon Boulevard), Tiburon, 435-6300; Contemporary Mexican: Striking vistas of the Belvedere hills, the north bay and distant San Francisco skyline. **VVV**

HARBOR VILLAGE, #4 Embarcadero Center (Front), 398-8883; Chinese: An impressive bay view with the Bay Bridge as a focal point. **VV**

HORNBLOWER DINING CRUISES, Pier 33, The Embarcadero, 434-0300; American/Continental: The best view restaurant in northern California; it's a movable visual feast as the good ship *City of San Francisco* sails about the bay. **VVVV**

JULIUS' CASTLE, 1541 Montgomery (Union), 362- 3042; Continental: A stellar vista of the waterfront and bay from Telegraph Hill. **VVV**

MAXWELL'S PLUM, Ghirardelli Square (North Point), 441-4140; American/Continental: A nice panorama of the bayfront. **VV**

THE MOONRAKER, 105 Rockaway Beach Avenue, Pacifica, 359-0303; Continental: Our agents weren't enthusiastic about the food, but the vista is great. Yes, it would be rude to take a lunch. **VV**

PACIFIC CAFE, Ghirardelli Square, 775-1173; seafood: Some of the tables offer glimpses of the bay. **V**

THE ROTUNDA AT NEIMAN-MARCUS, 150 Stockton (Geary) 362-4777; American/California: Attention shoppers, you can watch other shoppers while lunching inside this handsome glass silo; some tables have views of nearby Union Square. **VV**

SAM'S ANCHOR CAFE, 27 Main Street (Tiburon Boulevard), Tiburon, 435-4527; Seafood: Sam's outdoor deck offers a vision of the north bay and the far spires of San Francisco.

SCOMA'S, Pier 47 (Fisherman's Wharf), 771-4383; Seafood: A low-level bayfront view. **V**

SCOTT'S SEAFOOD, #3 Embarcadero Center (Drumm), 981-0622; Seafood: Scott's corner location in the Embarcadero complex offers some bay glimpses. **V**

SEAL ROCK INN, 545 Point Lobos (48th Avenue), 752-8000; American, mostly omelets: Have breakfast within sound and sight of the barking seals; don't forget to wave. **VV**

THE SHADOWS, 1349 Montgomery (Union, on Telegraph Hill), 982-5536; Contemporary French: A cozy Telegraph Hill view of city lights. **V**

SKATES, 100 Seawall Drive (University Avenue), Berkeley, 549-1900; American trendy: See the bay from the opposite shore; Skates is a raucous place but fortunately, noise can't drown out a vista. **VV**

TOKYO SUKIYAKI, 225 Jefferson (Fisherman's Wharf, near Taylor), 775-9030; Japanese: It offers somewhat of a Wharf View, but you may have to rise from your tatami mat to enjoy it. **V**

VICTOR'S, 335 Powell (in the Westin St. Francis, near Geary), 774-0253; California cuisine: Only the Carnelian Room rivals this panorama, and nothing rivals the skyroom opulence. **VVV**

THE WATERFRONT, Pier 7 (The Embarcadero), 391- 2696; Seafood/Continental: Generous bay views, and the seating is terraced, so everybody gets a peek. **VV**

DINING OUT—LITERALLY

Restaurants with outdoor dining and/or cocktail areas

Some places open their patios only when the weather is reasonable; others are heated and are almost always open, and a few serve only cocktails outside. There are nearly as many al fresco dining spots outside the city as in, so we've separated them.

BILL'S PLACE, 2315 CLEMENT (24th Avenue)

BULL'S TEXAS CAFE, 25 Van Ness Avenue (Market)

COMPADRES MEXICAN BAR & GRILL, Ghirardelli Square (North Point)

CULTURED SALAD, #3 Embarcadero Center (Sacramento)
ENRICO'S RESTAURANT, 504 Broadway (Columbus)
HAYES GARDEN CAFE, 482-A Hayes (Octavia)
HOLDING COMPANY, #2 Embarcadero Center (Front)
JULIE'S SUPPER CLUB, 1123 Folsom (Seventh)
LA FUENTE, #2 Embarcadero Center (Sacramento)
LAS MANANITAS, 850 Montgomery (Pacific Avenue)
MARY GULLI'S, 3661 Sacramento (Spruce)
OLD CLAM HOUSE, 299 Bayshore (Oakdale)
PATIO CAFE, 531 Castro (18th)
RAF CENTROGRIGLIA, 478 Green (Grant)
RUBY'S GOURMET PIZZA, 3249 Scott (Lombard)
RYAN'S, 4230 18th (Diamond)
SCOTT'S SEAFOOD, #3 Embarcadero Center (Drumm)
SEAL ROCK INN, 545 Point Lobos (48th Avenue)
SUISSE ITALIA, 101 California (Drumm)

Outside San Francisco

AUBERGE DU SOLEIL, 180 Rutherford Hill Road (Silverado), Rutherford
BAY WOLF CAFE & RESTAURANT, 3853 Piedmont Avenue (41st), Oakland
CASA MADRONA, 801 Bridgeway, Sausalito
DOMAINE CHANDON, California Drive (off Highway 29), Yountville
EL DORADO INN, 405 First Street West (Spain), Sonoma
GERTIE'S CHESAPEAKE BAY CAFE, 1919 Addison (Martin Luther King Jr. Way), Berkeley
GUAYMAS RESTAURANT, #5 Main Street (Tiburon Boulevard), Tiburon
THE LARK CREEK INN, 234 Magnolia Avenue, Larkspur
LES ARCADES, 133 East Napa (First Street), Sonoma
MAX'S OPERA CAFE, 1250 Old Bayshore (Broadway), Burlingame
MUSTARDS GRILL, 7399 St. Helena Highway, Yountville (patio for cocktails only)
SAM'S ANCHOR CAFE, 27 Main Street (Tiburon Boulevard), Tiburon
SAN BENITO HOUSE, 356 Main Street (Mill), Half Moon Bay
THORNHILL CAFE, 5761 Thornhill Drive (Grisborne), Oakland
TOURELLE CAFE AND RESTAURANT, 3565 Mount Diablo Boulevard (Oak Hill Road), Lafayette

Chapter Eleven
A GUIDE TO THE GUIDES
Reviews of other dining directories

Having gotten this far into *SAN FRANCISCO'S ULTIMATE DINING GUIDE*, you must realize that while it is certainly the ultimate, it is not perfect. *Restaurants of San Francisco* talks more about the food than we do, Paul Wallach's hefty 447-pager lists more restaurants and *Epicurean Rendezvous* is full of pretty colored pictures.

Of course, none of those guides are having as much fun as we are, and none have drawn from so many sources for their information. And some (good grief) accept advertising and say only nice things about the restaurants. (We found not one overcooked fish in *Epicurean Rendezvous*.)

We assume you've purchased this book by now, and haven't been standing for all this time in the bookstore. So we'll review some of the other guides currently on the market, and to make it more interesting, we'll rate them.

1. Restaurants of San Francisco by Patricia Unterman and Stan Sesser, Chronicle Books, San Francisco, © 1988.

If your focus is more on food than environment, you'll like this dining guide. Unterman and Sesser are employed as restaurant critics for the *San Francisco Chronicle*. With this backing, they always know where their next meal is coming from, and who is paying for it. Thus, they can spend a good part of their time pondering the proper pedigree of a pork chop, and they can probably tell you more about sweetbreads than you want to know.

They apparently dine anonymously most of the time (as we do), and their reviews are detailed and seemingly impartial. Yes, we know Ms. Unterman owns Hayes Street Grill and it earned two stars in Sesser's write-up. But we don't have a problem with that, because it's well-established as a good seafood restaurant. And no, we're not being nice because Pat and Stan are bosom dining critics; we've never met them.

One fault: the authors should put down their forks occasionally and talk more about the restaurant. Environment is an important part of dining.

2. Best Restaurants of San Francisco, edited by Jacqueline Killeen, published in cooperation with *San Francisco Focus* Magazine, 101 Productions, San Francisco, © 1986.

Our second-place book shares the Unterman-Sesser advantage; drawing on the staff and resources of *San Francisco Focus*, it receives input from full-time restaurant critics.

The reviews indicate an intimacy with the Bay Area restaurant scene, and the book is dressed up with sketches and an occasional menu, an improvement over the austere look of the Chronicle tome.

It's a book to sit down and read through, if you have the time after you've finished the one in your hands. In addition to individual listings (by district, which is a drawback to an out-of-towner), it discusses neighborhood dining trends or types of restaurants, such as listing some of the better Asian places along Clement, or suggesting where to find some interesting *trattorias* in the city.

3. Good Eats: A Design and Food Guide to Bay Area Restaurants by Herb McLaughlin, Peanut Butter Publishing, Seattle, Washington, © 1987.

McLaughlin offers an interesting new approach as a restaurant critic. An architect, he views a dining parlor from a design as well as a culinary standpoint, rating both the look and the taste of the place. *Good Eats* is the best-written of the dining guides, from a literary sense. It's a book to be read more for entertainment than for information. His menu descriptions lack specifics, and his arbitrary groupings ("The Classics", "Haute Design", "So Bad It's Good") make it difficult to find a particular restaurant.

4. 200 Good Restaurants by Russ Riera, Creative Arts Book Company, Berkeley, © 1986.

Riera has been writing restaurant reviews since 1970, as he modestly advises us in the introduction, and his copy reveals considerably knowledge of the Bay Area dining scene. We like the straightforward organization of his guide. Each listing is separated into menu items, the atmosphere, a bit about the owners and the prices.

Although the book is informative, his writing lacks vigor. He's not tempted by clever cynicism the way the rest of us are, and his attempts at humor are flatter than a crepe. "At one German restaurant I was at, the dumplings were so heavy, it took two hands to lift the fork." Stick with the straight stuff, Russ.

5. Zagat San Francisco Restaurant Survey, Published by Zagat Survey, New York, © 1987.

The Zagat books are successful mini-guides based on survey forms turned in by volunteer critics. The advantage of a pure survey is that it offers readers the undiluted opinions of fellow diners. But there's a disadvantage; it contains no input from seasoned restaurant critics, who may be more open-minded and fair than volunteer "civilian" judges. (We tempered our civilian panel with input from folks in the restaurant and lodging field.)

We like the fact that the guide is small, portable and simply arranged. If you memorize a few codes, it packs a fair dab of basic info. And it's alphabetized. Some guides list restaurants according to location or type, requiring readers to spend too much time in the index. (We even had trouble finding the index in one guide.)

The reviews are punchy, but they lack detail. One receives only a rapid-fire series of quick takes. There's nothing on hours, credit cards, bar service or appropriate dress. True, phone numbers are listed, but out-of-towners don't always have easy access to telephones (particularly along middle Market Street, where people may be living in the phone booths).

6. The Thrifty Gourmet by Sharon Silva and Frank Viviano, Chronicle Books, San Francisco, © 1987.

This little book is really better than its sixth place listing suggests; it probably should have a special category. It isn't useful as an overall dining guide, because it talks only about budget dinners. But for the person looking for "250 Great Dinners in the Bay Area for $6.95 or Less," it's excellent.

The write-ups are based on specific meals, an interesting approach. And they're thorough and entertaining; the authors demonstrate a considerable knowledge of food, particularly ethnic fare. We like the fact that they often go into the background of the various dishes they describe.

7. Paul Wallach's Guide to Restaurants of San Francisco and Northern California, Peregrine Smith Books, Salt Lake City, Utah, © 1985.

Wallach, whose offices are in Glendale, appears to know everybody in San Francisco. With an endorsement from former Mayor Dianne Feinstein, and a "panel of experts" that includes Bob Mondavi and Cyril Magnin, we didn't know whether to read his book or salute it. (We couldn't even get Mayor Art Agnos to endorse his favorite Greek restaurant.)

Wallach's encyclopedic guide assaults us with overkill. He reviews more than a thousand restaurants, and his introduction is nearly as long as the entire Zagat Survey.

"My love affair with restaurants began when I was about six years old..." begins his fifteen-page intro. Then he puts his readers in the same age group. He patiently advises them how to properly enter a restaurant (gentleman first, unless a host or hostess is leading the way), explains how to split a check, and cautions them not to over-order. And his lack of familiarity with our turf is evident. He refers to Greens as an "East Bay" restaurant and talks of Square One's view of Golden Gate Park. Pretty good trick for a place that's located near the waterfront; try Walton Park, Mr. Wallach.

The final three guides contain advertising, either from the restaurants themselves or from other groups. Write-ups are essentially puff pieces with little value as dining critiques. But they are useful for information purposes. Two of them re-print menus; that's certainly helpful when you're pondering where to eat tonight.

8. Epicurean Rendezvous, edited by Maia Madden, published by AM/PM Guides, San Francisco, © 1987.

Well, it's certainly a pretty little thing. *Epicurean Rendezvous* is a slick, full color publication listing the "100 Finest Restaurants in Northern California," which have received the publisher's prestigious "Noblesse Cuisine and Service Award." The book claims to accept no advertising from restaurants. However, other ads subsidize the guide; it sells for only $5.

The listings are pretty, topped with smiling faces of owners and chefs, and featuring full-color dining room shots. And of course the "reviews" are pure puffery.

9. Cityguide by Bella Levin-Whelan and Dan Whelan, Danella Publications, Sausalito © 1987.

This is essentially a menu guide, with a somewhat detailed write-up above each cafe. The "review" is uncompromisingly complimentary, and it follows a set formula. It begins with a brief description of the restaurant and its owners, then proceeds with an intimate description of "our most recent meal there." The step-by-step account of each memorable feast is so detailed that you can almost picture the authors chewing.

The sample menus with prices offer useful information. The back of the book is a scattergun of listings and ads, ranging from Hawaii's Kona Village to lingerie parlors.

10. San Francisco Epicure by Maria Theresa Caen, Peanut Butter Publishing, Seattle, © 1986.

The subtitle sums it up: "A Menu Guide to the San Francisco Bay Area's Finest Restaurants." There's little copy in the book; just a brief, complimentary paragraph or two and a typical menu. Each listing begins with a quote about that particular restaurant by another critic or perhaps a well-fed customer. In some instances, the restaurant owner or manager contributes the quote. It's a coffee table-sized book, but with a limp cover.